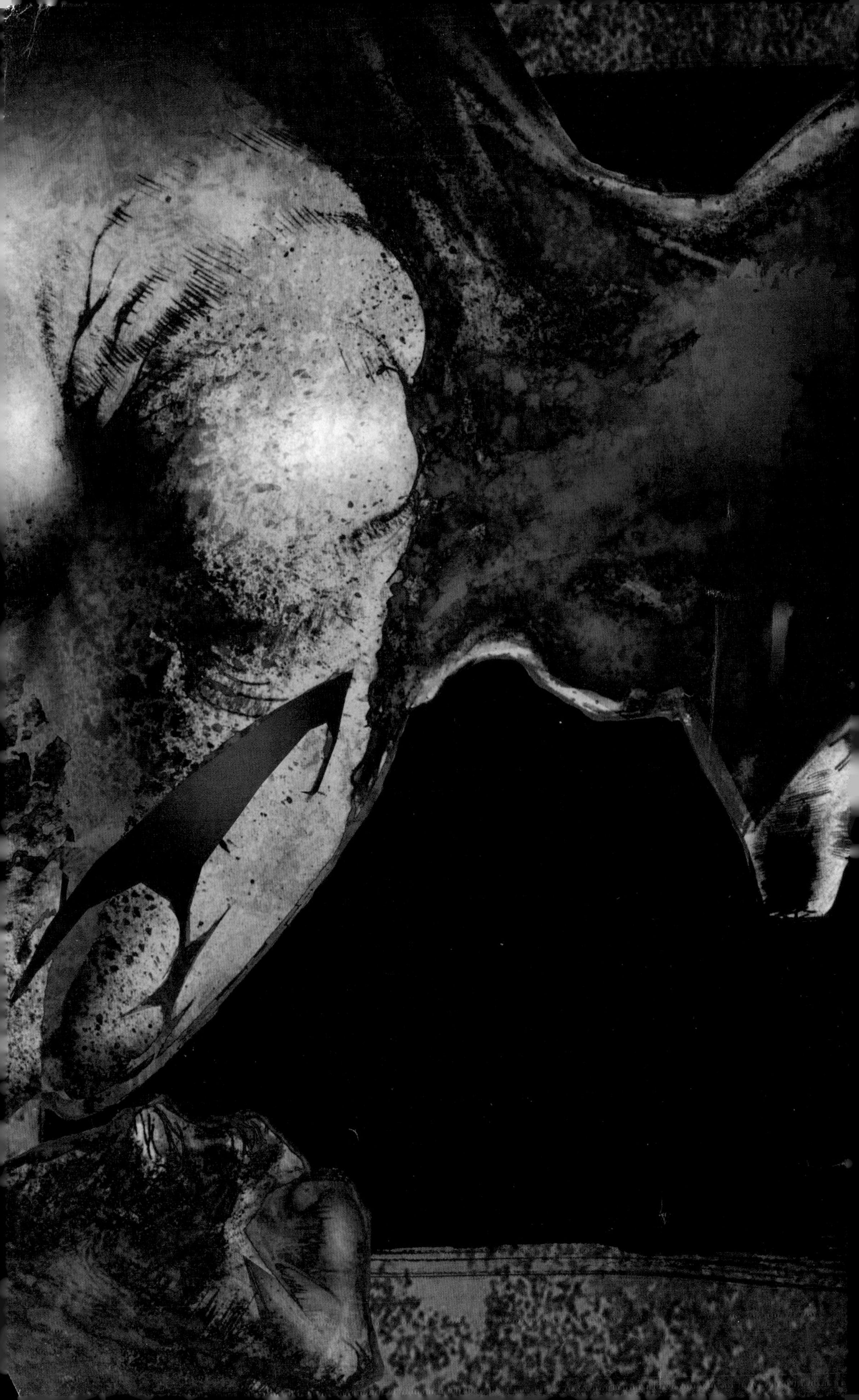

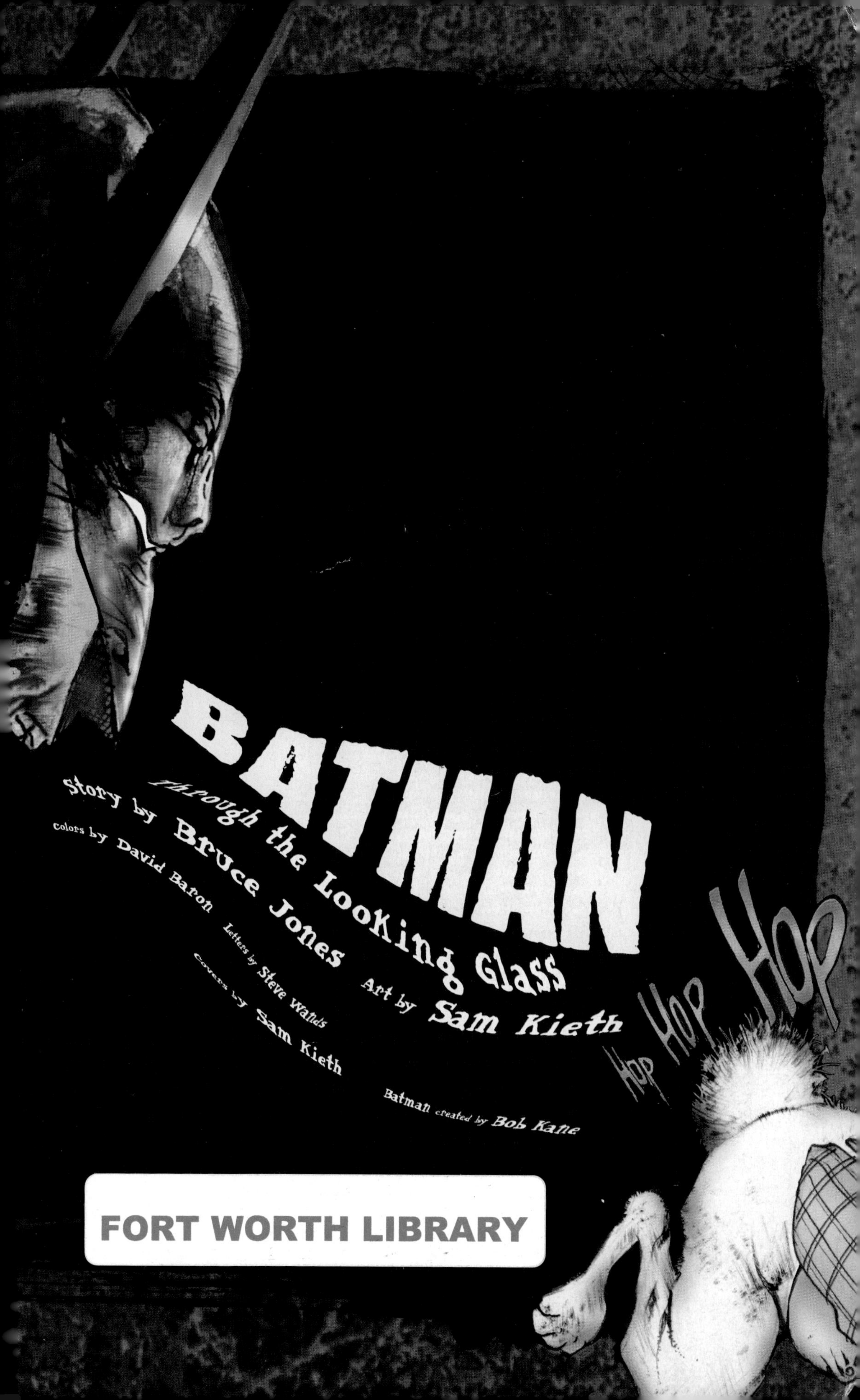
Hop Hop Hop

BATMAN
through the Looking Glass

Story by Bruce Jones Art by Sam Kieth

Colors by David Baron Letters by Steve Wands

Covers by Sam Kieth

Batman created by Bob Kane

Mike Carlin   Editor - Original Series
Robbin Brosterman   Design Director - Books
Louis Prandi   Publication Design

Bob Harras   VP - Editor-in-Chief

Diane Nelson   President
Dan DiDio and Jim Lee   Co-Publishers
Geoff Johns   Chief Creative Officer
John Rood   Executive VP - Sales, Marketing and Business Development
Amy Genkins   Senior VP - Business and Legal Affairs
Nairi Gardiner   Senior VP - Finance
Jeff Boison   VP - Publishing Operations
Mark Chiarello   VP - Art Direction and Design
John Cunningham   VP - Marketing
Terri Cunningham   VP - Talent Relations and Services
Alison Gill   Senior VP - Manufacturing and Operations
Hank Kanalz   Senior VP - Digital
Jay Kogan   VP - Business and Legal Affairs, Publishing
Jack Mahan   VP - Business Affairs, Talent
Nick Napolitano   VP - Manufacturing Administration
Sue Pohja   VP - Book Sales
Courtney Simmons   Senior VP - Publicity
Bob Wayne   Senior VP - Sales

Library of Congress Cataloging-in-Publication Data

Jones, Bruce, 1944-
  Batman : through the looking glass / Bruce Jones, Sam Kieth.
     p. cm.
  ISBN 978-1-4012-2553-7
  1. Graphic novels. I. Kieth, Sam. II. Title. III. Title: Through the looking glass.
  PN6728.B36J65 2012
  741.5'973--dc23
                        2012032132

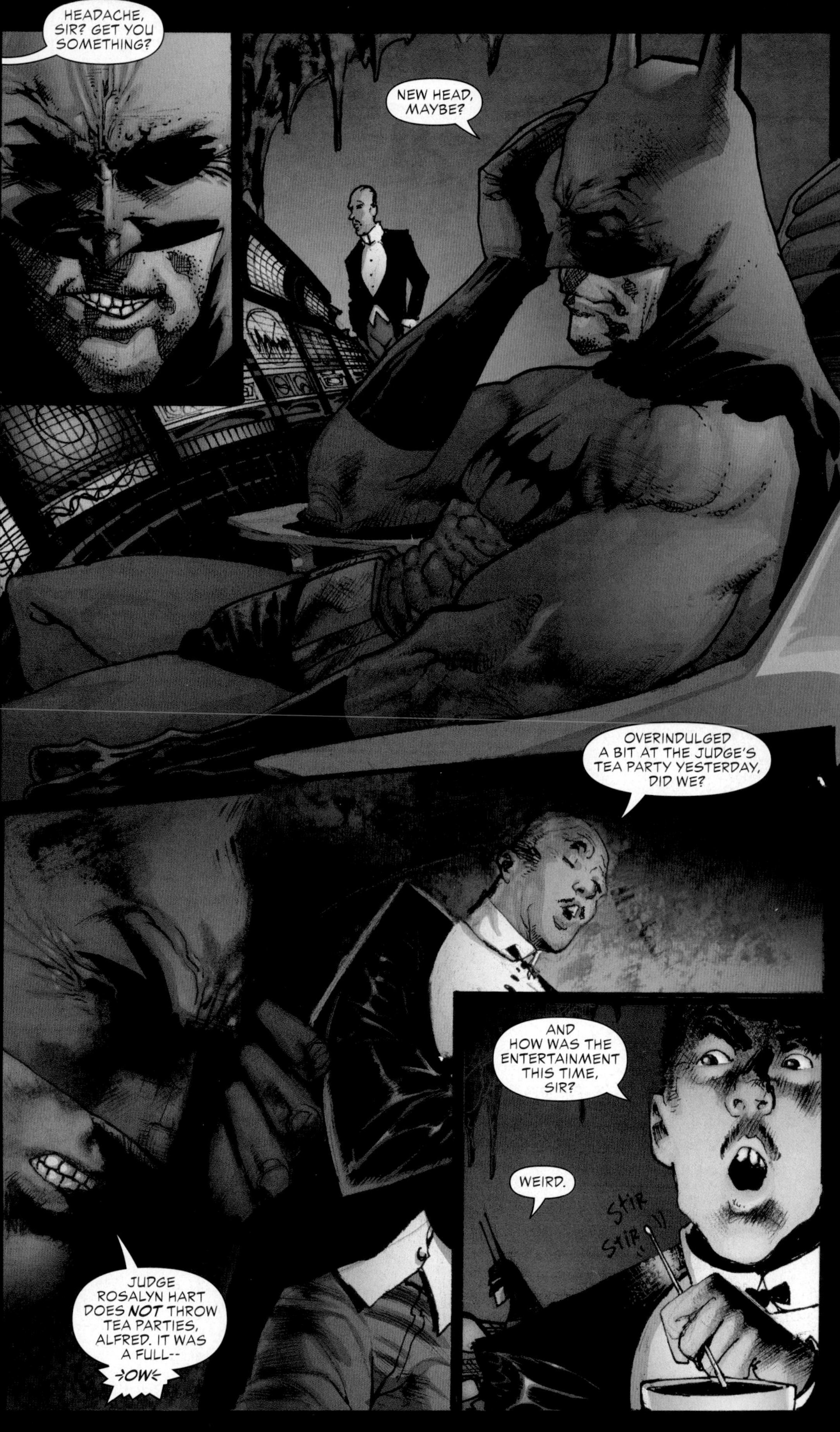
HEADACHE, SIR? GET YOU SOMETHING?
NEW HEAD, MAYBE?
OVERINDULGED A BIT AT THE JUDGE'S TEA PARTY YESTERDAY, DID WE?
JUDGE ROSALYN HART DOES **NOT** THROW TEA PARTIES, ALFRED. IT WAS A FULL--
OW
AND HOW WAS THE ENTERTAINMENT THIS TIME, SIR?
WEIRD.
STIR STIR

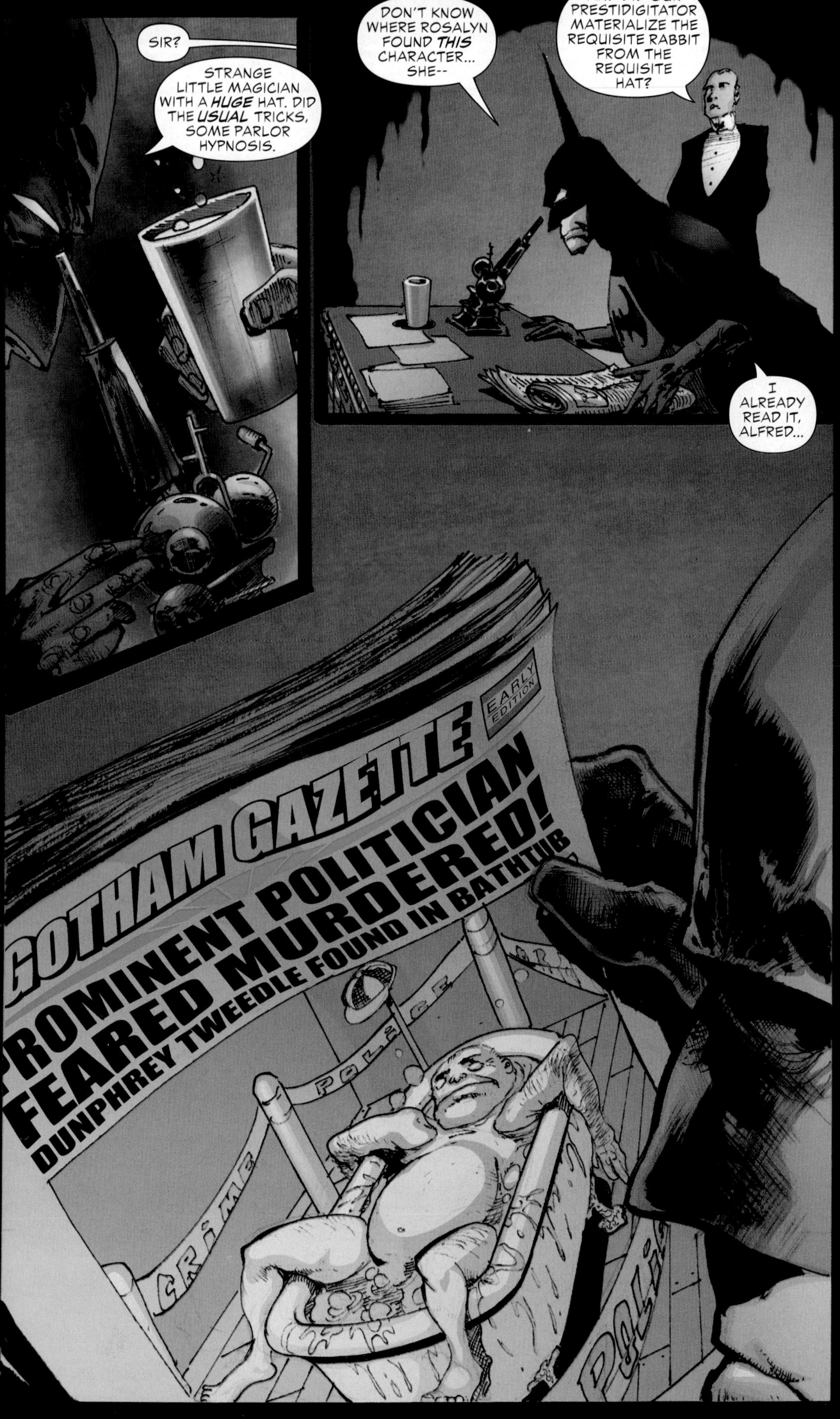
SIR?
STRANGE LITTLE MAGICIAN WITH A *HUGE* HAT. DID THE *USUAL* TRICKS, SOME PARLOR HYPNOSIS.
DON'T KNOW WHERE ROSALYN FOUND *THIS* CHARACTER... SHE--
AND DID OUR PRESTIDIGITATOR MATERIALIZE THE REQUISITE RABBIT FROM THE REQUISITE HAT?
I ALREADY READ IT, ALFRED...
GOTHAM GAZETTE
EARLY EDITION
PROMINENT POLITICIAN FEARED MURDERED!
DUNPHREY TWEEDLE FOUND IN BATHTUB

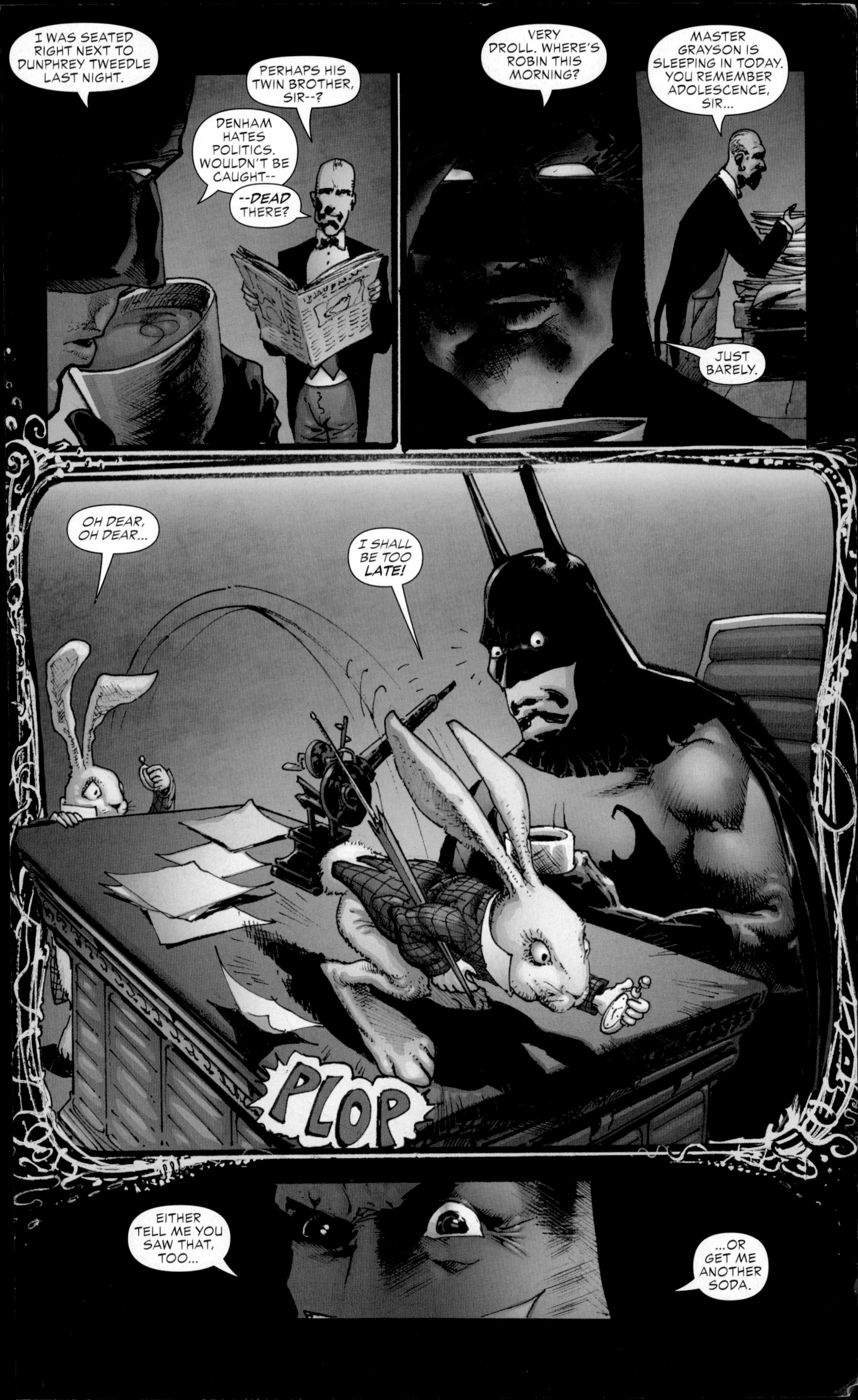
I WAS SEATED RIGHT NEXT TO DUNPHREY TWEEDLE LAST NIGHT.
PERHAPS HIS TWIN BROTHER, SIR--?
DENHAM HATES POLITICS. WOULDN'T BE CAUGHT--
--DEAD THERE?
VERY DROLL. WHERE'S ROBIN THIS MORNING?
MASTER GRAYSON IS SLEEPING IN TODAY. YOU REMEMBER ADOLESCENCE, SIR...
JUST BARELY.
OH DEAR, OH DEAR...
I SHALL BE TOO LATE!
PLOP
EITHER TELL ME YOU SAW THAT, TOO...
...OR GET ME ANOTHER SODA.

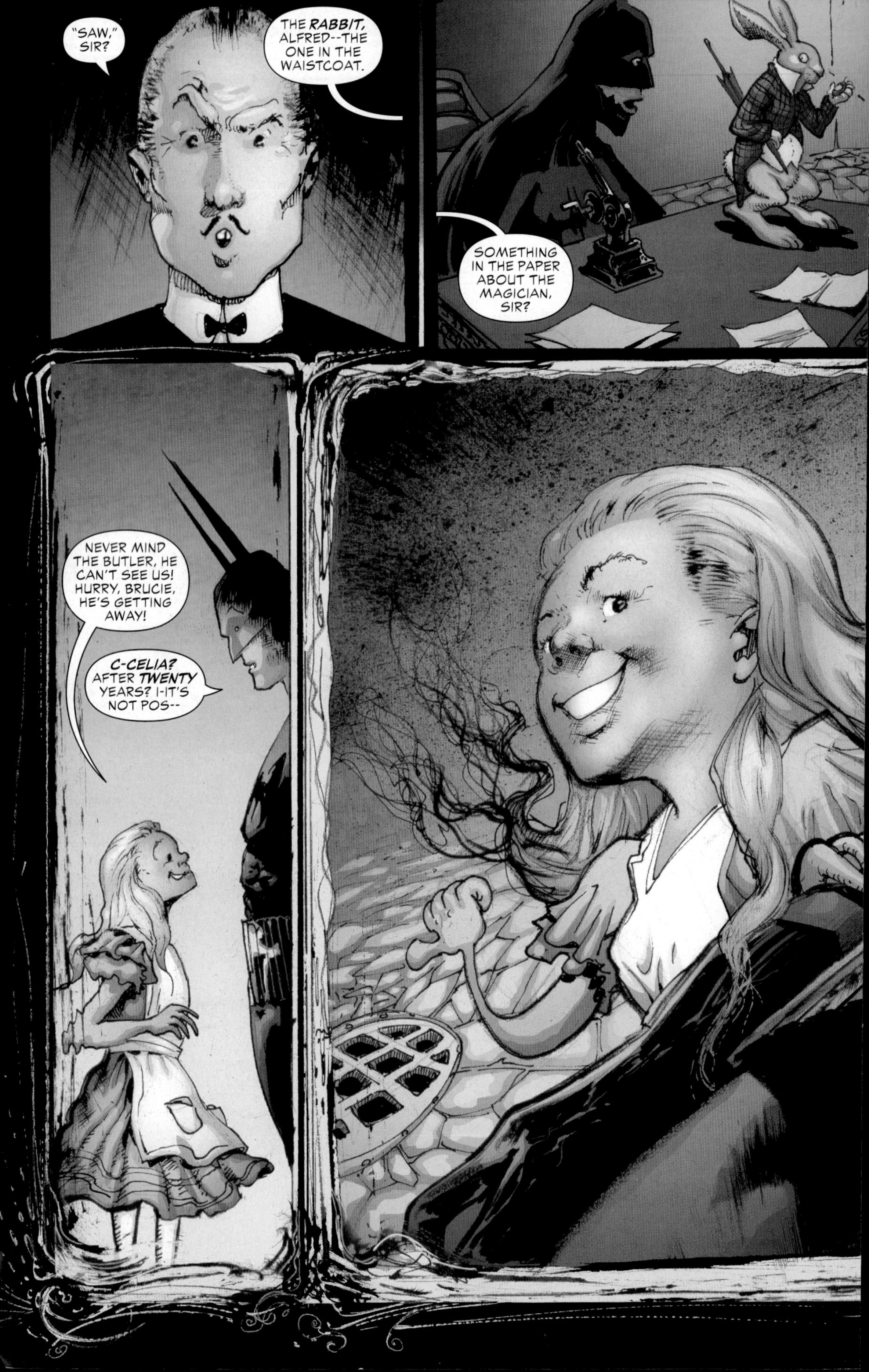
"SAW," SIR?
THE RABBIT, ALFRED--THE ONE IN THE WAISTCOAT.
SOMETHING IN THE PAPER ABOUT THE MAGICIAN, SIR?
NEVER MIND THE BUTLER, HE CAN'T SEE US! HURRY, BRUCIE, HE'S GETTING AWAY!
C-CELIA? AFTER TWENTY YEARS? I-IT'S NOT POS--

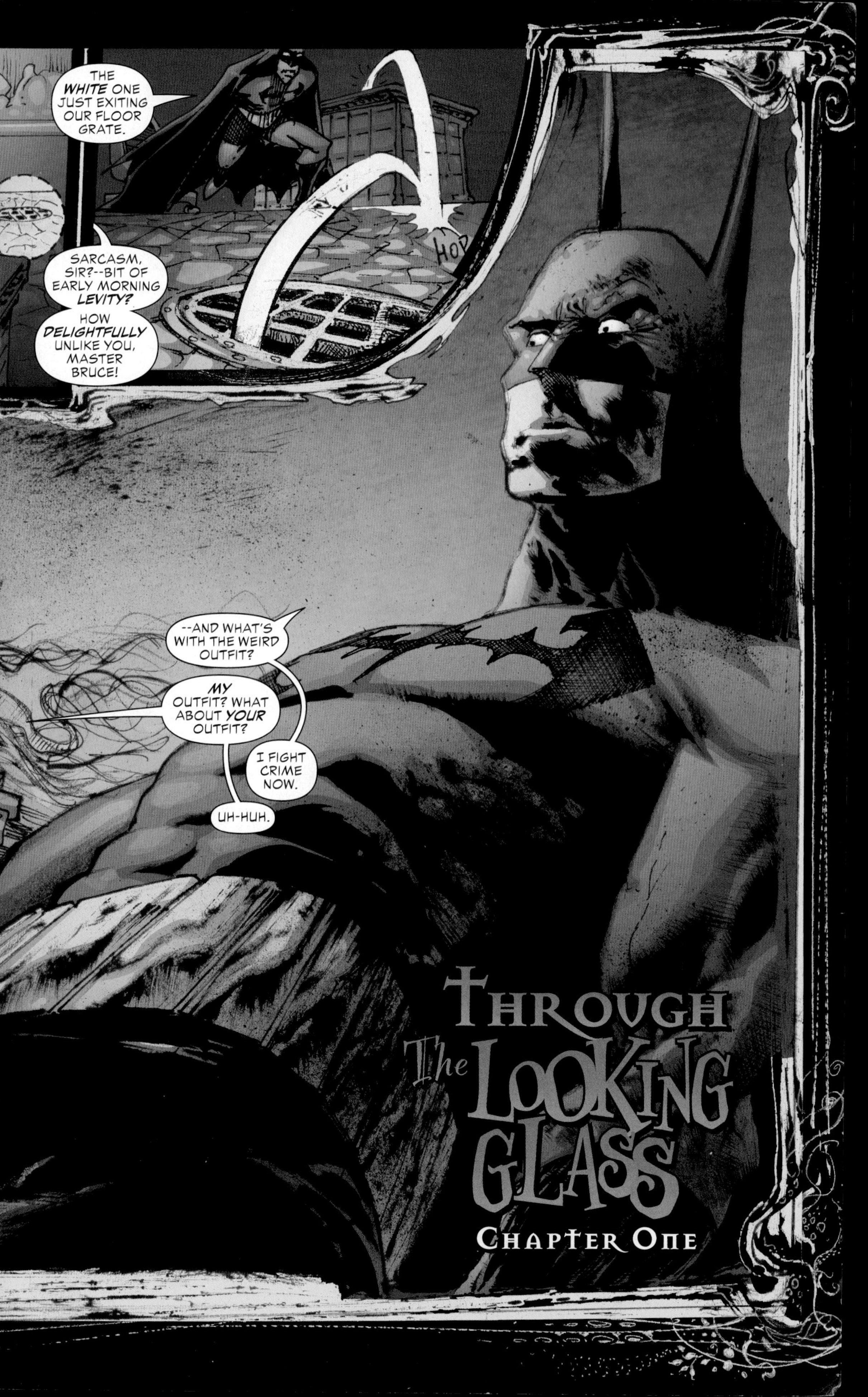
THE WHITE ONE JUST EXITING OUR FLOOR GRATE.
HOP
SARCASM, SIR?--BIT OF EARLY MORNING LEVITY?
HOW DELIGHTFULLY UNLIKE YOU, MASTER BRUCE!
--AND WHAT'S WITH THE WEIRD OUTFIT?
MY OUTFIT? WHAT ABOUT YOUR OUTFIT?
I FIGHT CRIME NOW.
UH-HUH.
THROUGH THE LOOKING GLASS
CHAPTER ONE

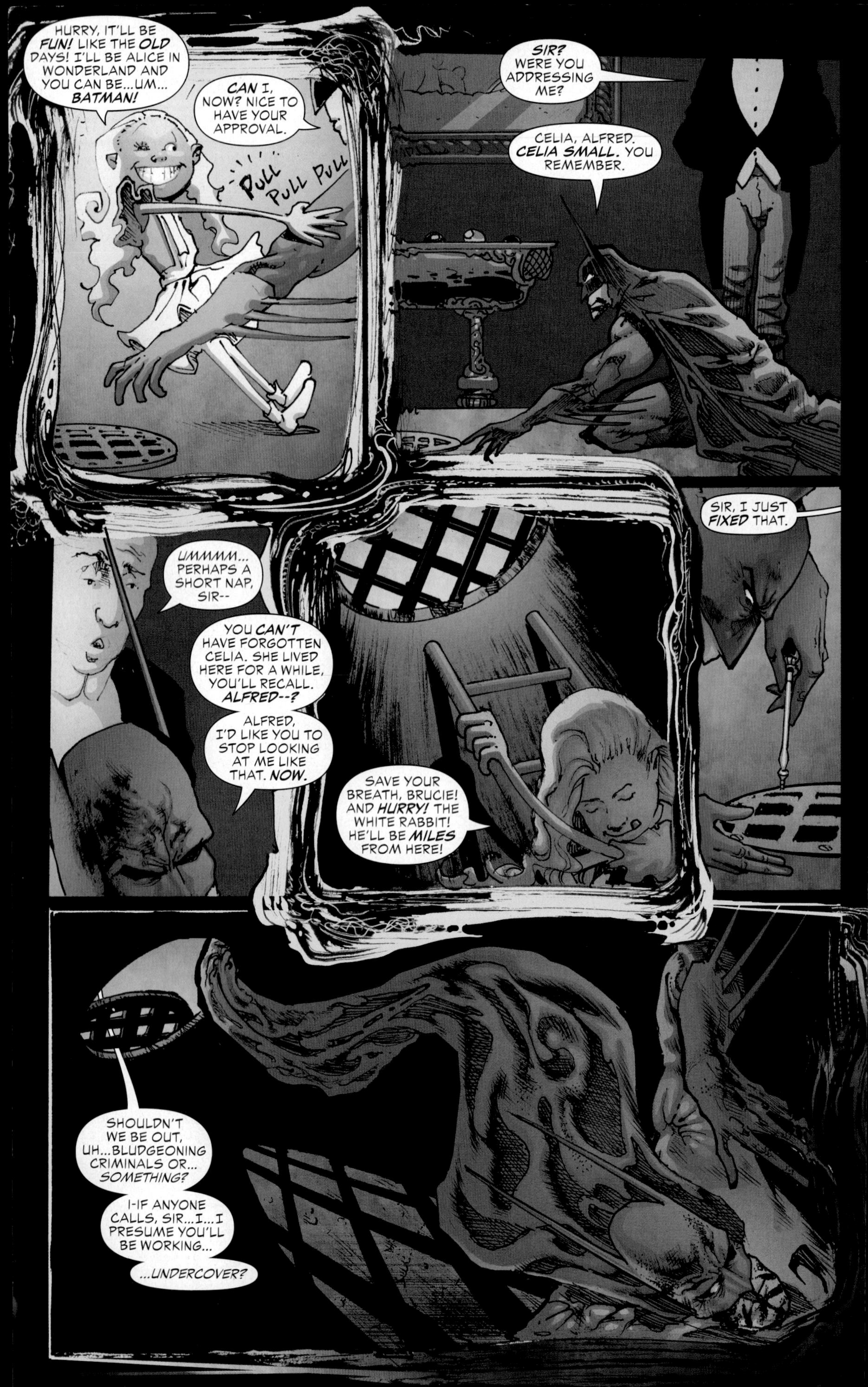
HURRY, IT'LL BE FUN! LIKE THE OLD DAYS! I'LL BE ALICE IN WONDERLAND AND YOU CAN BE...UM... BATMAN!
CAN I, NOW? NICE TO HAVE YOUR APPROVAL.
PULL PULL PULL
SIR? WERE YOU ADDRESSING ME?
CELIA, ALFRED. CELIA SMALL. YOU REMEMBER.
UMMMM... PERHAPS A SHORT NAP, SIR--
YOU CAN'T HAVE FORGOTTEN CELIA. SHE LIVED HERE FOR A WHILE, YOU'LL RECALL. ALFRED--?
ALFRED, I'D LIKE YOU TO STOP LOOKING AT ME LIKE THAT. NOW.
SAVE YOUR BREATH, BRUCIE! AND HURRY! THE WHITE RABBIT! HE'LL BE MILES FROM HERE!
SIR, I JUST FIXED THAT.
SHOULDN'T WE BE OUT, UH...BLUDGEONING CRIMINALS OR... SOMETHING?
I-IF ANYONE CALLS, SIR...I...I PRESUME YOU'LL BE WORKING...
...UNDERCOVER?

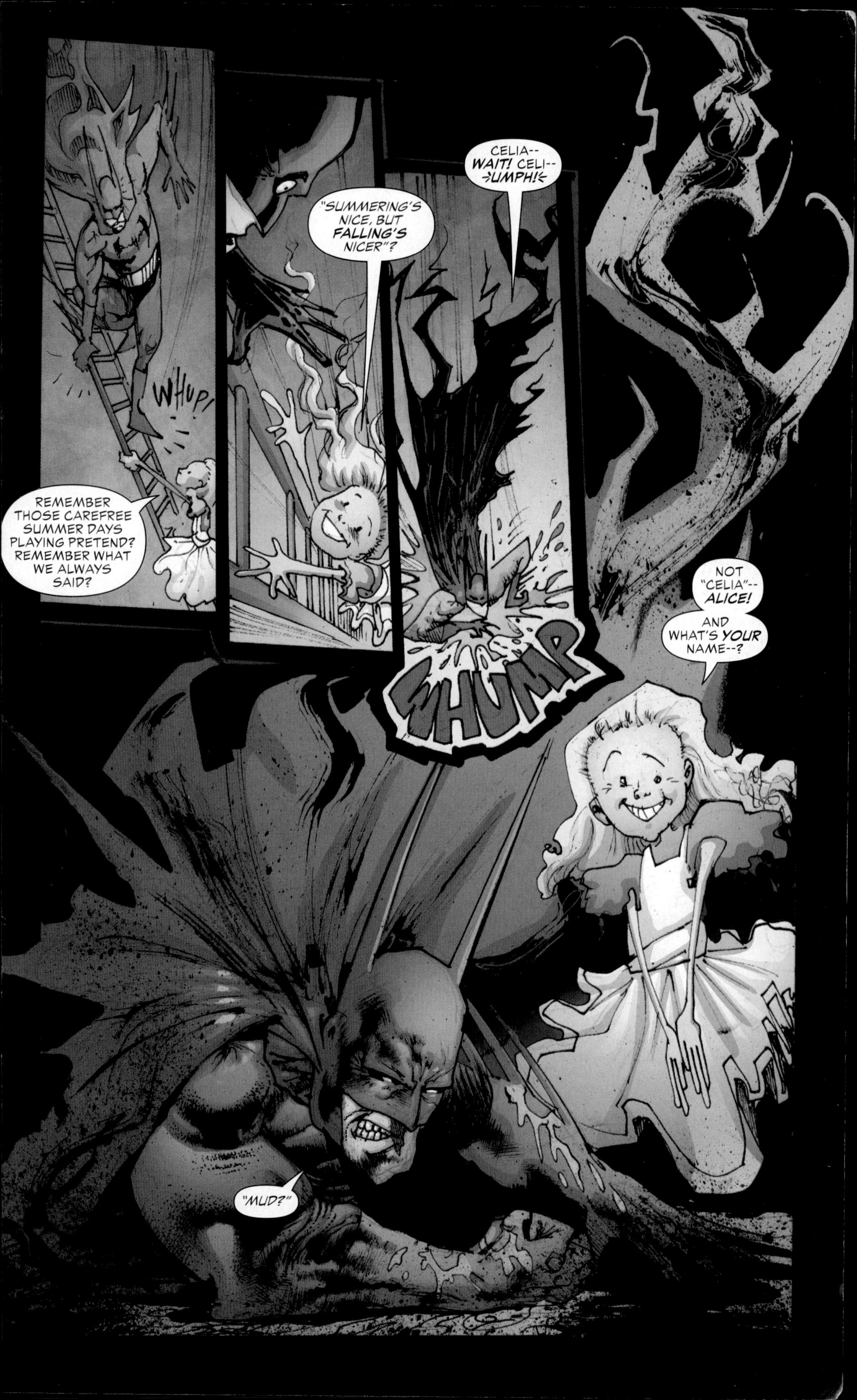
WHUP!
REMEMBER THOSE CAREFREE SUMMER DAYS PLAYING PRETEND? REMEMBER WHAT WE ALWAYS SAID?
"SUMMERING'S NICE, BUT FALLING'S NICER"?
CELIA-- WAIT! CELI-- UMPH!
WHUMP
NOT "CELIA"-- ALICE!
AND WHAT'S YOUR NAME--?
"MUD?"

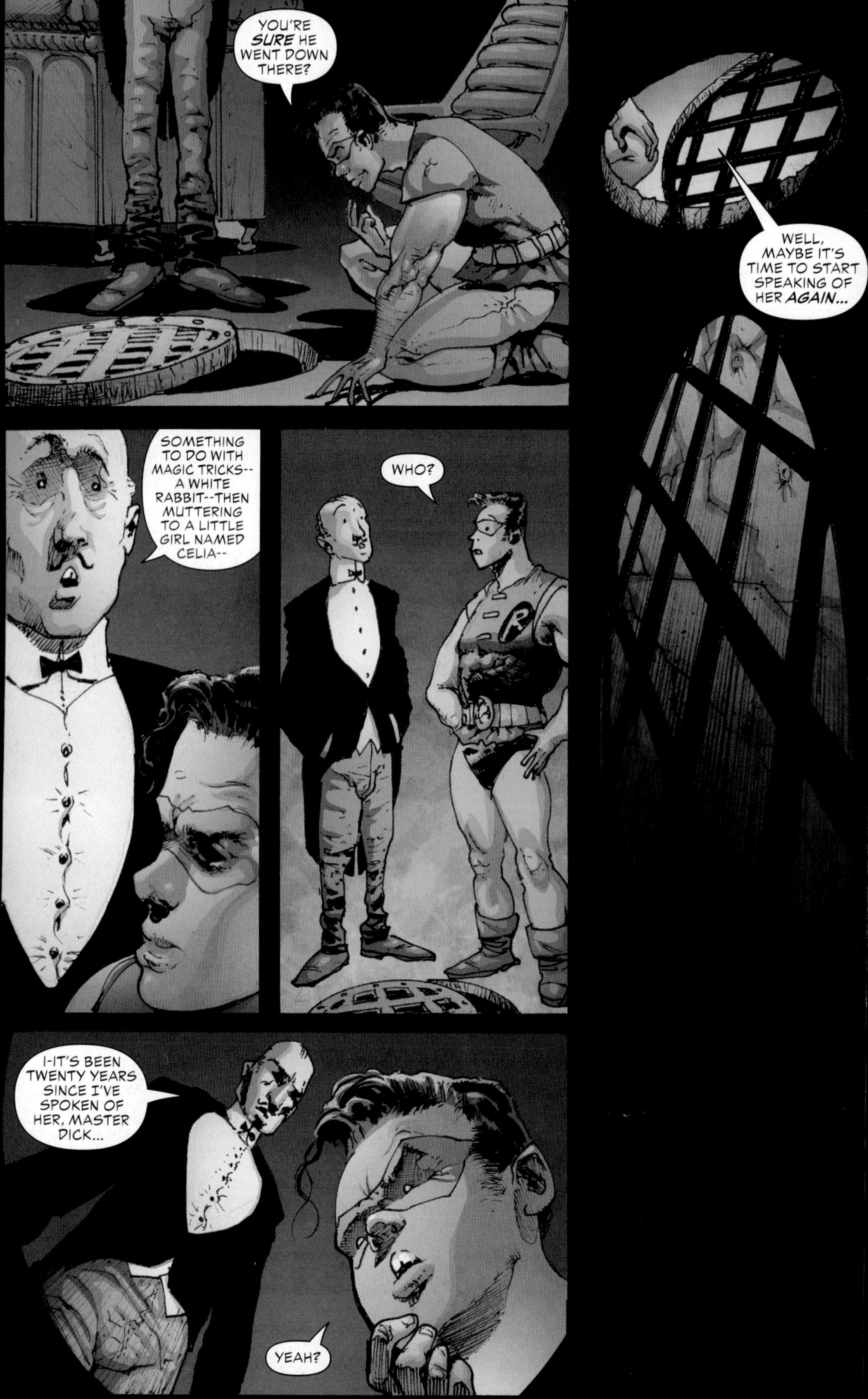
YOU'RE SURE HE WENT DOWN THERE?
SOMETHING TO DO WITH MAGIC TRICKS-- A WHITE RABBIT--THEN MUTTERING TO A LITTLE GIRL NAMED CELIA--
WHO?
I-IT'S BEEN TWENTY YEARS SINCE I'VE SPOKEN OF HER, MASTER DICK...
YEAH?
WELL, MAYBE IT'S TIME TO START SPEAKING OF HER AGAIN...

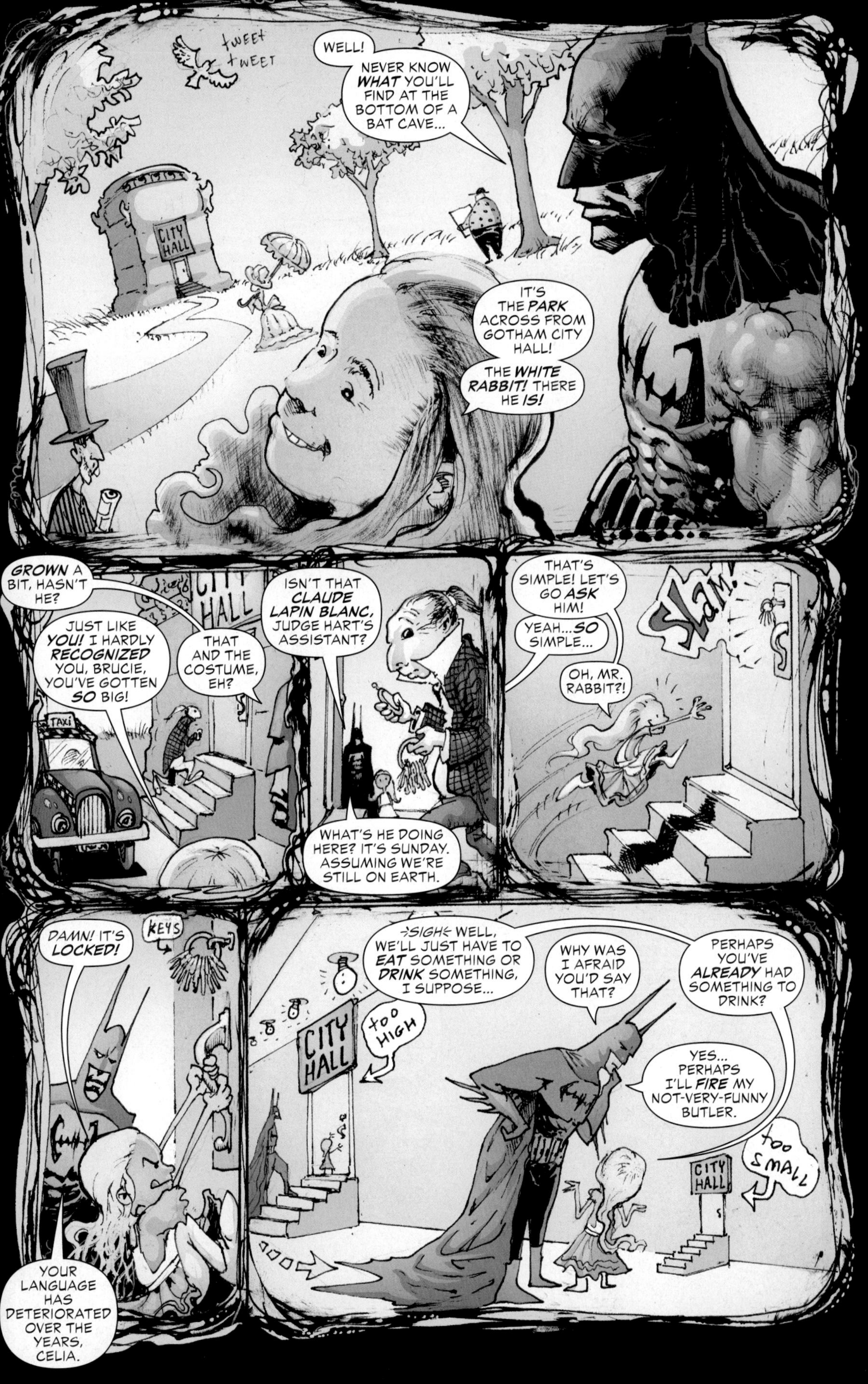
tweet tweet
WELL!
NEVER KNOW WHAT YOU'LL FIND AT THE BOTTOM OF A BAT CAVE...
CITY HALL
IT'S THE PARK ACROSS FROM GOTHAM CITY HALL!
THE WHITE RABBIT! THERE HE IS!
GROWN A BIT, HASN'T HE?
JUST LIKE YOU! I HARDLY RECOGNIZED YOU, BRUCIE, YOU'VE GOTTEN SO BIG!
THAT AND THE COSTUME, EH?
CITY HALL
TAXI
ISN'T THAT CLAUDE LAPIN BLANC, JUDGE HART'S ASSISTANT?
WHAT'S HE DOING HERE? IT'S SUNDAY. ASSUMING WE'RE STILL ON EARTH.
THAT'S SIMPLE! LET'S GO ASK HIM!
YEAH...SO SIMPLE...
OH, MR. RABBIT?!
SLAM!
DAMN! IT'S LOCKED!
KEYS
YOUR LANGUAGE HAS DETERIORATED OVER THE YEARS, CELIA.
SIGH WELL, WE'LL JUST HAVE TO EAT SOMETHING OR DRINK SOMETHING, I SUPPOSE...
WHY WAS I AFRAID YOU'D SAY THAT?
PERHAPS YOU'VE ALREADY HAD SOMETHING TO DRINK?
YES... PERHAPS I'LL FIRE MY NOT-VERY-FUNNY BUTLER.
CITY HALL
too HIGH
CITY HALL
too SMALL

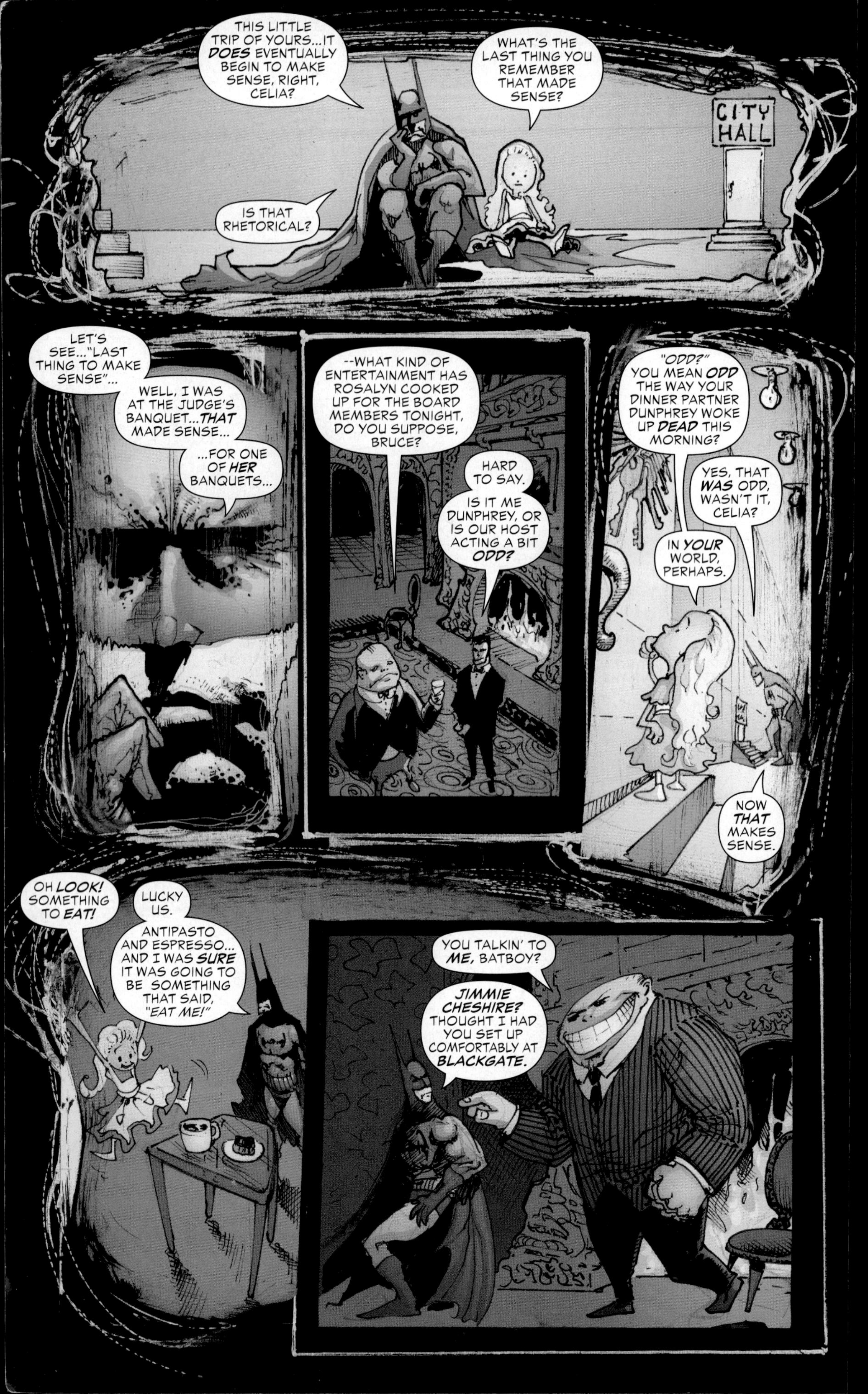
THIS LITTLE TRIP OF YOURS...IT DOES EVENTUALLY BEGIN TO MAKE SENSE, RIGHT, CELIA?
WHAT'S THE LAST THING YOU REMEMBER THAT MADE SENSE?
CITY HALL
IS THAT RHETORICAL?
LET'S SEE..."LAST THING TO MAKE SENSE"...
WELL, I WAS AT THE JUDGE'S BANQUET...THAT MADE SENSE...
...FOR ONE OF HER BANQUETS...
--WHAT KIND OF ENTERTAINMENT HAS ROSALYN COOKED UP FOR THE BOARD MEMBERS TONIGHT, DO YOU SUPPOSE, BRUCE?
HARD TO SAY.
IS IT ME DUNPHREY, OR IS OUR HOST ACTING A BIT ODD?
"ODD?" YOU MEAN ODD THE WAY YOUR DINNER PARTNER DUNPHREY WOKE UP DEAD THIS MORNING?
YES, THAT WAS ODD, WASN'T IT, CELIA?
IN YOUR WORLD, PERHAPS.
NOW THAT MAKES SENSE.
OH LOOK! SOMETHING TO EAT!
LUCKY US.
ANTIPASTO AND ESPRESSO... AND I WAS SURE IT WAS GOING TO BE SOMETHING THAT SAID, "EAT ME!"
YOU TALKIN' TO ME, BATBOY?
JIMMIE CHESHIRE? THOUGHT I HAD YOU SET UP COMFORTABLY AT BLACKGATE.

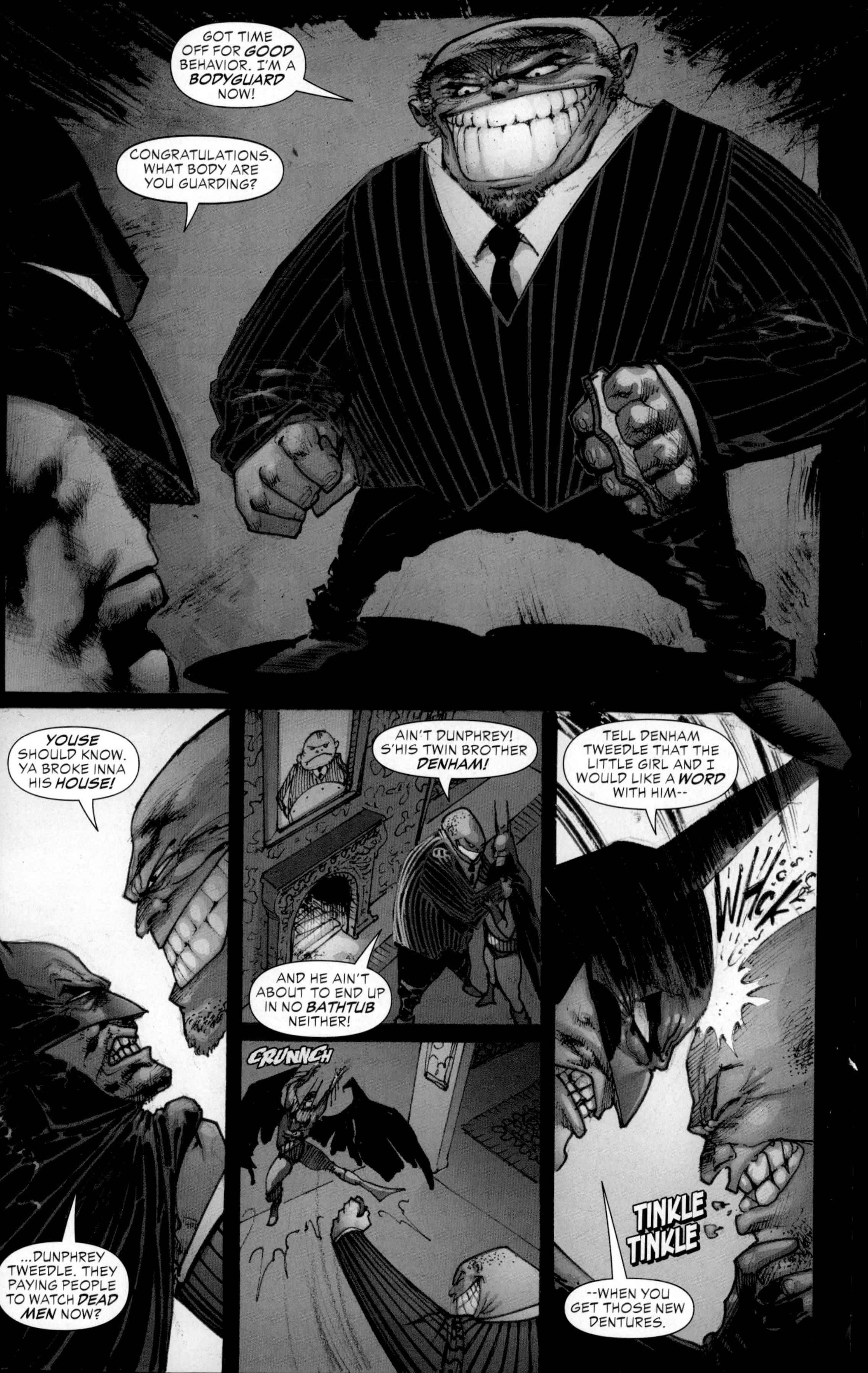
GOT TIME OFF FOR GOOD BEHAVIOR. I'M A BODYGUARD NOW!
CONGRATULATIONS. WHAT BODY ARE YOU GUARDING?
YOUSE SHOULD KNOW. YA BROKE INNA HIS HOUSE!
...DUNPHREY TWEEDLE. THEY PAYING PEOPLE TO WATCH DEAD MEN NOW?
AIN'T DUNPHREY! S'HIS TWIN BROTHER DENHAM!
AND HE AIN'T ABOUT TO END UP IN NO BATHTUB NEITHER!
CRUNNCH
TELL DENHAM TWEEDLE THAT THE LITTLE GIRL AND I WOULD LIKE A WORD WITH HIM--
WHACK
TINKLE TINKLE
--WHEN YOU GET THOSE NEW DENTURES.

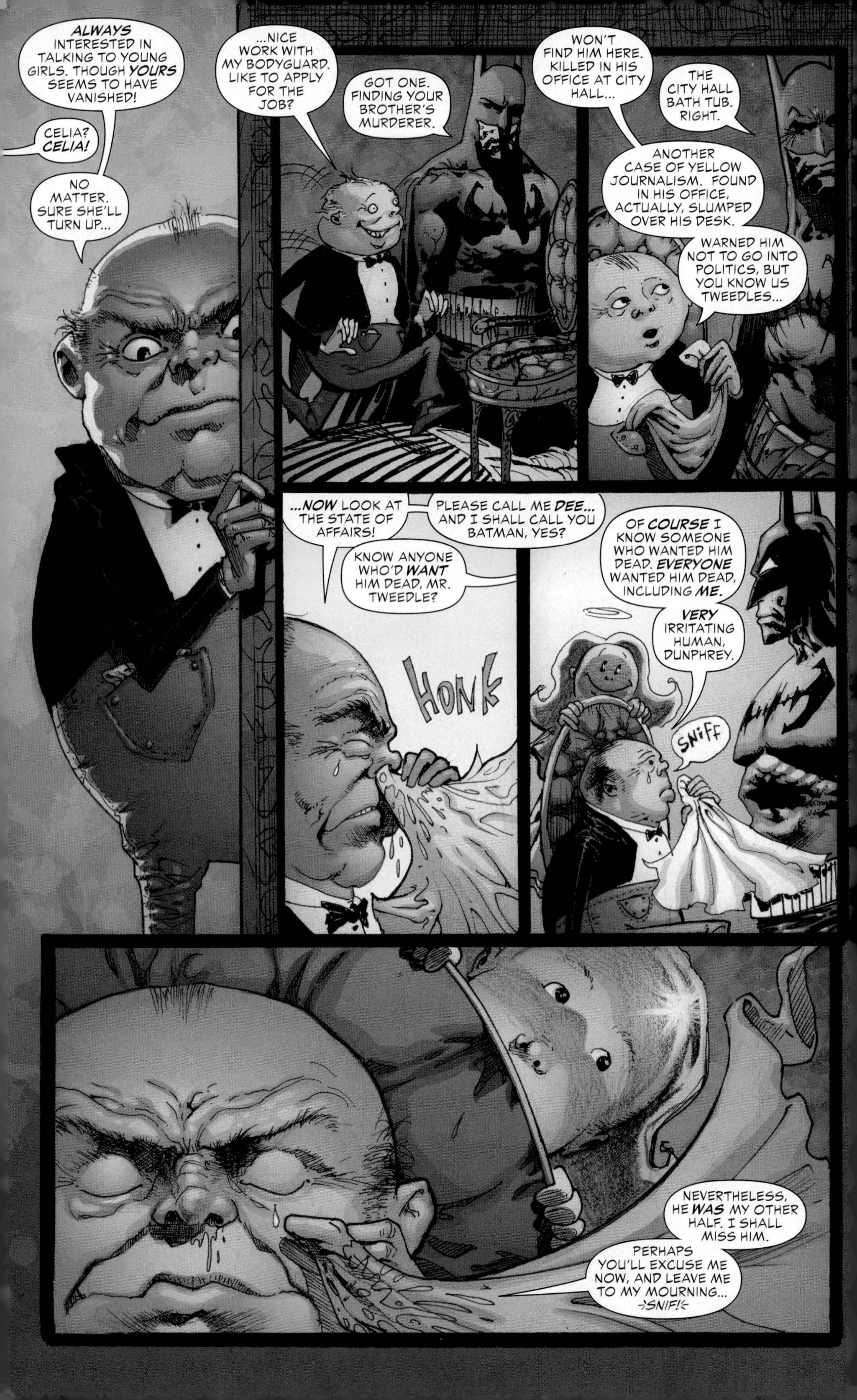
ALWAYS INTERESTED IN TALKING TO YOUNG GIRLS. THOUGH YOURS SEEMS TO HAVE VANISHED!
CELIA? CELIA!
NO MATTER. SURE SHE'LL TURN UP...
...NICE WORK WITH MY BODYGUARD. LIKE TO APPLY FOR THE JOB?
GOT ONE. FINDING YOUR BROTHER'S MURDERER.
WON'T FIND HIM HERE. KILLED IN HIS OFFICE AT CITY HALL...
THE CITY HALL BATH TUB. RIGHT.
ANOTHER CASE OF YELLOW JOURNALISM. FOUND IN HIS OFFICE, ACTUALLY, SLUMPED OVER HIS DESK.
WARNED HIM NOT TO GO INTO POLITICS, BUT YOU KNOW US TWEEDLES...
...NOW LOOK AT THE STATE OF AFFAIRS!
PLEASE CALL ME DEE... AND I SHALL CALL YOU BATMAN, YES?
KNOW ANYONE WHO'D WANT HIM DEAD, MR. TWEEDLE?
HONK
OF COURSE I KNOW SOMEONE WHO WANTED HIM DEAD. EVERYONE WANTED HIM DEAD, INCLUDING ME.
VERY IRRITATING HUMAN, DUNPHREY.
SNIFF
NEVERTHELESS, HE WAS MY OTHER HALF. I SHALL MISS HIM.
PERHAPS YOU'LL EXCUSE ME NOW, AND LEAVE ME TO MY MOURNING... SNIF!

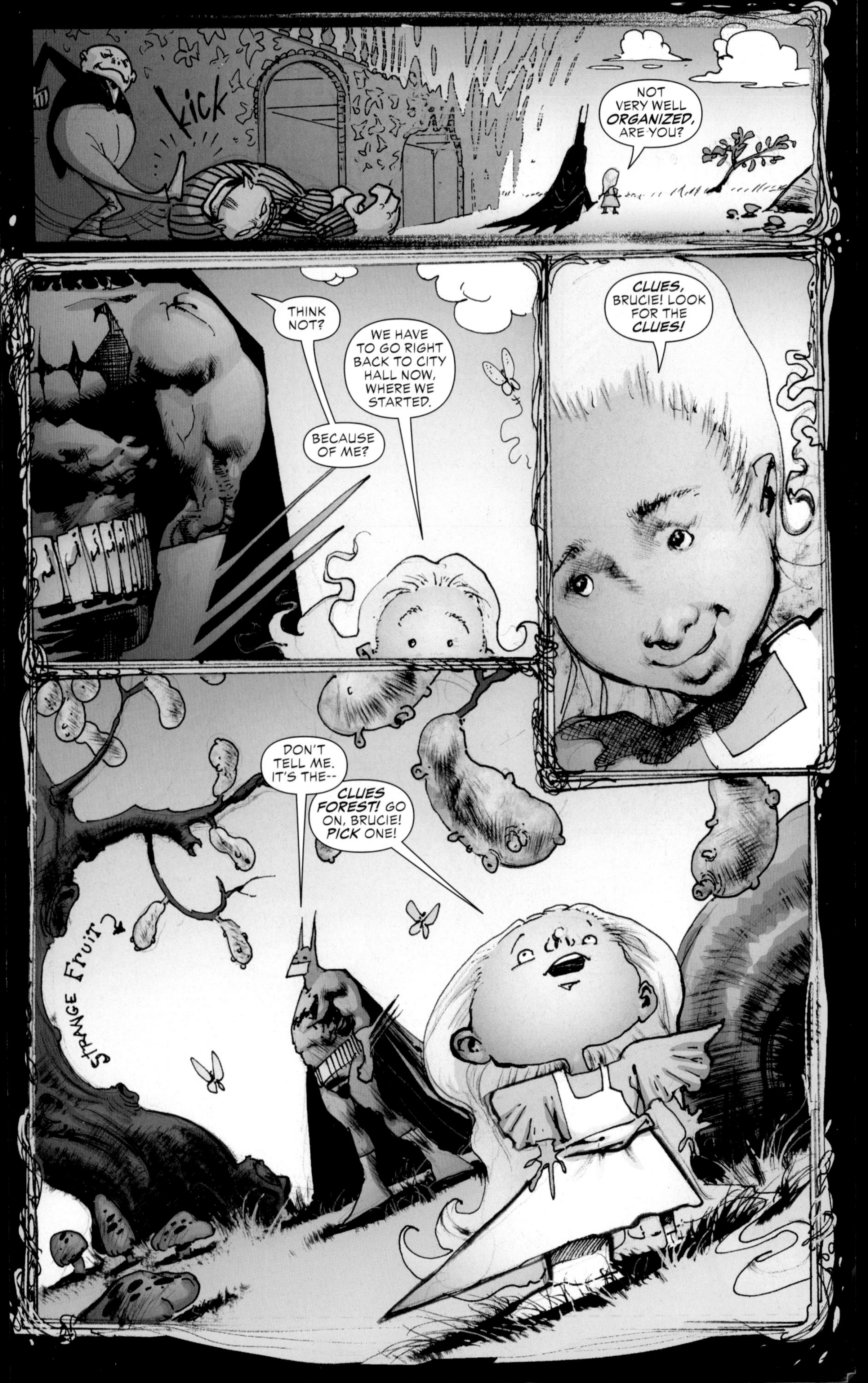
KICK
NOT VERY WELL ORGANIZED, ARE YOU?
THINK NOT?
BECAUSE OF ME?
WE HAVE TO GO RIGHT BACK TO CITY HALL NOW, WHERE WE STARTED.
CLUES, BRUCIE! LOOK FOR THE CLUES!
DON'T TELL ME. IT'S THE--
CLUES FOREST! GO ON, BRUCIE! PICK ONE!
STRANGE Fruit

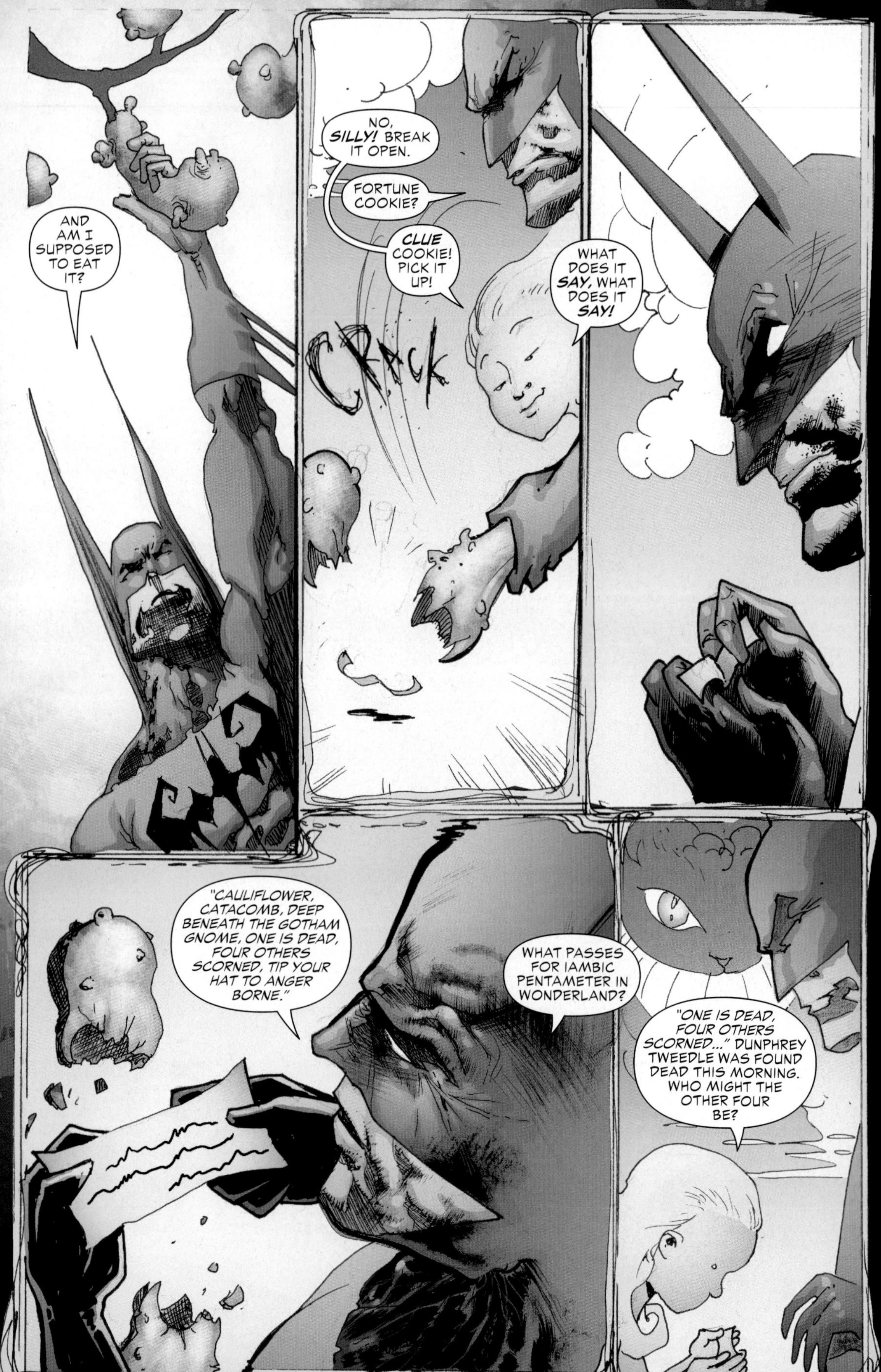
AND AM I SUPPOSED TO EAT IT?
FORTUNE COOKIE?
NO, SILLY! BREAK IT OPEN.
CLUE COOKIE! PICK IT UP!
CRACK
WHAT DOES IT SAY, WHAT DOES IT SAY!
"CAULIFLOWER, CATACOMB, DEEP BENEATH THE GOTHAM GNOME, ONE IS DEAD, FOUR OTHERS SCORNED, TIP YOUR HAT TO ANGER BORNE."
WHAT PASSES FOR IAMBIC PENTAMETER IN WONDERLAND?
"ONE IS DEAD, FOUR OTHERS SCORNED..." DUNPHREY TWEEDLE WAS FOUND DEAD THIS MORNING. WHO MIGHT THE OTHER FOUR BE?

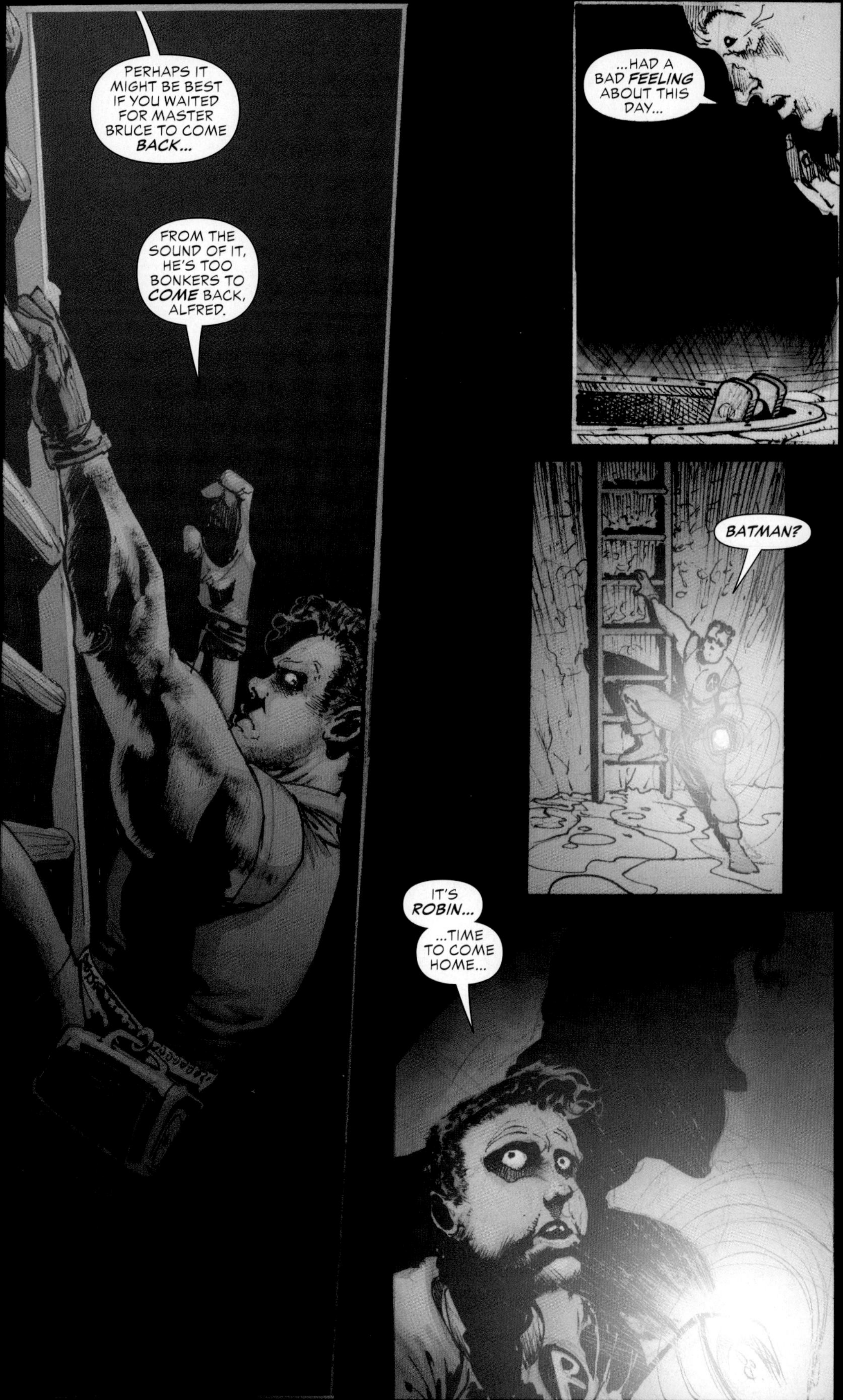
PERHAPS IT MIGHT BE BEST IF YOU WAITED FOR MASTER BRUCE TO COME BACK...
FROM THE SOUND OF IT, HE'S TOO BONKERS TO COME BACK, ALFRED.
...HAD A BAD FEELING ABOUT THIS DAY...
BATMAN?
IT'S ROBIN...
...TIME TO COME HOME...

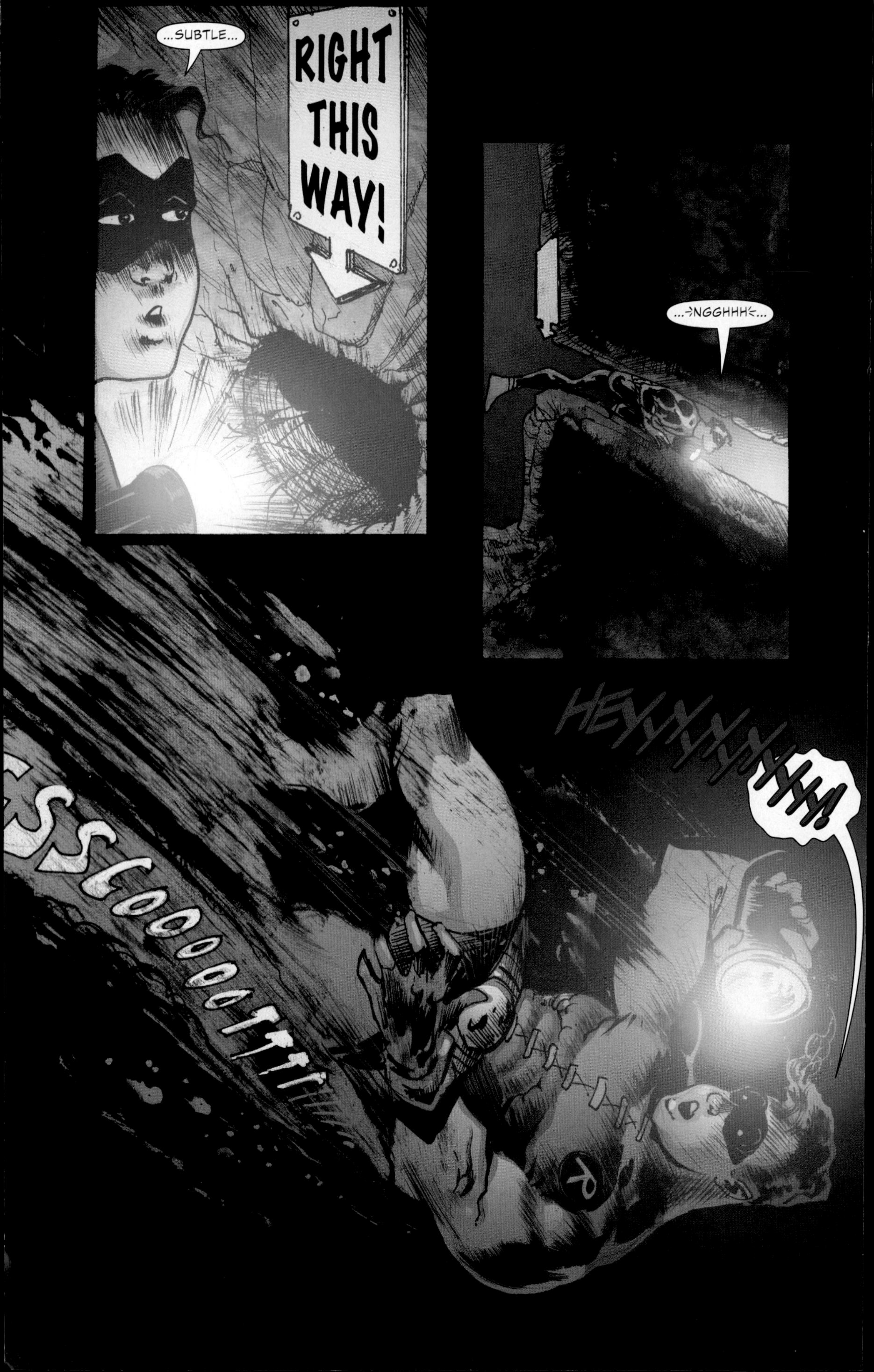
...SUBTLE...
RIGHT THIS WAY!
...NGGHHH...

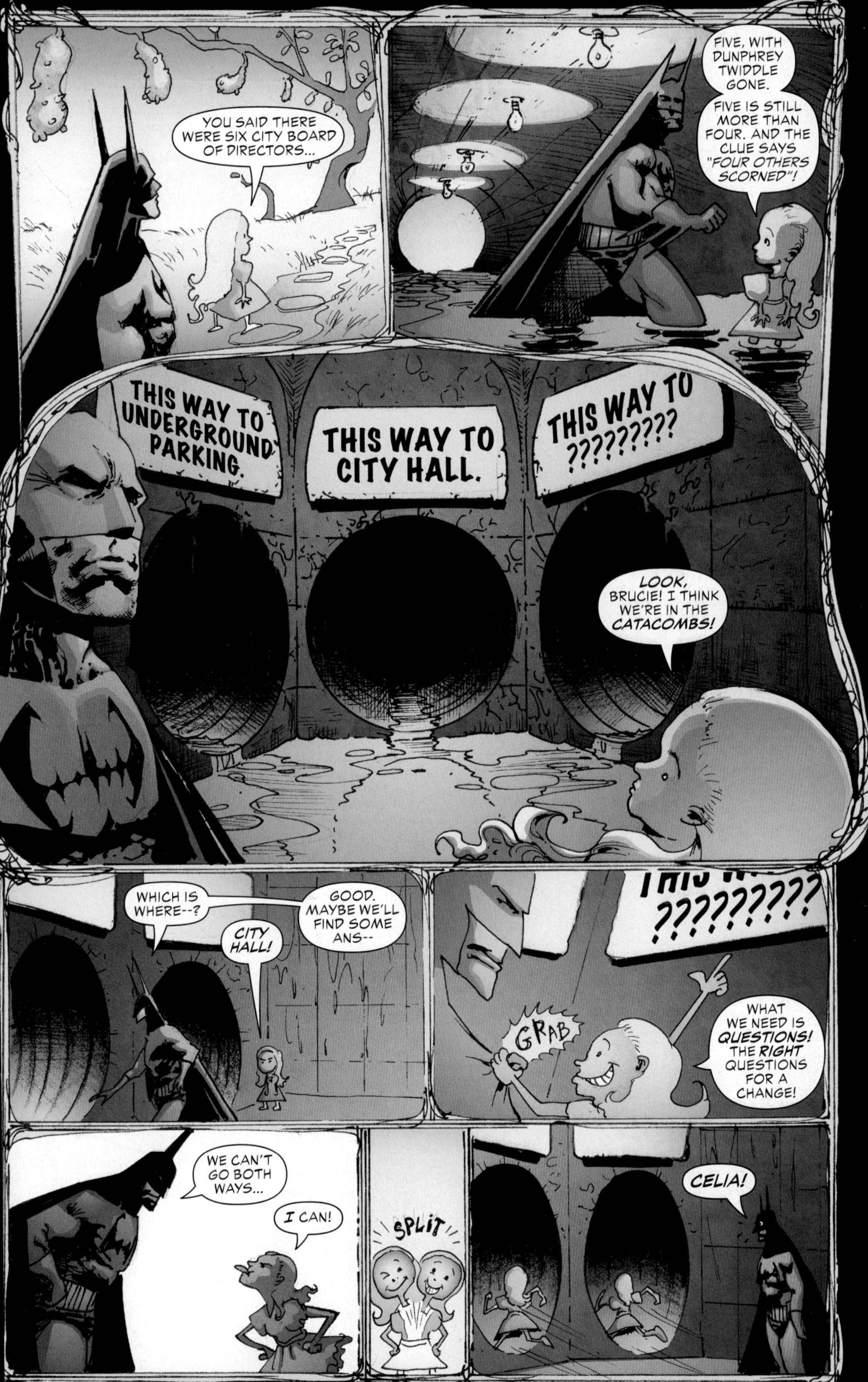
YOU SAID THERE WERE SIX CITY BOARD OF DIRECTORS...
FIVE, WITH DUNPHREY TWIDDLE GONE.
FIVE IS STILL MORE THAN FOUR. AND THE CLUE SAYS "FOUR OTHERS SCORNED"!
THIS WAY TO UNDERGROUND PARKING.
THIS WAY TO CITY HALL.
THIS WAY TO ?????????
LOOK, BRUCIE! I THINK WE'RE IN THE CATACOMBS!
WHICH IS WHERE--?
CITY HALL!
GOOD. MAYBE WE'LL FIND SOME ANS--
?????????
GRAB
WHAT WE NEED IS QUESTIONS! THE RIGHT QUESTIONS FOR A CHANGE!
WE CAN'T GO BOTH WAYS...
I CAN!
SPLIT
CELIA!

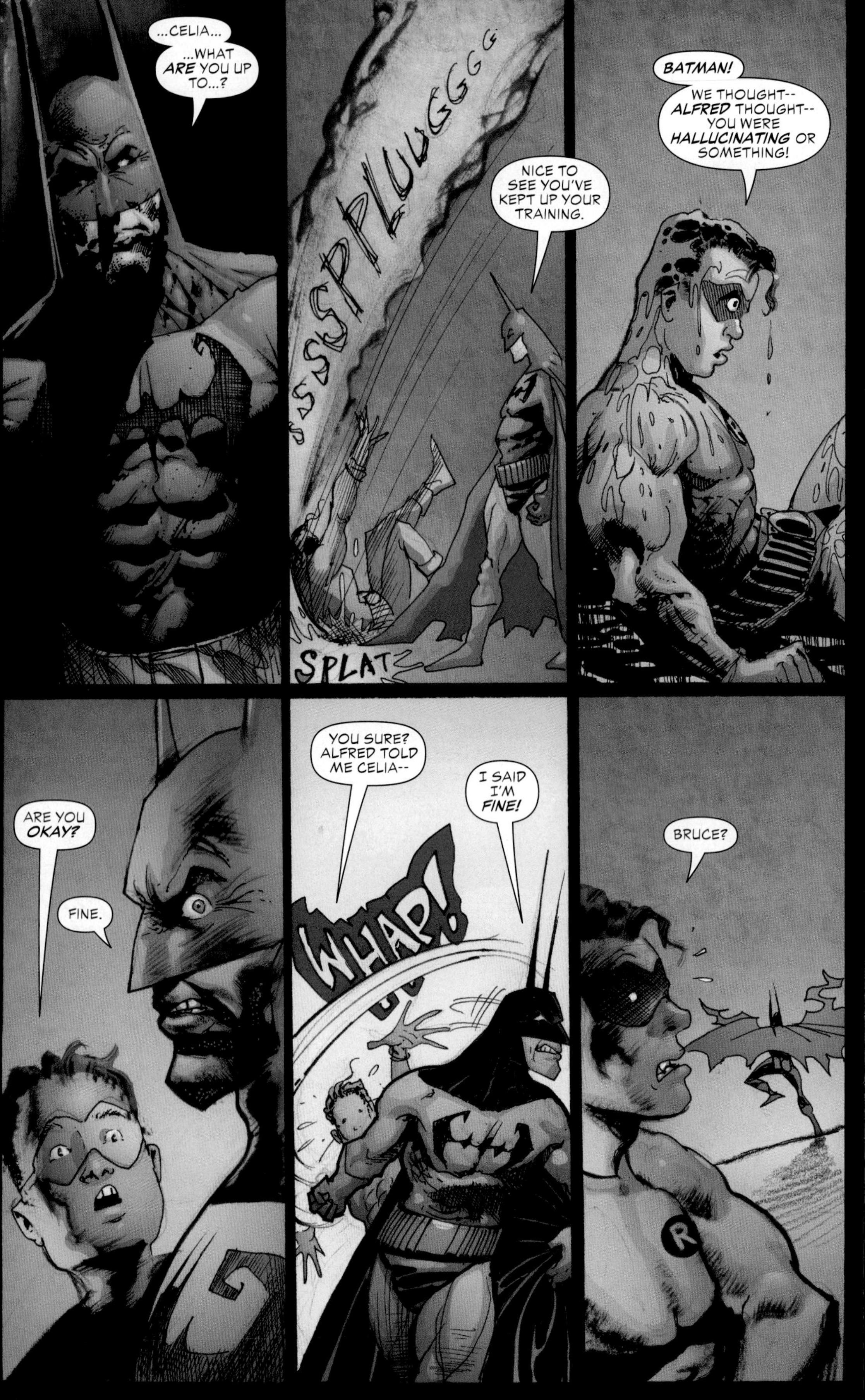
...CELIA...
...WHAT ARE YOU UP TO...?
SSSSSPLUGGGG
SPLAT
NICE TO SEE YOU'VE KEPT UP YOUR TRAINING.
BATMAN!
WE THOUGHT-- ALFRED THOUGHT-- YOU WERE HALLUCINATING OR SOMETHING!
ARE YOU OKAY?
FINE.
YOU SURE? ALFRED TOLD ME CELIA--
I SAID I'M FINE!
WHAP!
BRUCE?

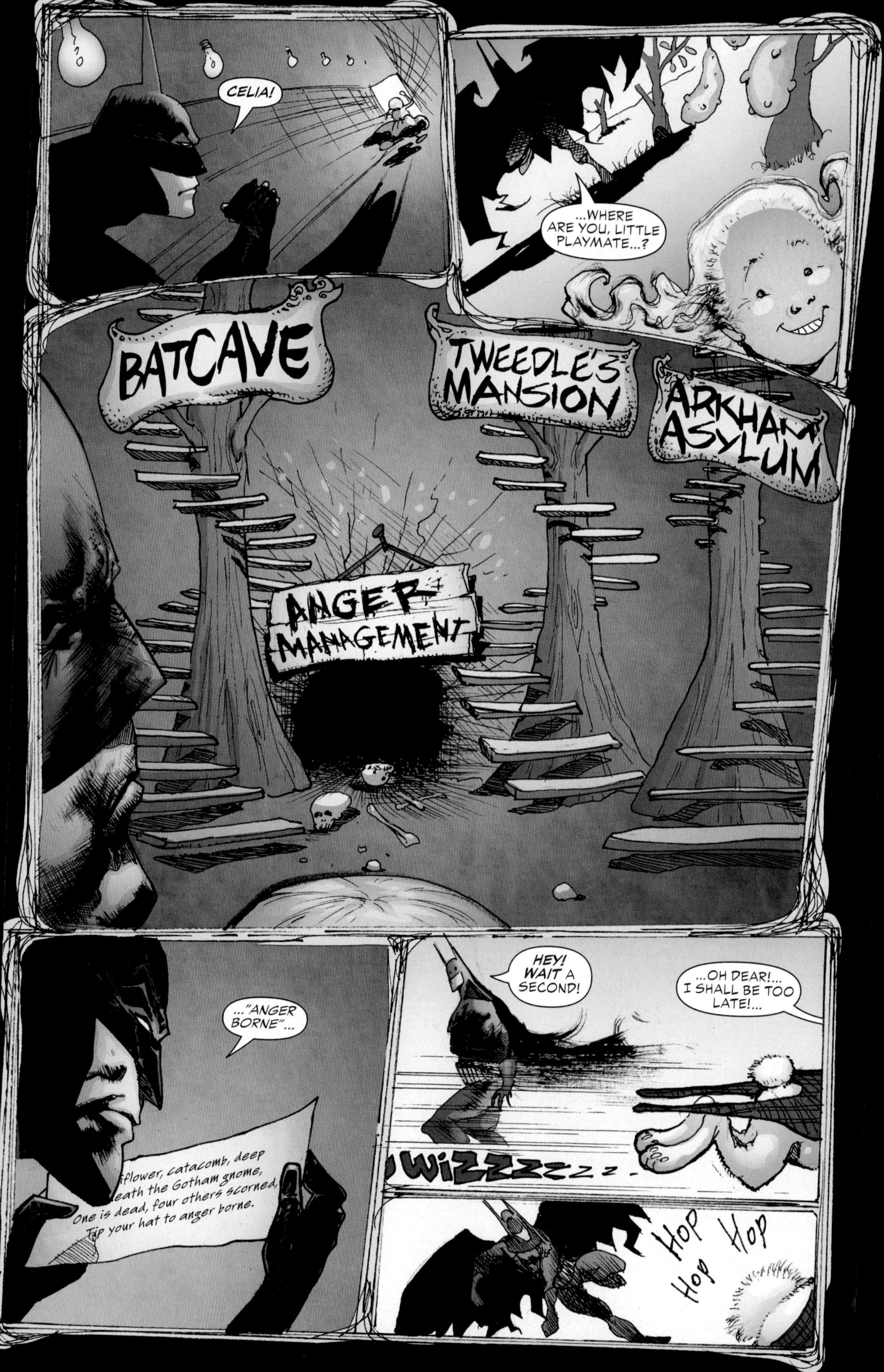
CELIA!
...WHERE ARE YOU, LITTLE PLAYMATE...?
BATCAVE
TWEEDLE'S MANSION
ARKHAM ASYLUM
ANGER MANAGEMENT
..."ANGER BORNE"...
iflower, catacomb, deep
eath the Gotham gnome,
One is dead, four others scorned,
Tip your hat to anger borne.
HEY! WAIT A SECOND!
...OH DEAR!... I SHALL BE TOO LATE!...
WIZZZZZZZ
HOP HOP HOP

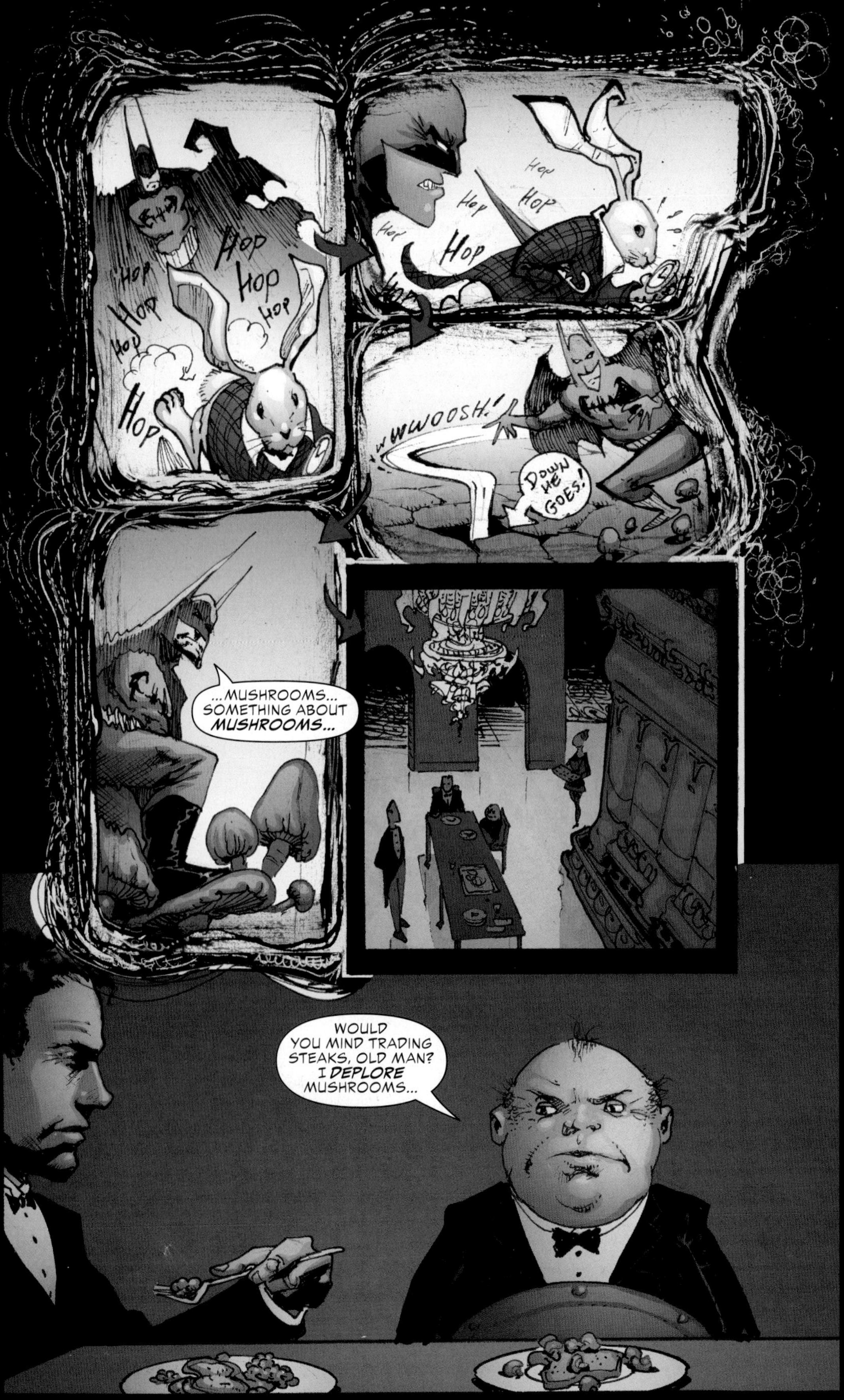
HOP
HOP
HOP
HOP
HOP
HOP
HOP
HOP
HOP
HOP
HOP
WWWOOSH!
DOWN HE GOES!
...MUSHROOMS...
SOMETHING ABOUT
MUSHROOMS...
WOULD
YOU MIND TRADING
STEAKS, OLD MAN?
I DEPLORE
MUSHROOMS...

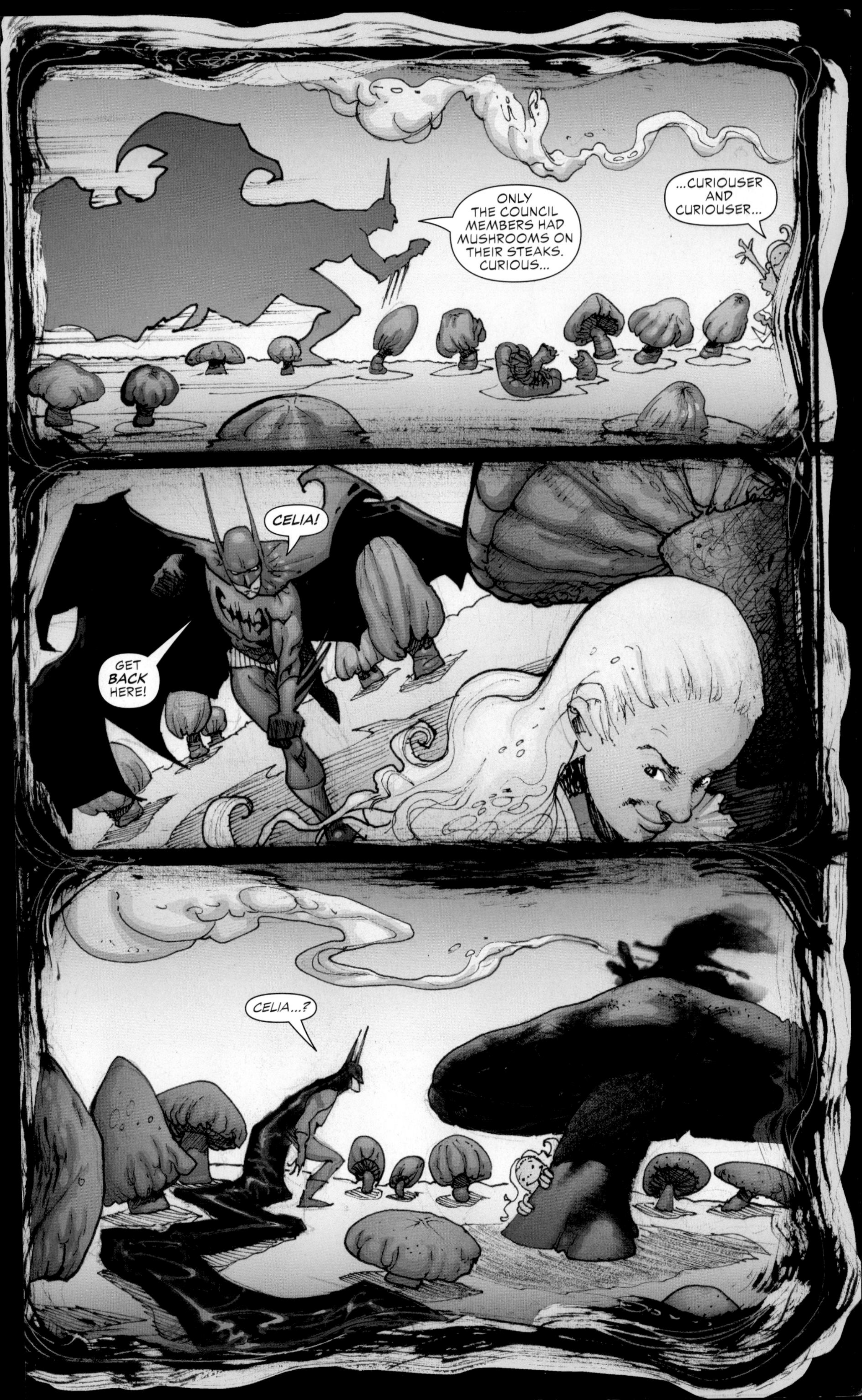
ONLY THE COUNCIL MEMBERS HAD MUSHROOMS ON THEIR STEAKS. CURIOUS...
...CURIOUSER AND CURIOUSER...
CELIA!
GET BACK HERE!
CELIA...?

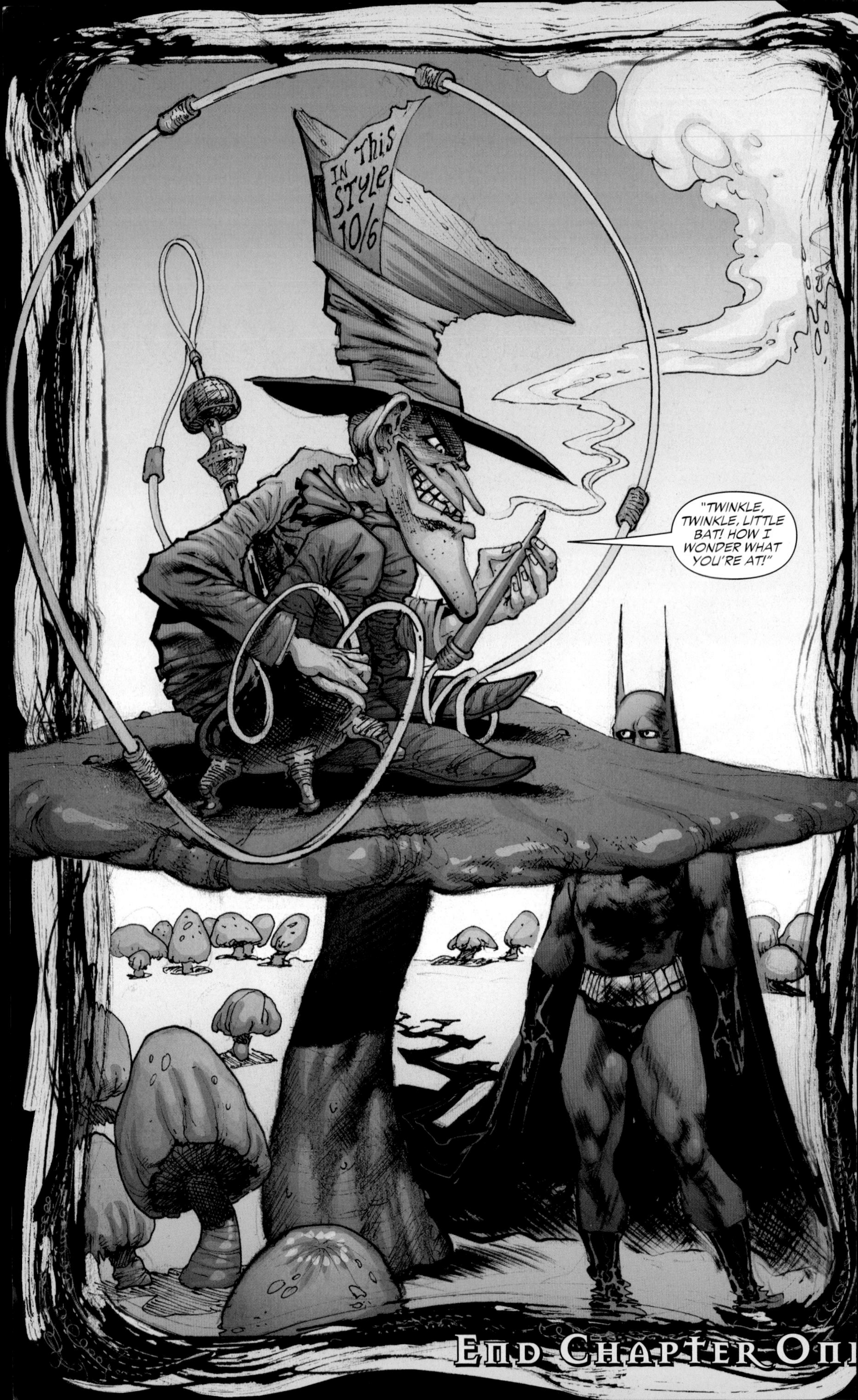
IN THIS STYLE 10/6
"TWINKLE, TWINKLE, LITTLE BAT! HOW I WONDER WHAT YOU'RE AT!"
END CHAPTER ONE

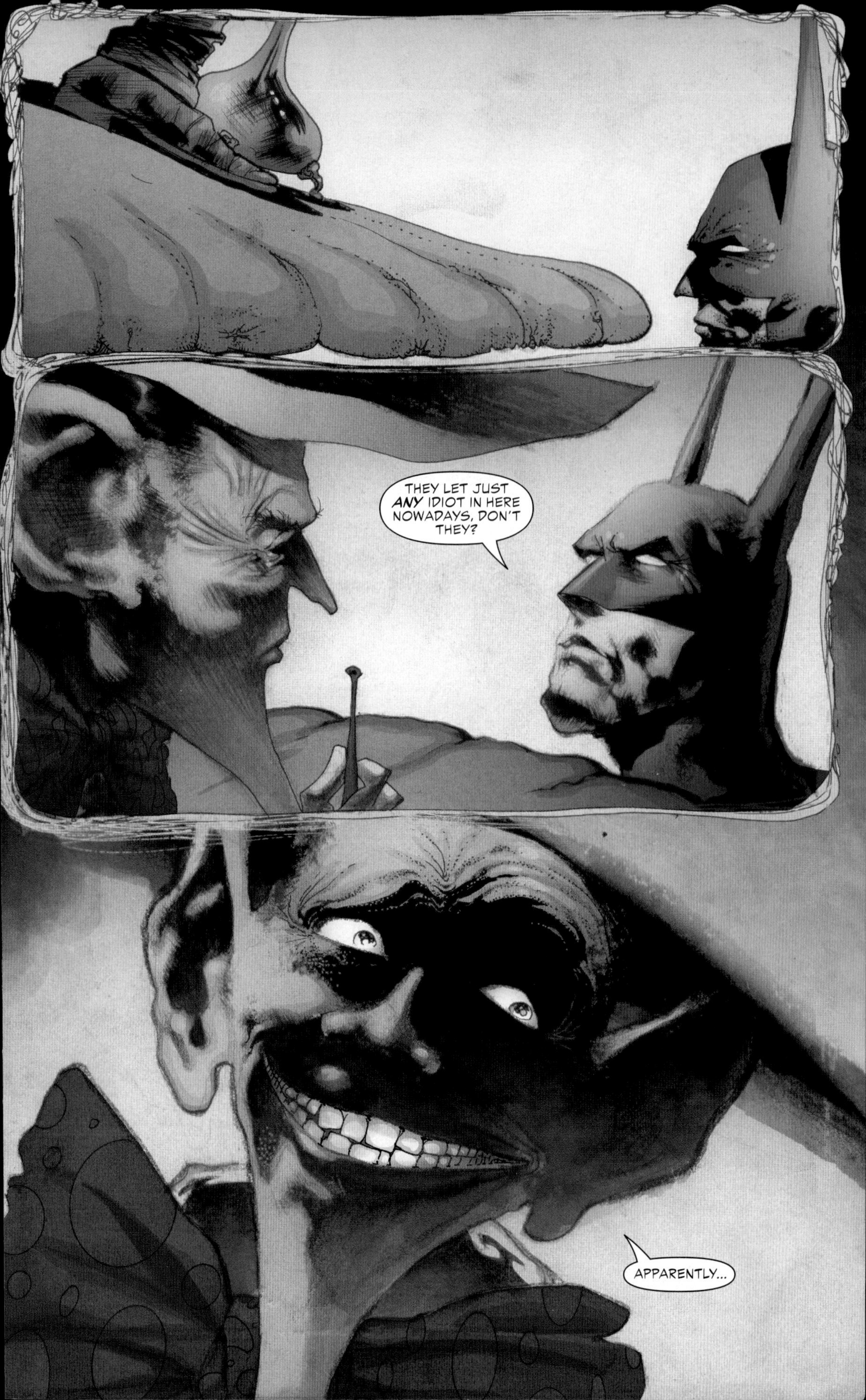
THEY LET JUST ANY IDIOT IN HERE NOWADAYS, DON'T THEY?
APPARENTLY...

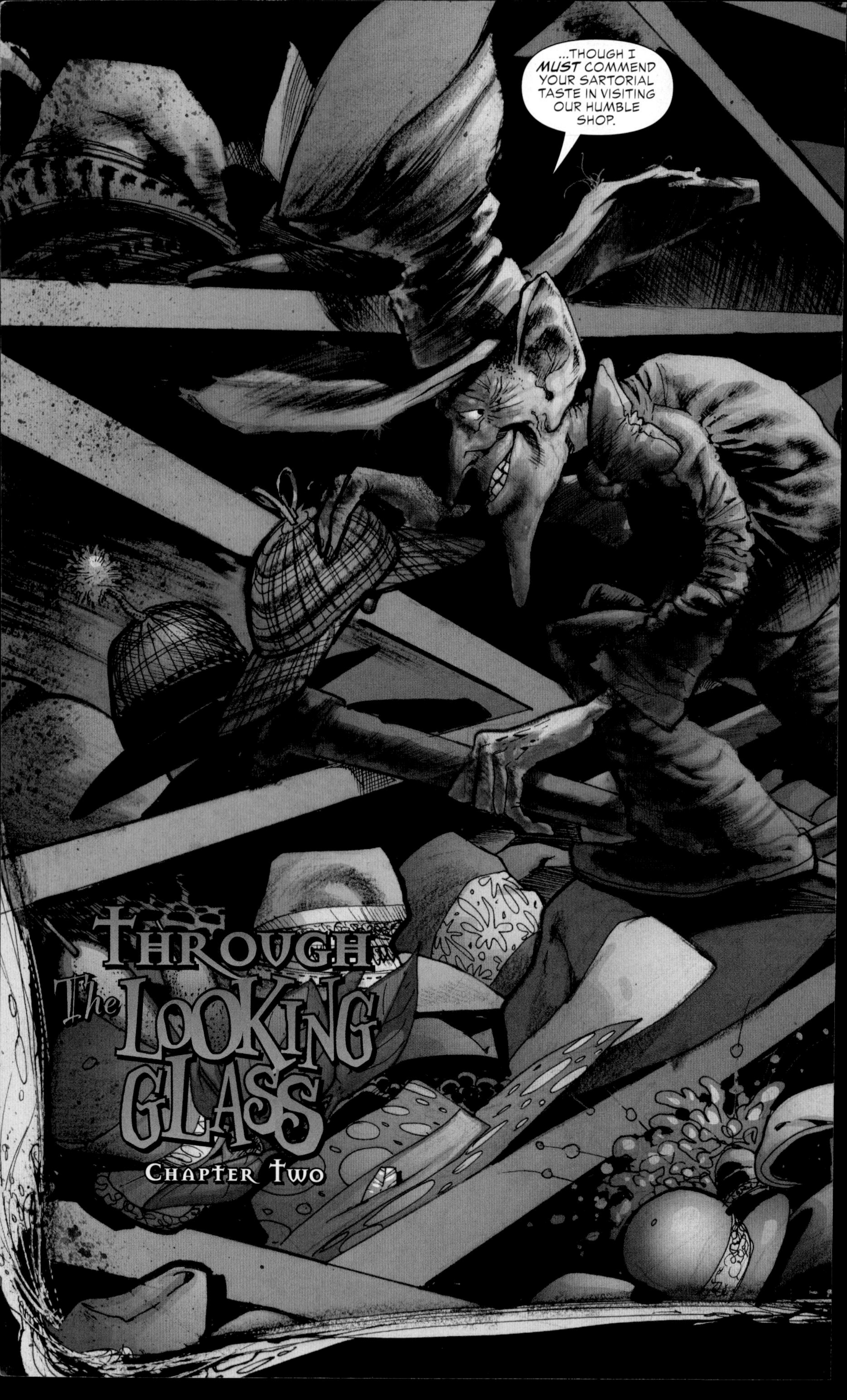
...THOUGH I MUST COMMEND YOUR SARTORIAL TASTE IN VISITING OUR HUMBLE SHOP.
THROUGH THE LOOKING GLASS
CHAPTER TWO

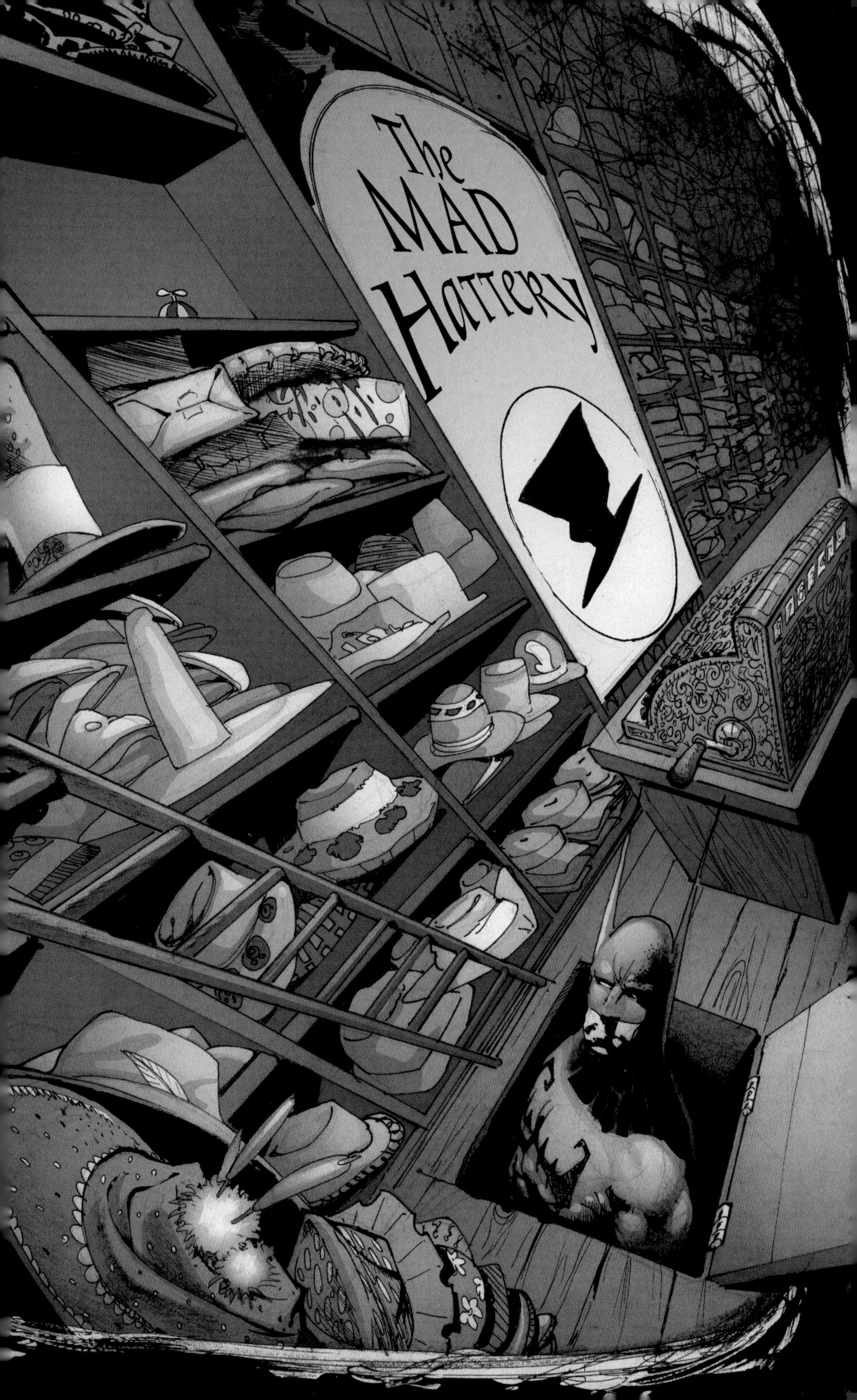
The MAD Hattery

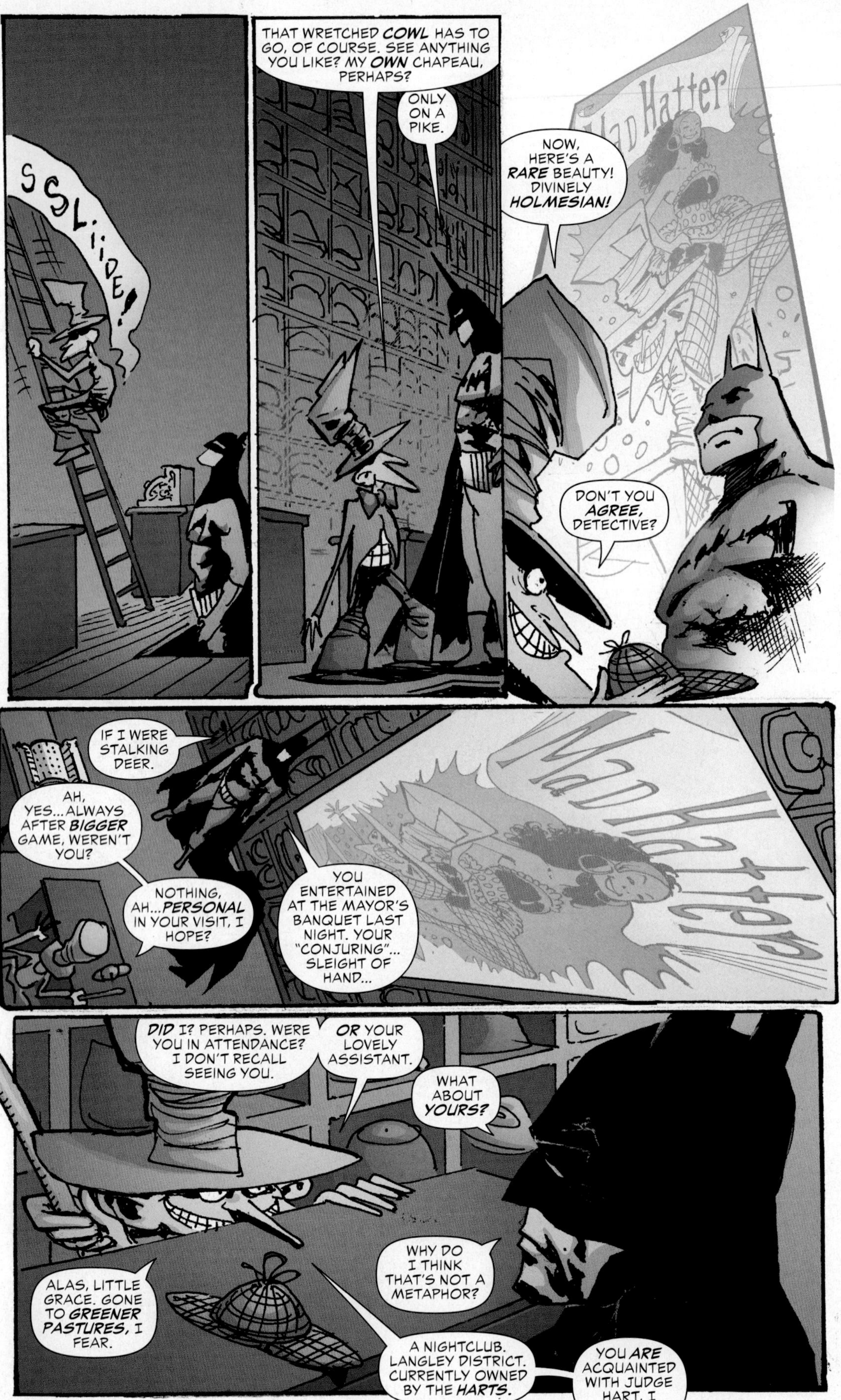
SSLiiiDE!
THAT WRETCHED COWL HAS TO GO, OF COURSE. SEE ANYTHING YOU LIKE? MY OWN CHAPEAU, PERHAPS?
ONLY ON A PIKE.
NOW, HERE'S A RARE BEAUTY! DIVINELY HOLMESIAN!
Mad Hatter
DON'T YOU AGREE, DETECTIVE?
IF I WERE STALKING DEER.
AH, YES...ALWAYS AFTER BIGGER GAME, WEREN'T YOU?
NOTHING, AH...PERSONAL IN YOUR VISIT, I HOPE?
YOU ENTERTAINED AT THE MAYOR'S BANQUET LAST NIGHT. YOUR "CONJURING"... SLEIGHT OF HAND...
Mad Hatter
DID I? PERHAPS. WERE YOU IN ATTENDANCE? I DON'T RECALL SEEING YOU.
OR YOUR LOVELY ASSISTANT.
WHAT ABOUT YOURS?
ALAS, LITTLE GRACE. GONE TO GREENER PASTURES, I FEAR.
WHY DO I THINK THAT'S NOT A METAPHOR?
A NIGHTCLUB. LANGLEY DISTRICT. CURRENTLY OWNED BY THE HARTS.
YOU ARE ACQUAINTED WITH JUDGE HART, I PRESUME?

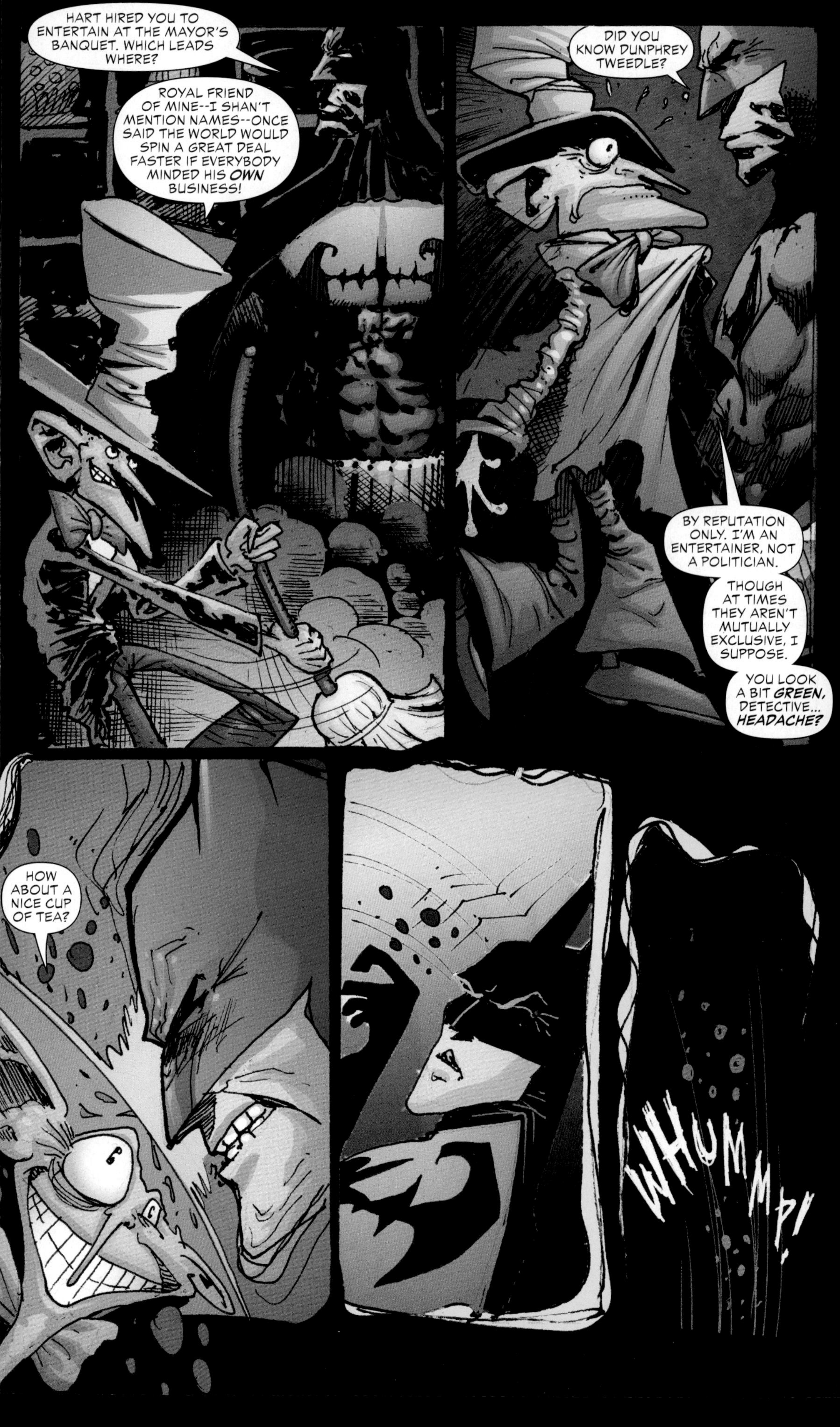
HART HIRED YOU TO ENTERTAIN AT THE MAYOR'S BANQUET. WHICH LEADS WHERE?
ROYAL FRIEND OF MINE--I SHAN'T MENTION NAMES--ONCE SAID THE WORLD WOULD SPIN A GREAT DEAL FASTER IF EVERYBODY MINDED HIS *OWN* BUSINESS!
DID YOU KNOW DUNPHREY TWEEDLE?
BY REPUTATION ONLY. I'M AN ENTERTAINER, NOT A POLITICIAN.
THOUGH AT TIMES THEY AREN'T MUTUALLY EXCLUSIVE, I SUPPOSE.
YOU LOOK A BIT *GREEN,* DETECTIVE... *HEADACHE?*
HOW ABOUT A NICE CUP OF TEA?
WHUMMP!

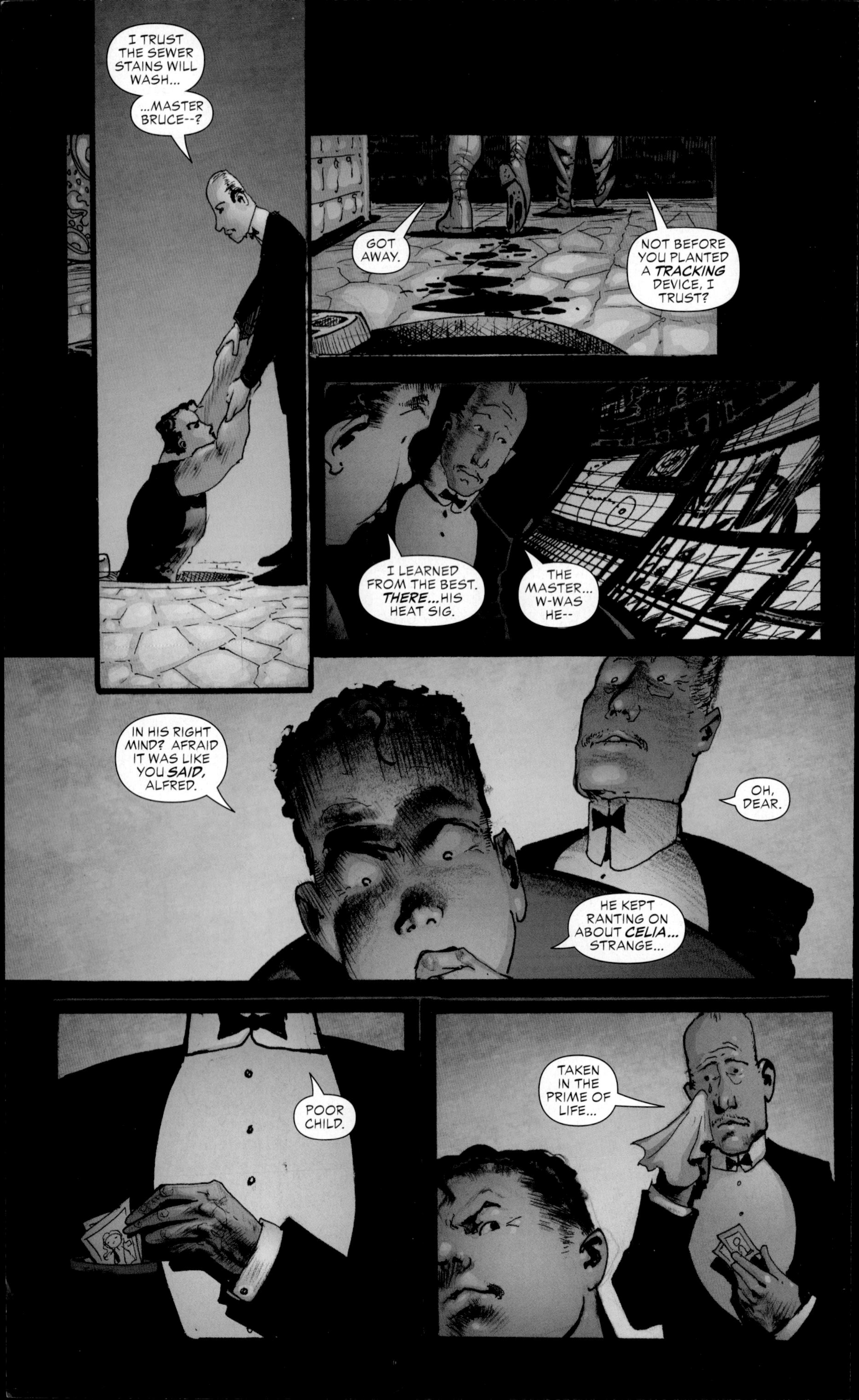
I TRUST THE SEWER STAINS WILL WASH...
...MASTER BRUCE--?
GOT AWAY.
NOT BEFORE YOU PLANTED A **TRACKING** DEVICE, I TRUST?
I LEARNED FROM THE BEST. **THERE...**HIS HEAT SIG.
THE MASTER... W-WAS HE--
IN HIS RIGHT MIND? AFRAID IT WAS LIKE YOU **SAID,** ALFRED.
OH, DEAR.
HE KEPT RANTING ON ABOUT **CELIA...** STRANGE...
POOR CHILD.
TAKEN IN THE PRIME OF LIFE...

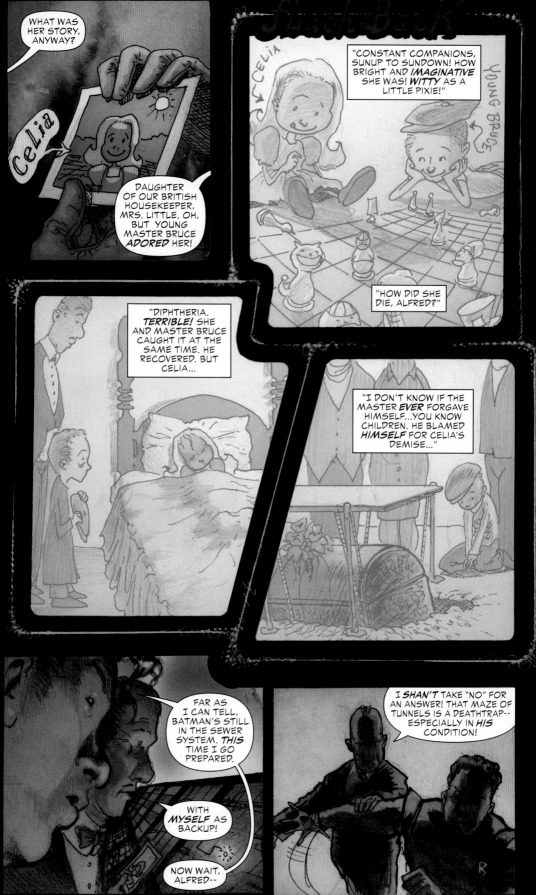

WHAT WAS HER STORY, ANYWAY?

Celia

DAUGHTER OF OUR BRITISH HOUSEKEEPER, MRS. LITTLE. OH, BUT YOUNG MASTER BRUCE *ADORED* HER!

CELIA

YOUNG BRUCE

"CONSTANT COMPANIONS, SUNUP TO SUNDOWN! HOW BRIGHT AND *IMAGINATIVE* SHE WAS! *WITTY* AS A LITTLE PIXIE!"

"HOW DID SHE DIE, ALFRED?"

"DIPHTHERIA. *TERRIBLE!* SHE AND MASTER BRUCE CAUGHT IT AT THE SAME TIME. HE RECOVERED. BUT CELIA..."

"I DON'T KNOW IF THE MASTER *EVER* FORGAVE HIMSELF...YOU KNOW CHILDREN. HE BLAMED *HIMSELF* FOR CELIA'S DEMISE..."

FAR AS I CAN TELL, BATMAN'S STILL IN THE SEWER SYSTEM. *THIS* TIME I GO PREPARED.

WITH *MYSELF* AS BACKUP!

NOW WAIT, ALFRED--

I *SHAN'T* TAKE "NO" FOR AN ANSWER! THAT MAZE OF TUNNELS IS A DEATHTRAP-- ESPECIALLY IN *HIS* CONDITION!

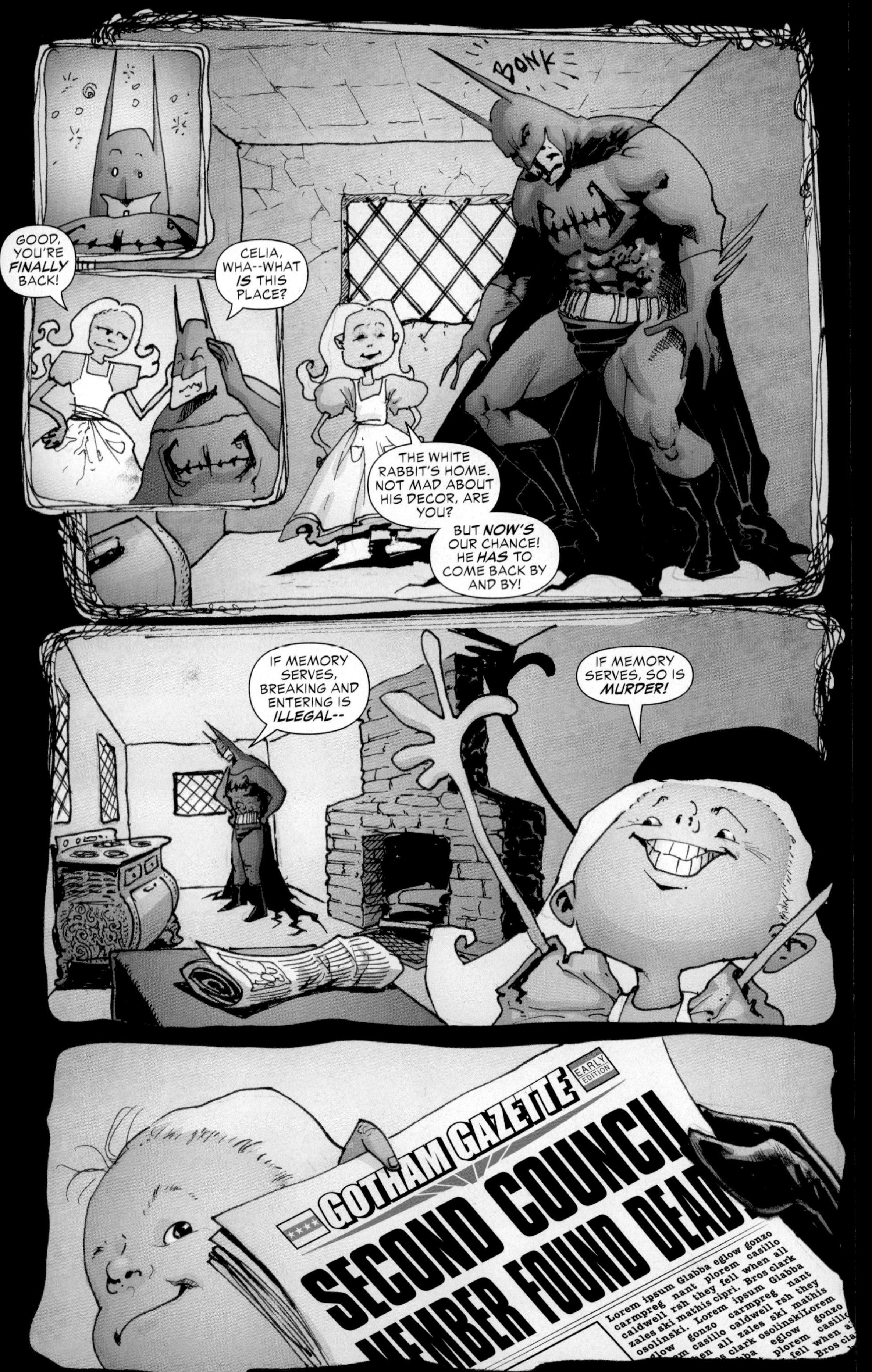
BONK
GOOD, YOU'RE *FINALLY* BACK!
CELIA, WHA--WHAT *IS* THIS PLACE?
THE WHITE RABBIT'S HOME. NOT MAD ABOUT HIS DECOR, ARE YOU?
BUT *NOW'S* OUR CHANCE! HE *HAS* TO COME BACK BY AND BY!
IF MEMORY SERVES, BREAKING AND ENTERING IS *ILLEGAL*--
IF MEMORY SERVES, SO IS *MURDER!*
GOTHAM GAZETTE
EARLY EDITION
SECOND COUNCIL
MEMBER FOUND DEAD

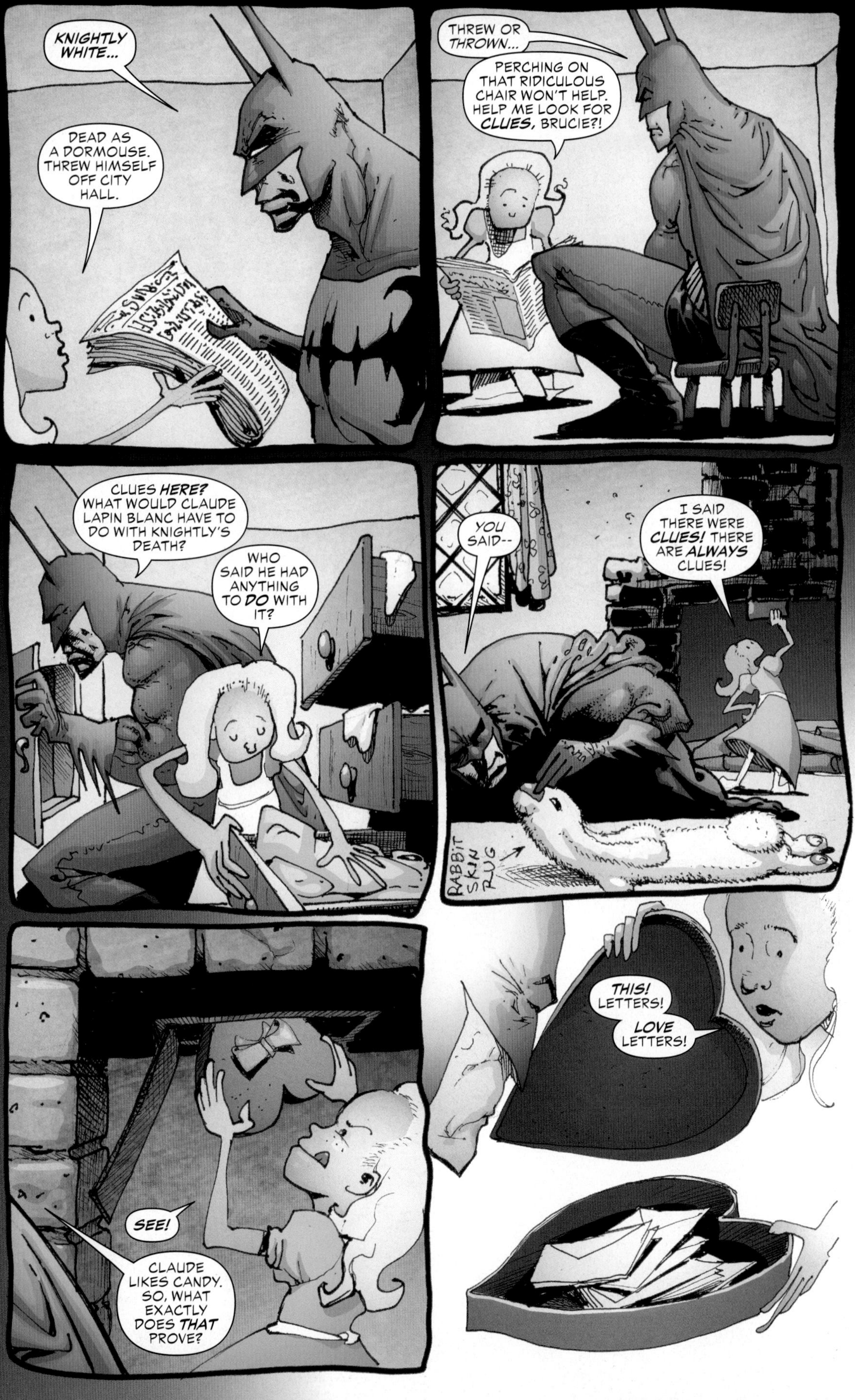
KNIGHTLY WHITE...
DEAD AS A DORMOUSE. THREW HIMSELF OFF CITY HALL.
THREW OR THROWN...
PERCHING ON THAT RIDICULOUS CHAIR WON'T HELP. HELP ME LOOK FOR CLUES, BRUCIE?!
CLUES HERE? WHAT WOULD CLAUDE LAPIN BLANC HAVE TO DO WITH KNIGHTLY'S DEATH?
WHO SAID HE HAD ANYTHING TO DO WITH IT?
YOU SAID--
I SAID THERE WERE CLUES! THERE ARE ALWAYS CLUES!
RABBIT SKIN RUG
SEE!
CLAUDE LIKES CANDY. SO, WHAT EXACTLY DOES THAT PROVE?
THIS! LETTERS!
LOVE LETTERS!

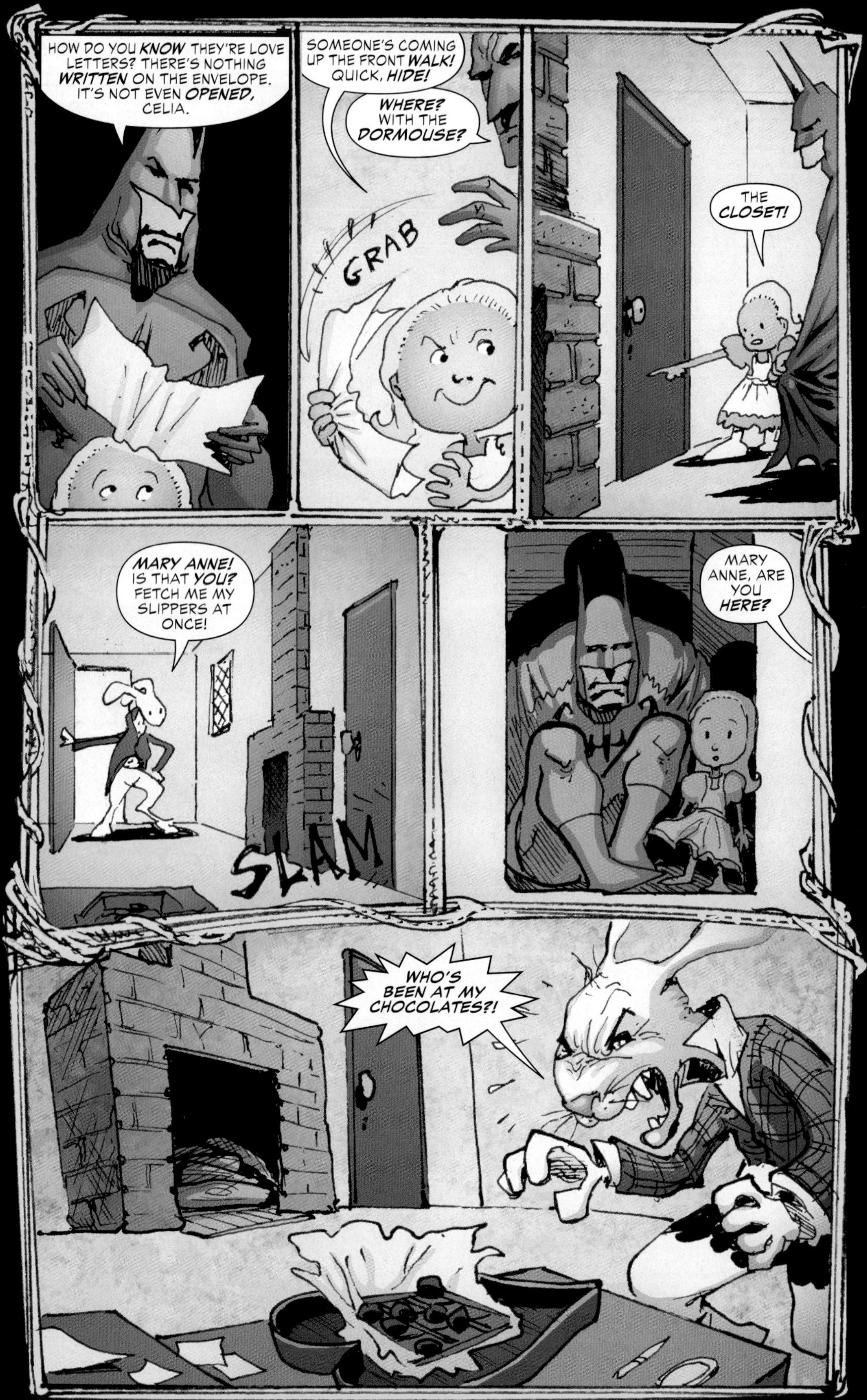
HOW DO YOU KNOW THEY'RE LOVE LETTERS? THERE'S NOTHING WRITTEN ON THE ENVELOPE. IT'S NOT EVEN OPENED, CELIA.
SOMEONE'S COMING UP THE FRONT WALK! QUICK, HIDE!
WHERE? WITH THE DORMOUSE?
GRAB
THE CLOSET!
MARY ANNE! IS THAT YOU? FETCH ME MY SLIPPERS AT ONCE!
SLAM
MARY ANNE, ARE YOU HERE?
WHO'S BEEN AT MY CHOCOLATES?!

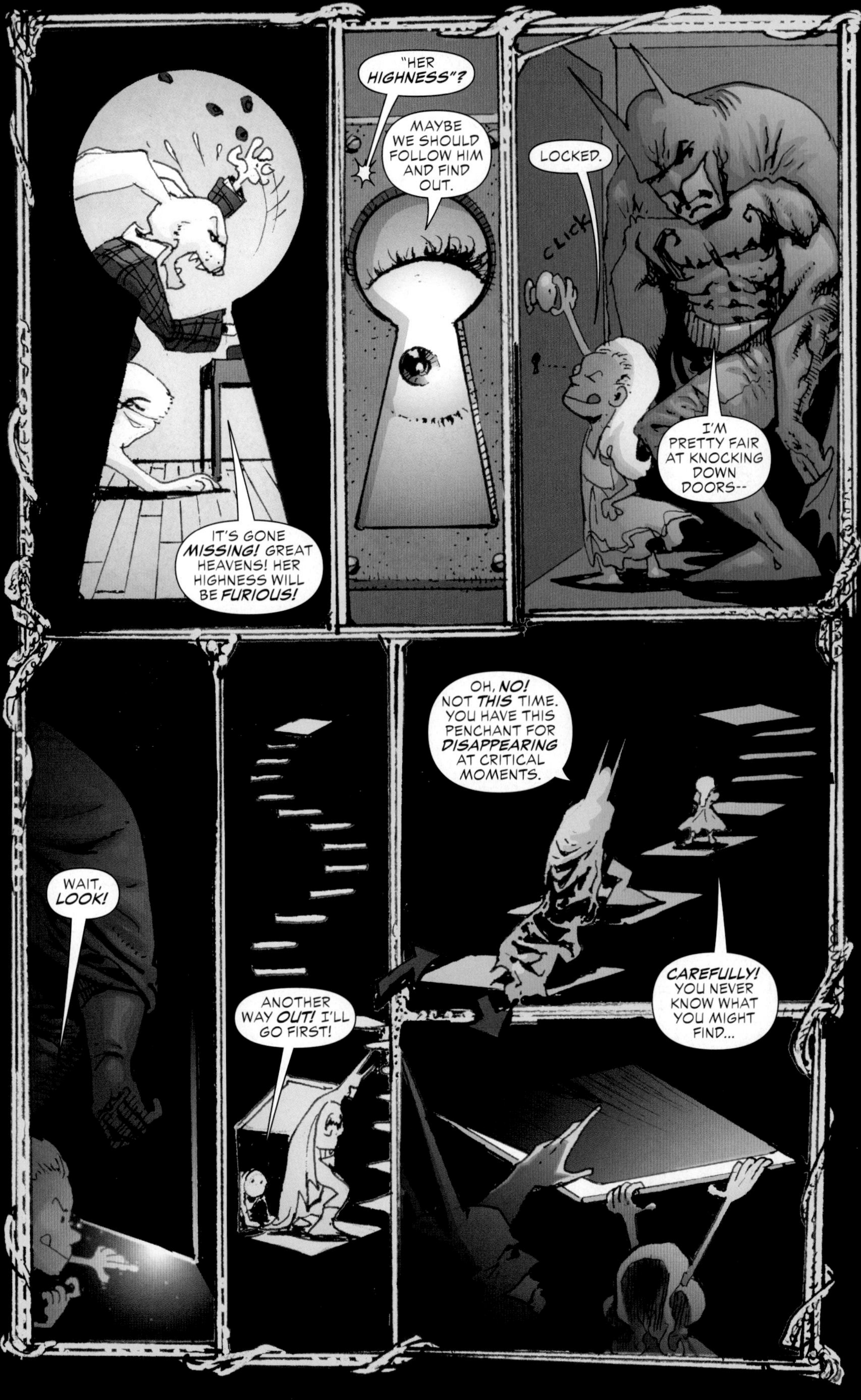
IT'S GONE *MISSING!* GREAT HEAVENS! HER HIGHNESS WILL BE *FURIOUS!*
"HER *HIGHNESS*"?
MAYBE WE SHOULD FOLLOW HIM AND FIND OUT.
LOCKED.
CLICK
I'M PRETTY FAIR AT KNOCKING DOWN DOORS--
WAIT, *LOOK!*
ANOTHER WAY *OUT!* I'LL GO FIRST!
OH, *NO!* NOT *THIS* TIME. YOU HAVE THIS PENCHANT FOR *DISAPPEARING* AT CRITICAL MOMENTS.
CAREFULLY! YOU NEVER KNOW WHAT YOU MIGHT FIND...

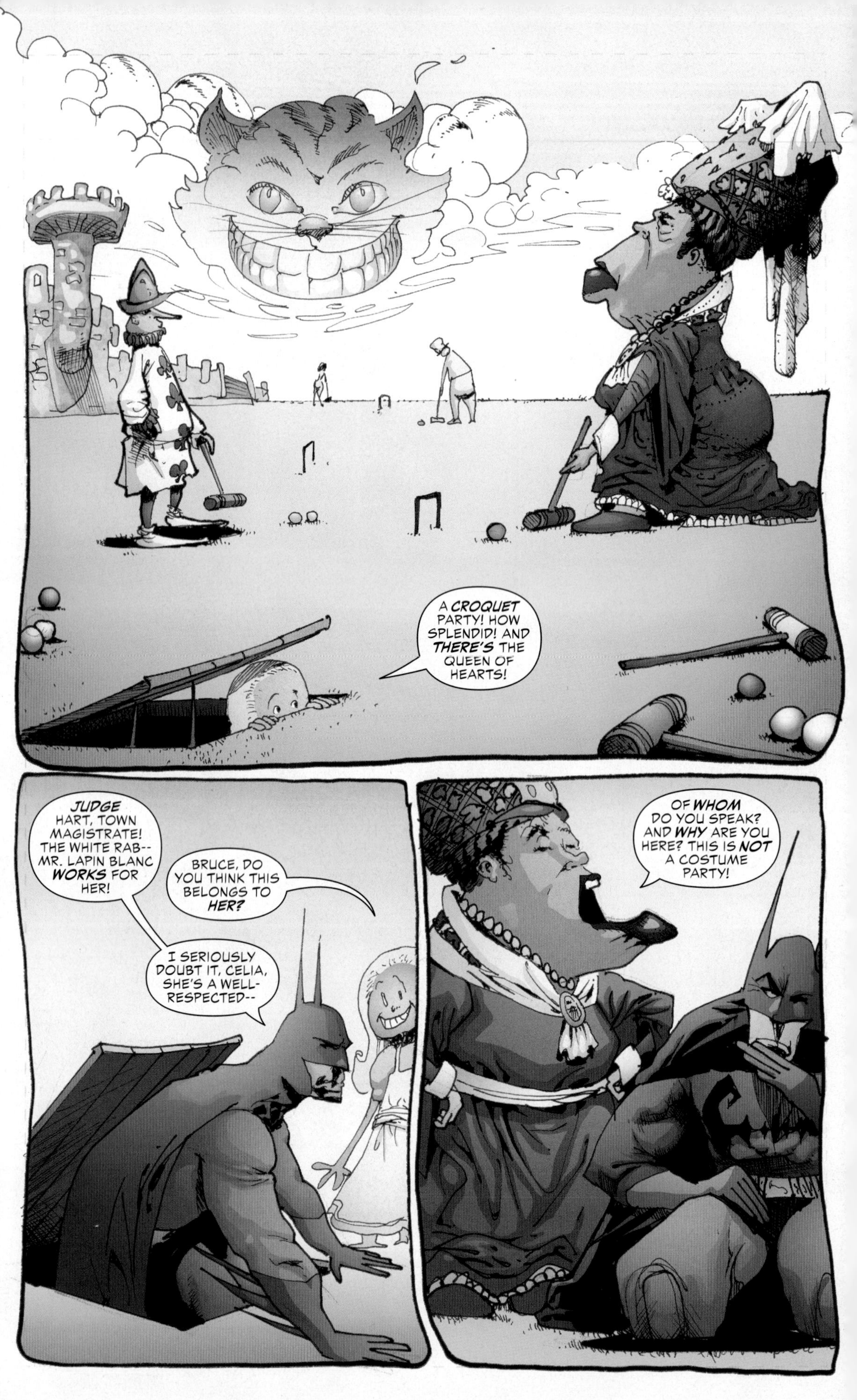
A CROQUET PARTY! HOW SPLENDID! AND THERE'S THE QUEEN OF HEARTS!
JUDGE HART, TOWN MAGISTRATE! THE WHITE RAB-- MR. LAPIN BLANC WORKS FOR HER!
BRUCE, DO YOU THINK THIS BELONGS TO HER?
I SERIOUSLY DOUBT IT, CELIA, SHE'S A WELL-RESPECTED--
OF WHOM DO YOU SPEAK? AND WHY ARE YOU HERE? THIS IS NOT A COSTUME PARTY!

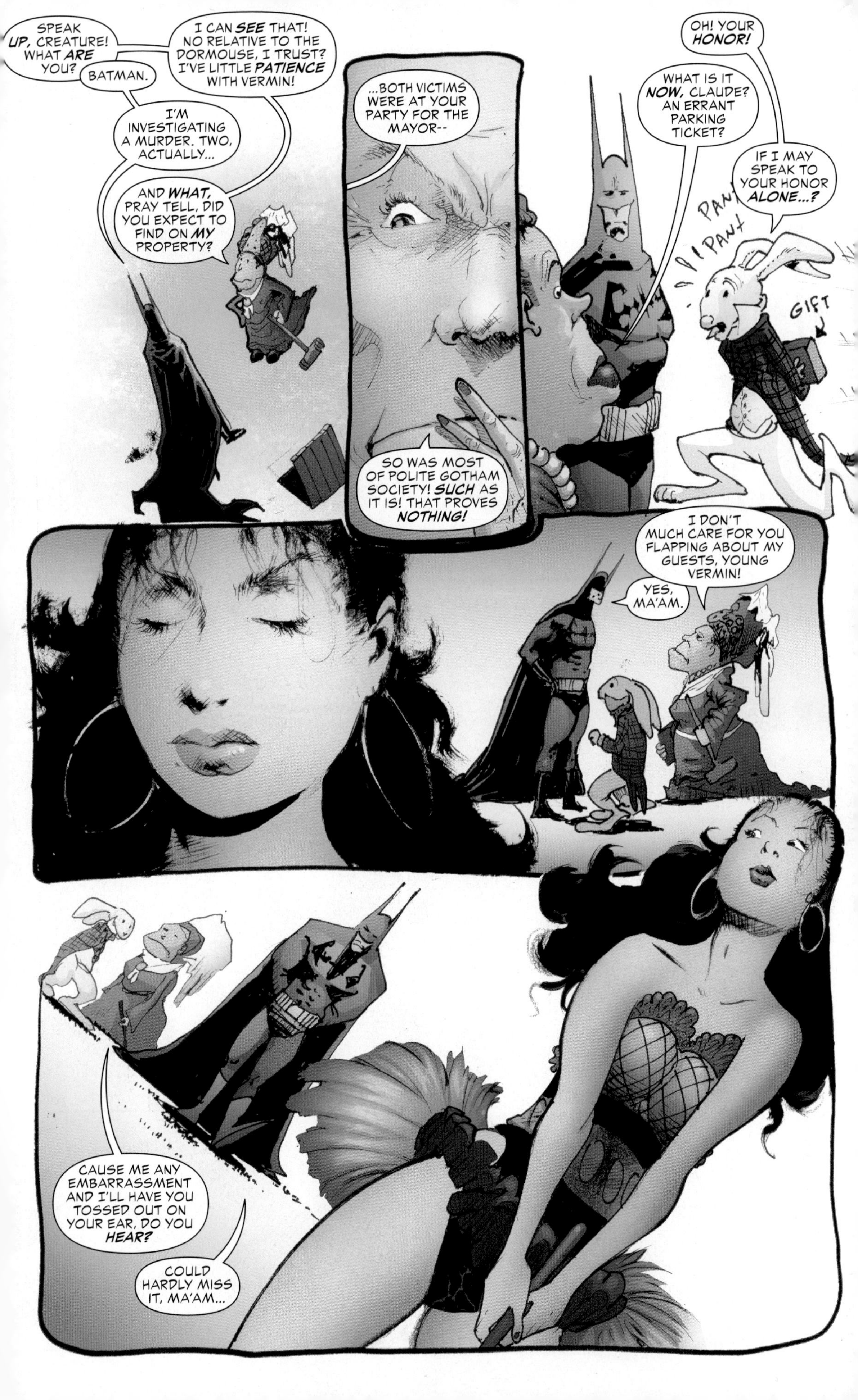
SPEAK UP, CREATURE! WHAT ARE YOU?
BATMAN.
I CAN SEE THAT! NO RELATIVE TO THE DORMOUSE, I TRUST? I'VE LITTLE PATIENCE WITH VERMIN!
I'M INVESTIGATING A MURDER. TWO, ACTUALLY...
AND WHAT, PRAY TELL, DID YOU EXPECT TO FIND ON MY PROPERTY?
...BOTH VICTIMS WERE AT YOUR PARTY FOR THE MAYOR--
SO WAS MOST OF POLITE GOTHAM SOCIETY! SUCH AS IT IS! THAT PROVES NOTHING!
OH! YOUR HONOR!
WHAT IS IT NOW, CLAUDE? AN ERRANT PARKING TICKET?
IF I MAY SPEAK TO YOUR HONOR ALONE...?
PANT PANT
GIFT
I DON'T MUCH CARE FOR YOU FLAPPING ABOUT MY GUESTS, YOUNG VERMIN!
YES, MA'AM.
CAUSE ME ANY EMBARRASSMENT AND I'LL HAVE YOU TOSSED OUT ON YOUR EAR, DO YOU HEAR?
COULD HARDLY MISS IT, MA'AM...

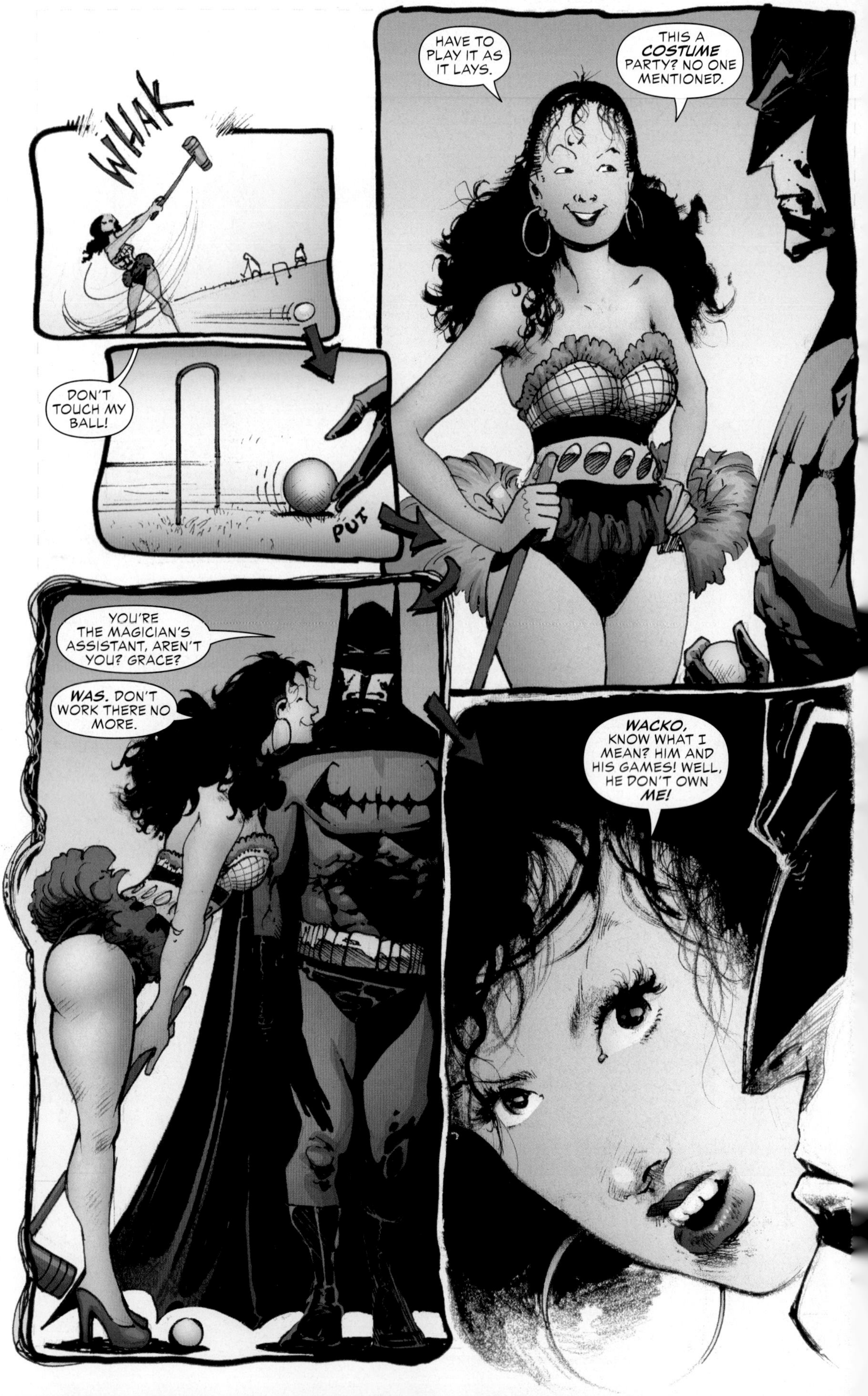
WHAK
DON'T TOUCH MY BALL!
PUT
HAVE TO PLAY IT AS IT LAYS.
THIS A COSTUME PARTY? NO ONE MENTIONED.
YOU'RE THE MAGICIAN'S ASSISTANT, AREN'T YOU? GRACE?
WAS. DON'T WORK THERE NO MORE.
WACKO, KNOW WHAT I MEAN? HIM AND HIS GAMES! WELL, HE DON'T OWN ME!

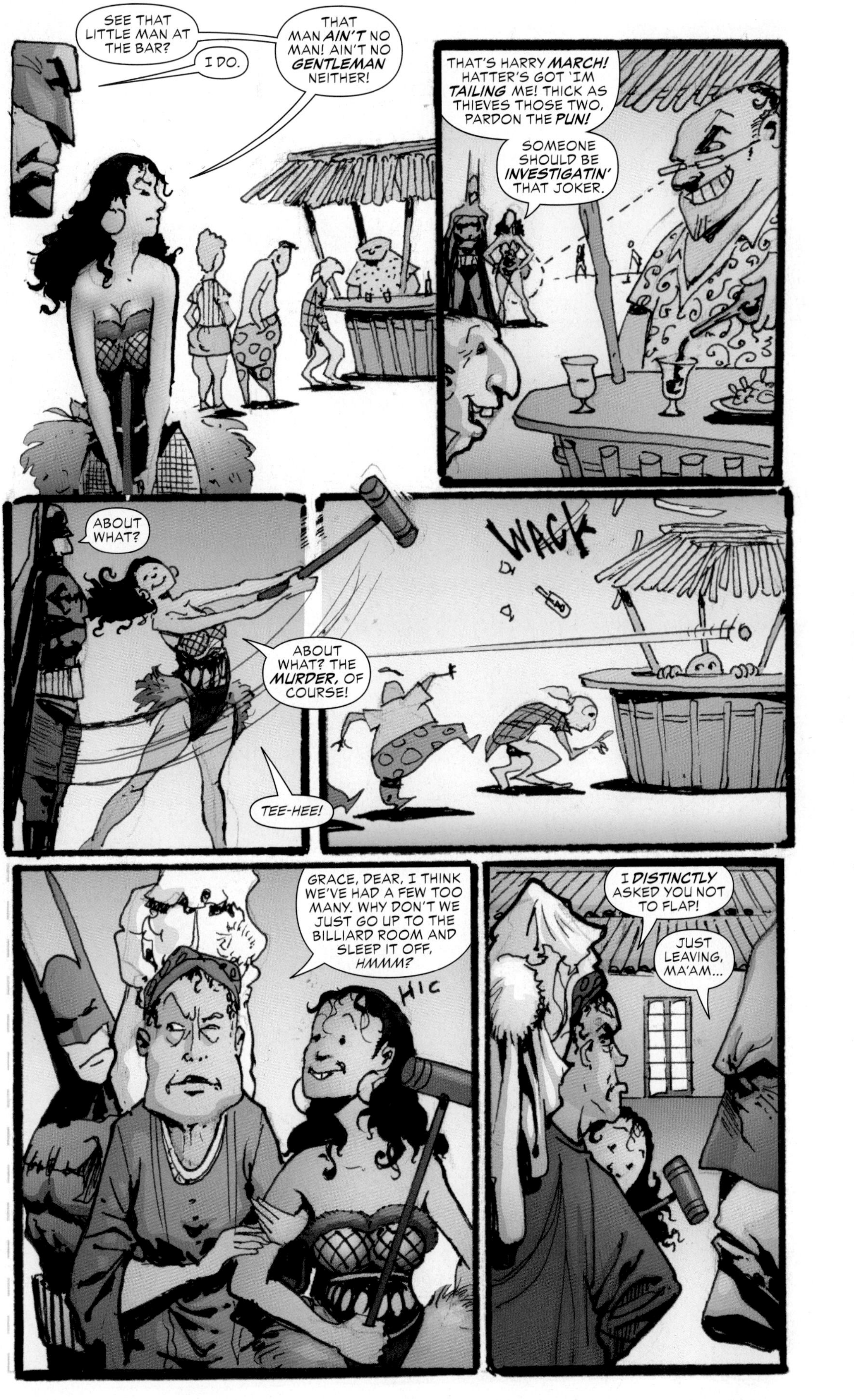

SEE THAT LITTLE MAN AT THE BAR?
THAT MAN AIN'T NO MAN! AIN'T NO GENTLEMAN NEITHER!
I DO.
THAT'S HARRY MARCH! HATTER'S GOT 'IM TAILING ME! THICK AS THIEVES THOSE TWO, PARDON THE PUN!
SOMEONE SHOULD BE INVESTIGATIN' THAT JOKER.
ABOUT WHAT?
ABOUT WHAT? THE MURDER, OF COURSE!
TEE-HEE!
WACK
GRACE, DEAR, I THINK WE'VE HAD A FEW TOO MANY. WHY DON'T WE JUST GO UP TO THE BILLIARD ROOM AND SLEEP IT OFF, HMMM?
HIC
I DISTINCTLY ASKED YOU NOT TO FLAP!
JUST LEAVING, MA'AM...

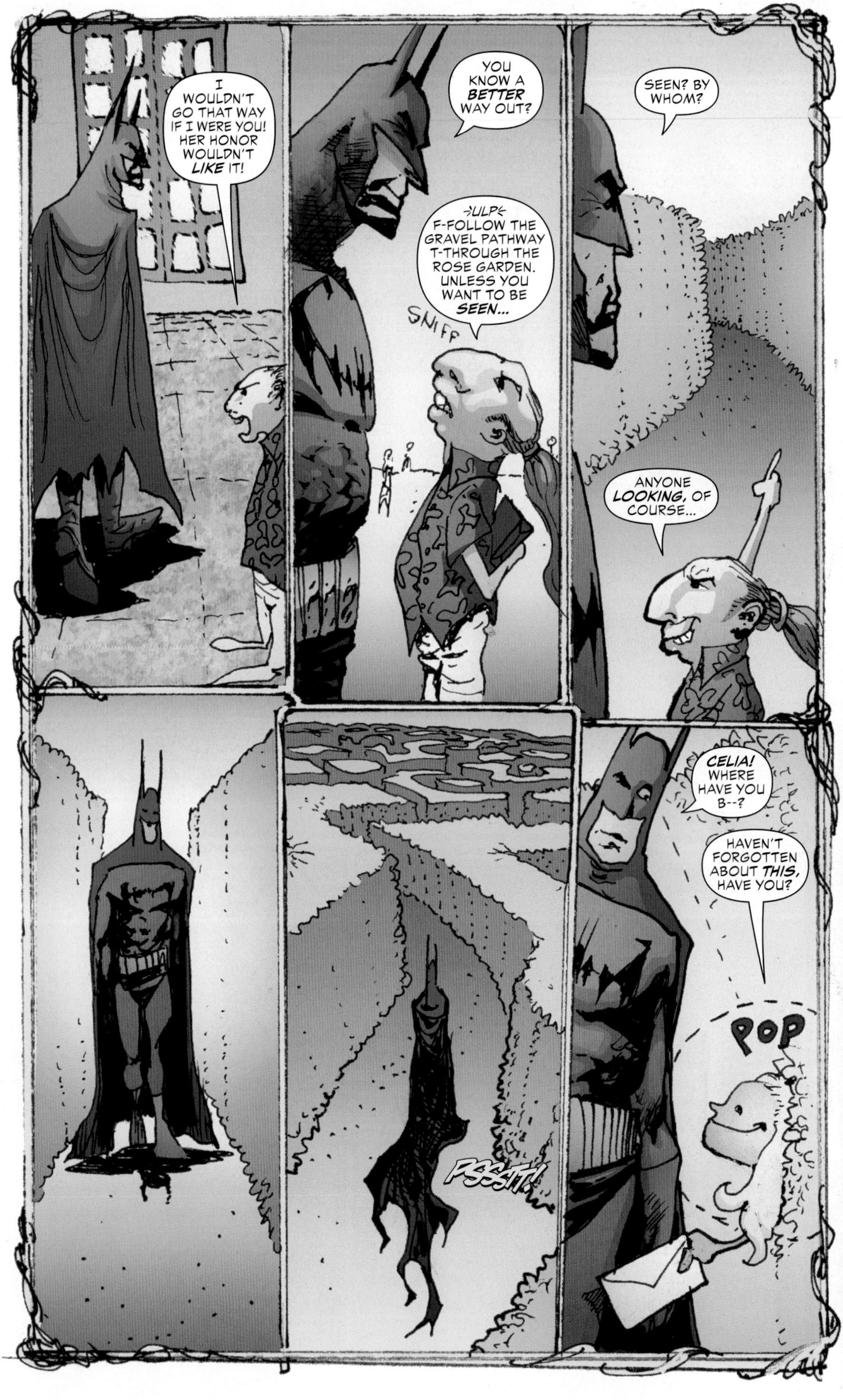
I WOULDN'T GO THAT WAY IF I WERE YOU! HER HONOR WOULDN'T LIKE IT!
YOU KNOW A BETTER WAY OUT?
>ULP< F-FOLLOW THE GRAVEL PATHWAY T-THROUGH THE ROSE GARDEN. UNLESS YOU WANT TO BE SEEN...
SNIFF
SEEN? BY WHOM?
ANYONE LOOKING, OF COURSE...
PSSSTT!
CELIA! WHERE HAVE YOU B--?
HAVEN'T FORGOTTEN ABOUT THIS, HAVE YOU?
POP

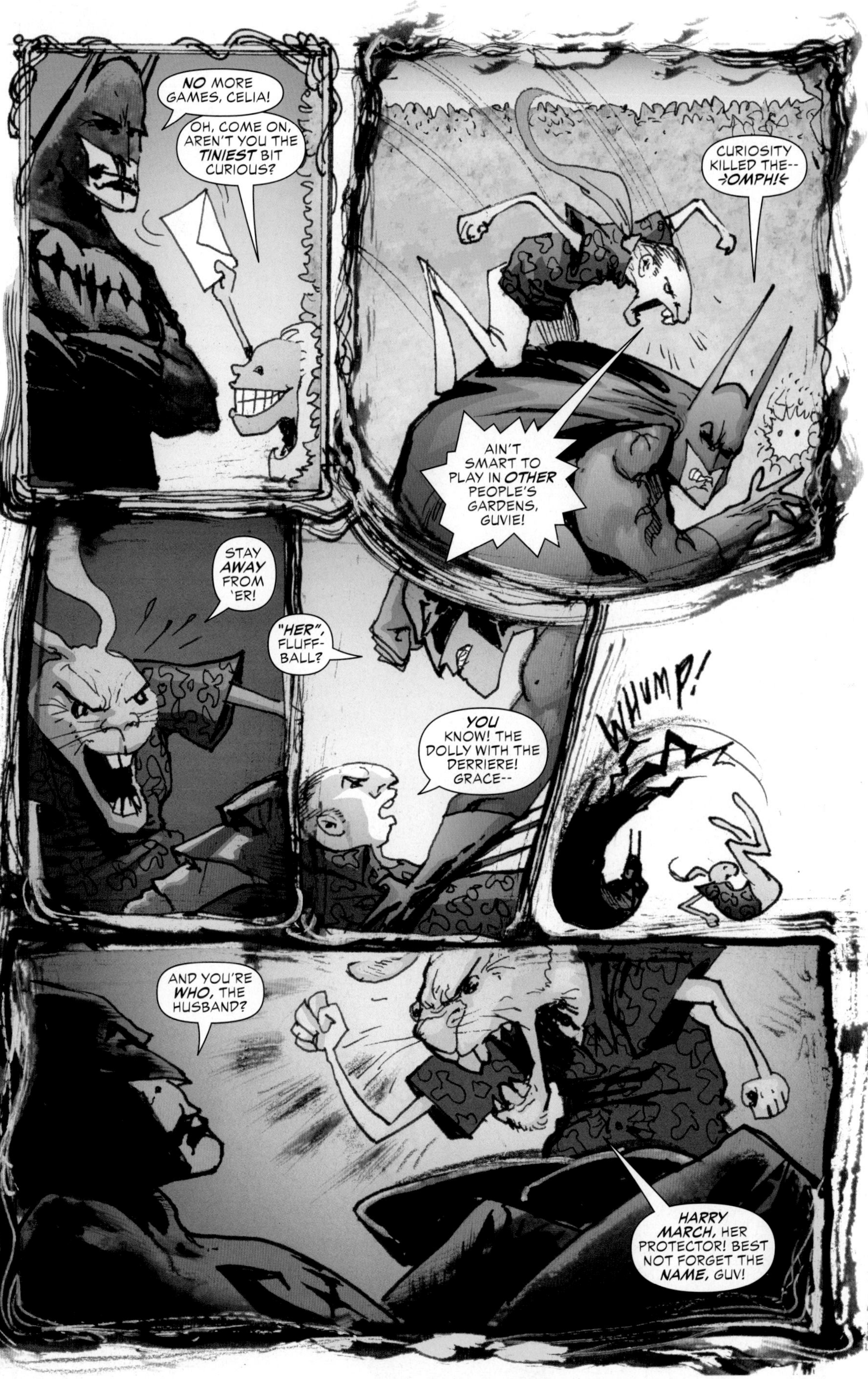
NO MORE GAMES, CELIA!
OH, COME ON, AREN'T YOU THE TINIEST BIT CURIOUS?
CURIOSITY KILLED THE-- OMPH!
AIN'T SMART TO PLAY IN OTHER PEOPLE'S GARDENS, GUVIE!
STAY AWAY FROM 'ER!
"HER", FLUFF-BALL?
YOU KNOW! THE DOLLY WITH THE DERRIERE! GRACE--
WHUMP!
AND YOU'RE WHO, THE HUSBAND?
HARRY MARCH, HER PROTECTOR! BEST NOT FORGET THE NAME, GUV!

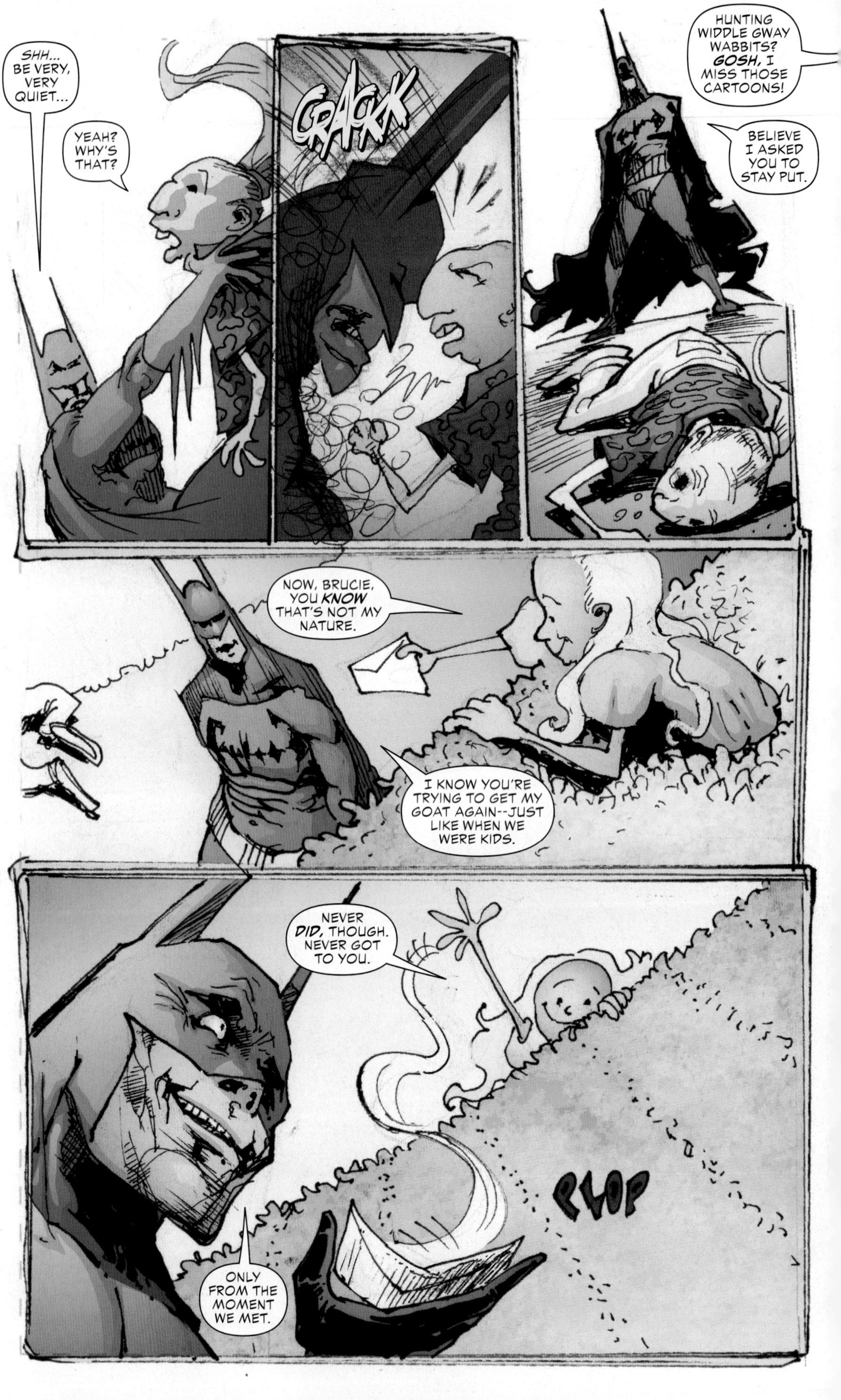

SHH... BE VERY, VERY QUIET...
YEAH? WHY'S THAT?
CRACK
HUNTING WIDDLE GWAY WABBITS? GOSH, I MISS THOSE CARTOONS!
BELIEVE I ASKED YOU TO STAY PUT.
NOW, BRUCIE, YOU KNOW THAT'S NOT MY NATURE.
I KNOW YOU'RE TRYING TO GET MY GOAT AGAIN--JUST LIKE WHEN WE WERE KIDS.
NEVER DID, THOUGH. NEVER GOT TO YOU.
PLOP
ONLY FROM THE MOMENT WE MET.

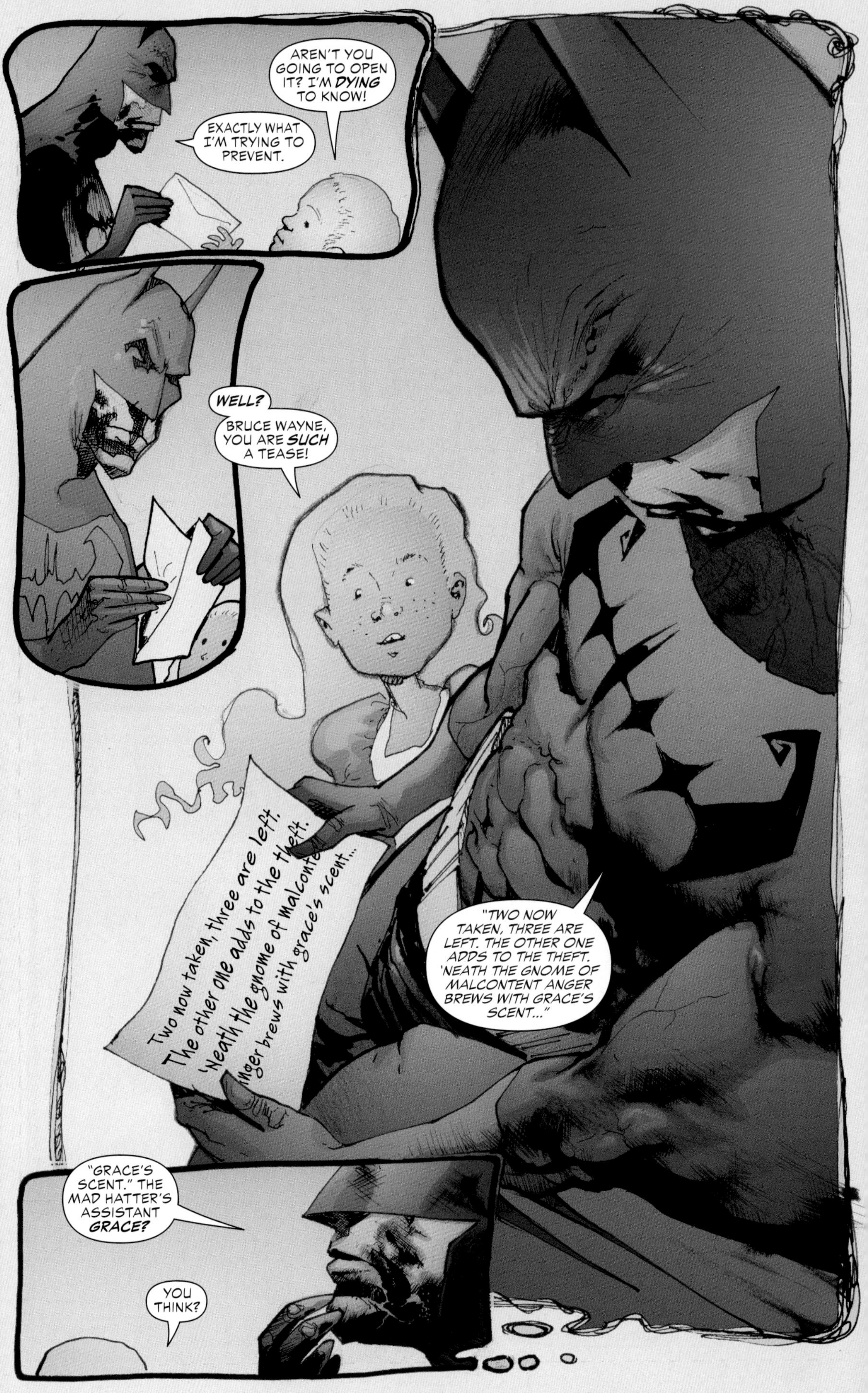

AREN'T YOU GOING TO OPEN IT? I'M DYING TO KNOW!
EXACTLY WHAT I'M TRYING TO PREVENT.
WELL?
BRUCE WAYNE, YOU ARE SUCH A TEASE!
Two now taken, three are left. The other one adds to the theft. 'Neath the gnome of malcontent anger brews with grace's scent...
"TWO NOW TAKEN, THREE ARE LEFT. THE OTHER ONE ADDS TO THE THEFT. 'NEATH THE GNOME OF MALCONTENT ANGER BREWS WITH GRACE'S SCENT..."
"GRACE'S SCENT." THE MAD HATTER'S ASSISTANT GRACE?
YOU THINK?

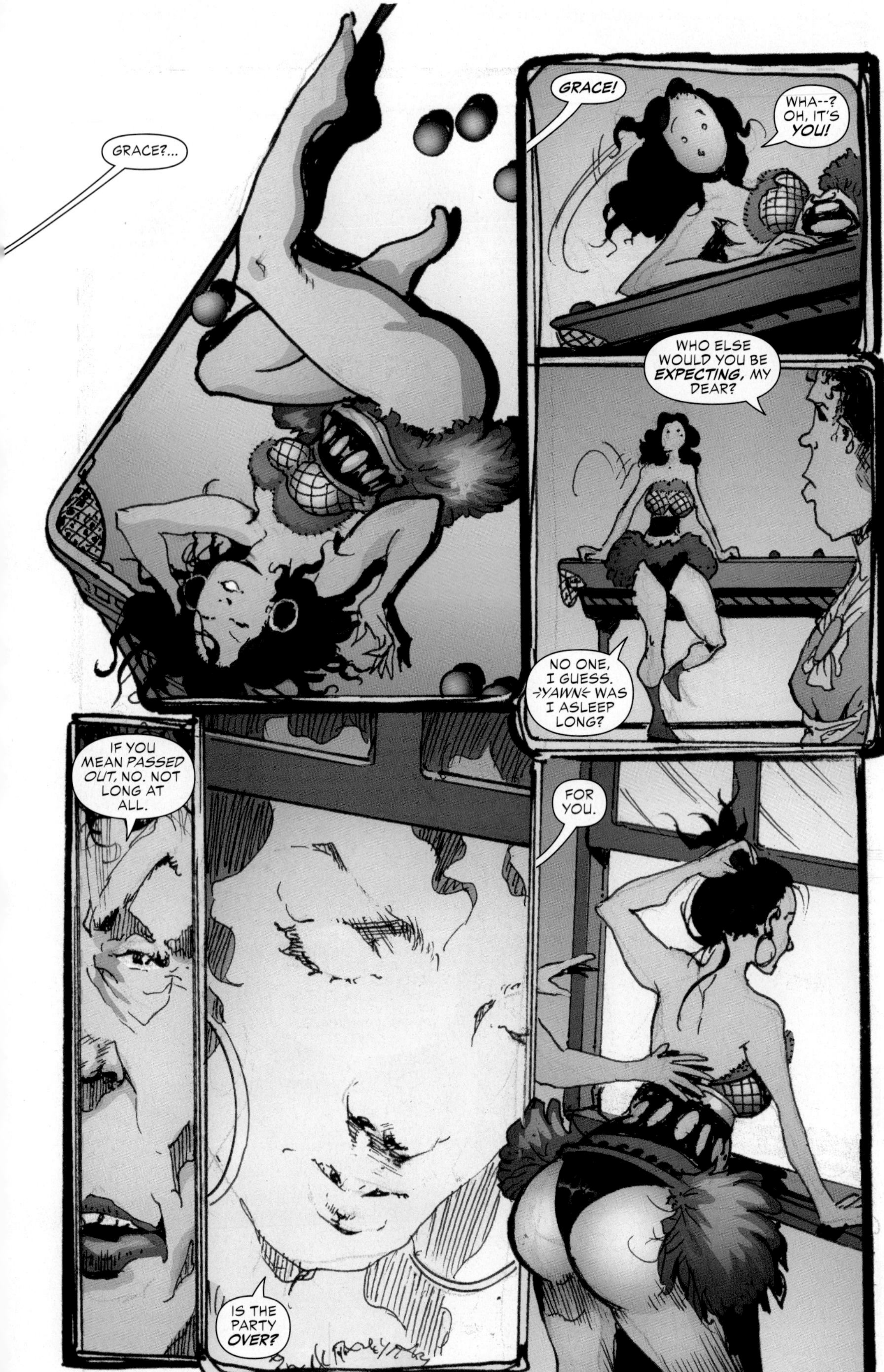
GRACE?...
GRACE!
WHA--? OH, IT'S YOU!
WHO ELSE WOULD YOU BE EXPECTING, MY DEAR?
NO ONE, I GUESS. >YAWN< WAS I ASLEEP LONG?
IF YOU MEAN PASSED OUT, NO. NOT LONG AT ALL.
IS THE PARTY OVER?
FOR YOU.

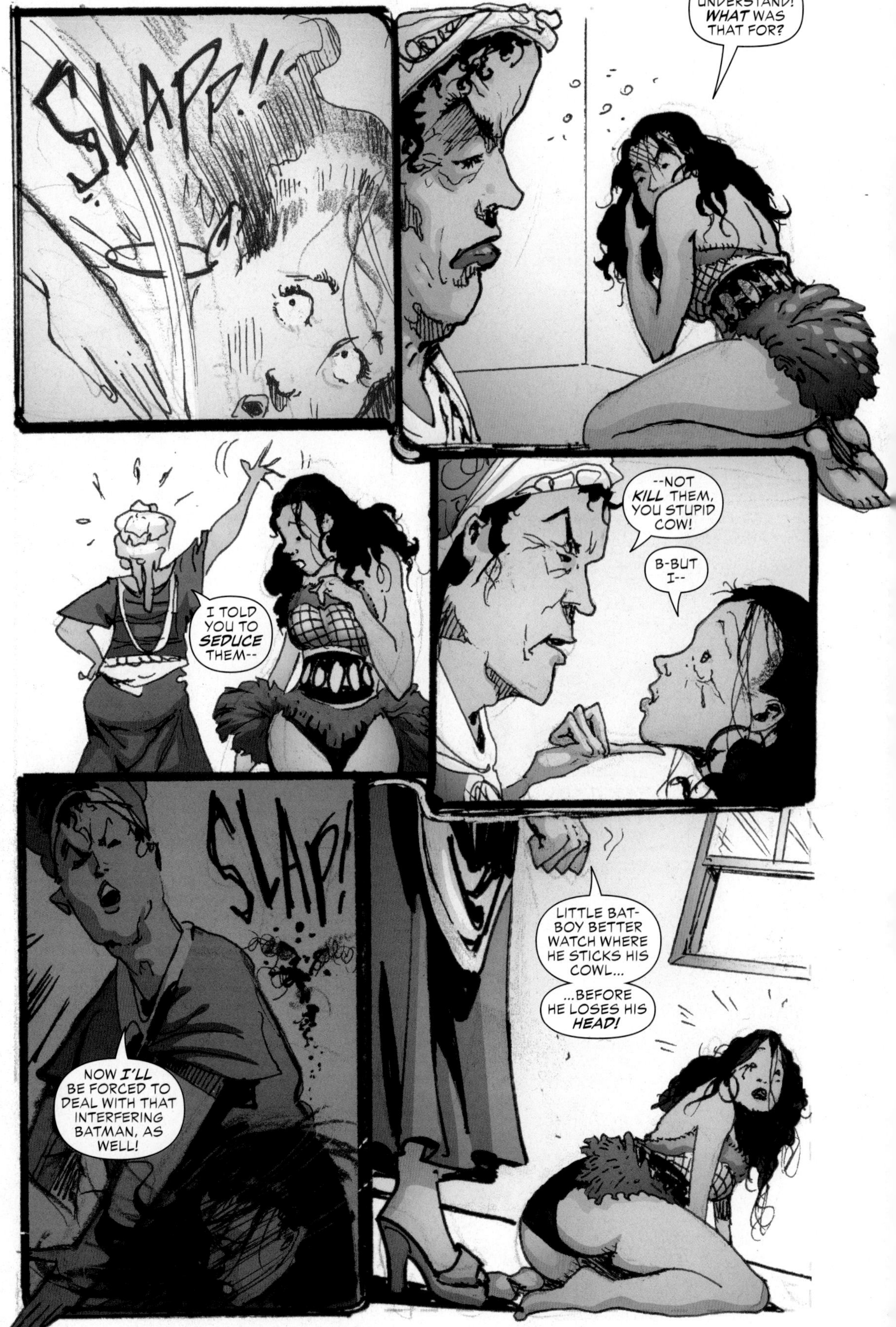
SLAPP!!
I-I DON'T UNDERSTAND! WHAT WAS THAT FOR?
I TOLD YOU TO SEDUCE THEM--
--NOT KILL THEM, YOU STUPID COW!
B-BUT I--
SLAP!
NOW I'LL BE FORCED TO DEAL WITH THAT INTERFERING BATMAN, AS WELL!
LITTLE BAT-BOY BETTER WATCH WHERE HE STICKS HIS COWL...
...BEFORE HE LOSES HIS HEAD!

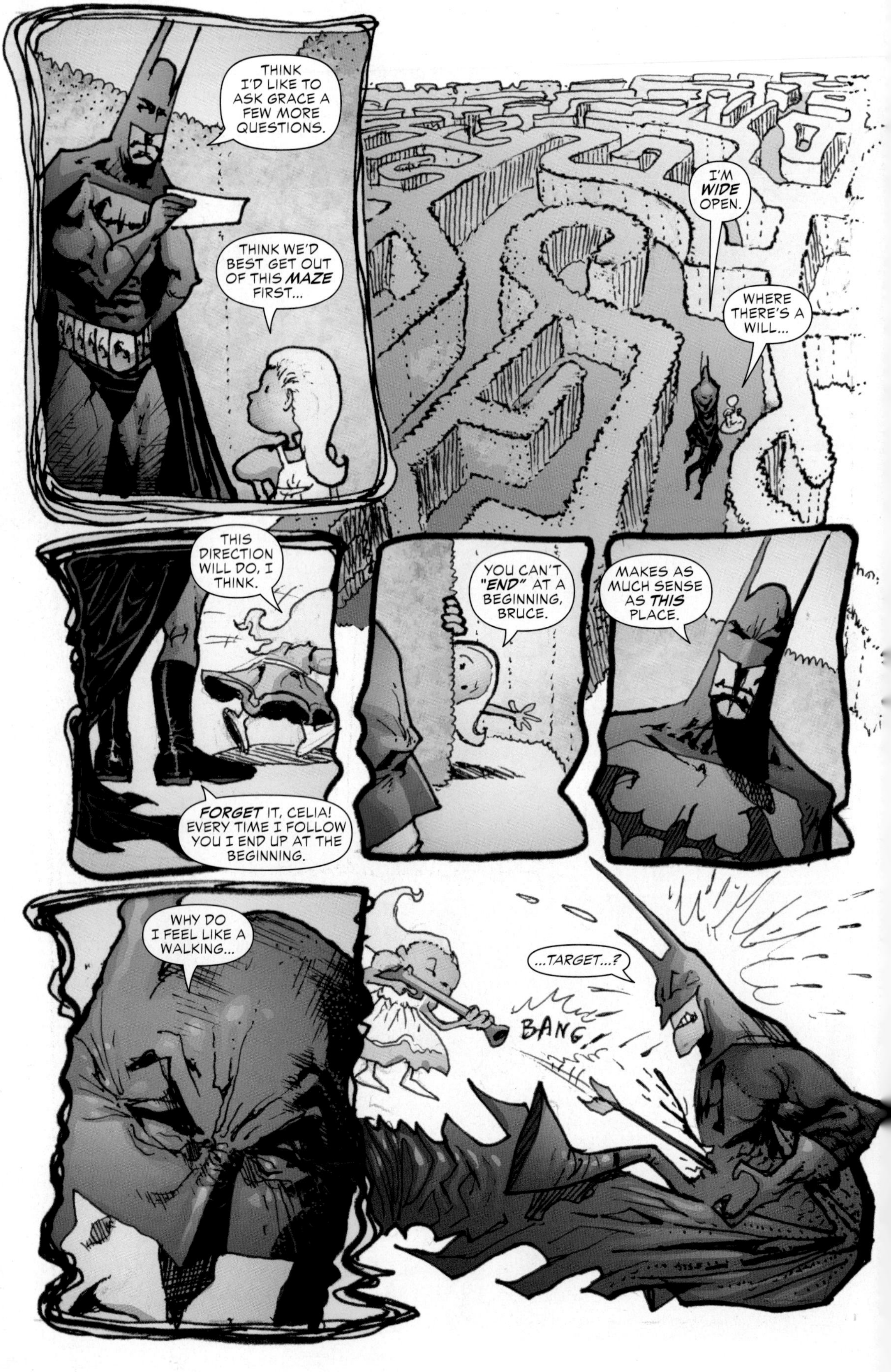
THINK I'D LIKE TO ASK GRACE A FEW MORE QUESTIONS.
THINK WE'D BEST GET OUT OF THIS MAZE FIRST...
I'M WIDE OPEN.
WHERE THERE'S A WILL...
THIS DIRECTION WILL DO, I THINK.
FORGET IT, CELIA! EVERY TIME I FOLLOW YOU I END UP AT THE BEGINNING.
YOU CAN'T "END" AT A BEGINNING, BRUCE.
MAKES AS MUCH SENSE AS THIS PLACE.
WHY DO I FEEL LIKE A WALKING...
...TARGET...?
BANG!

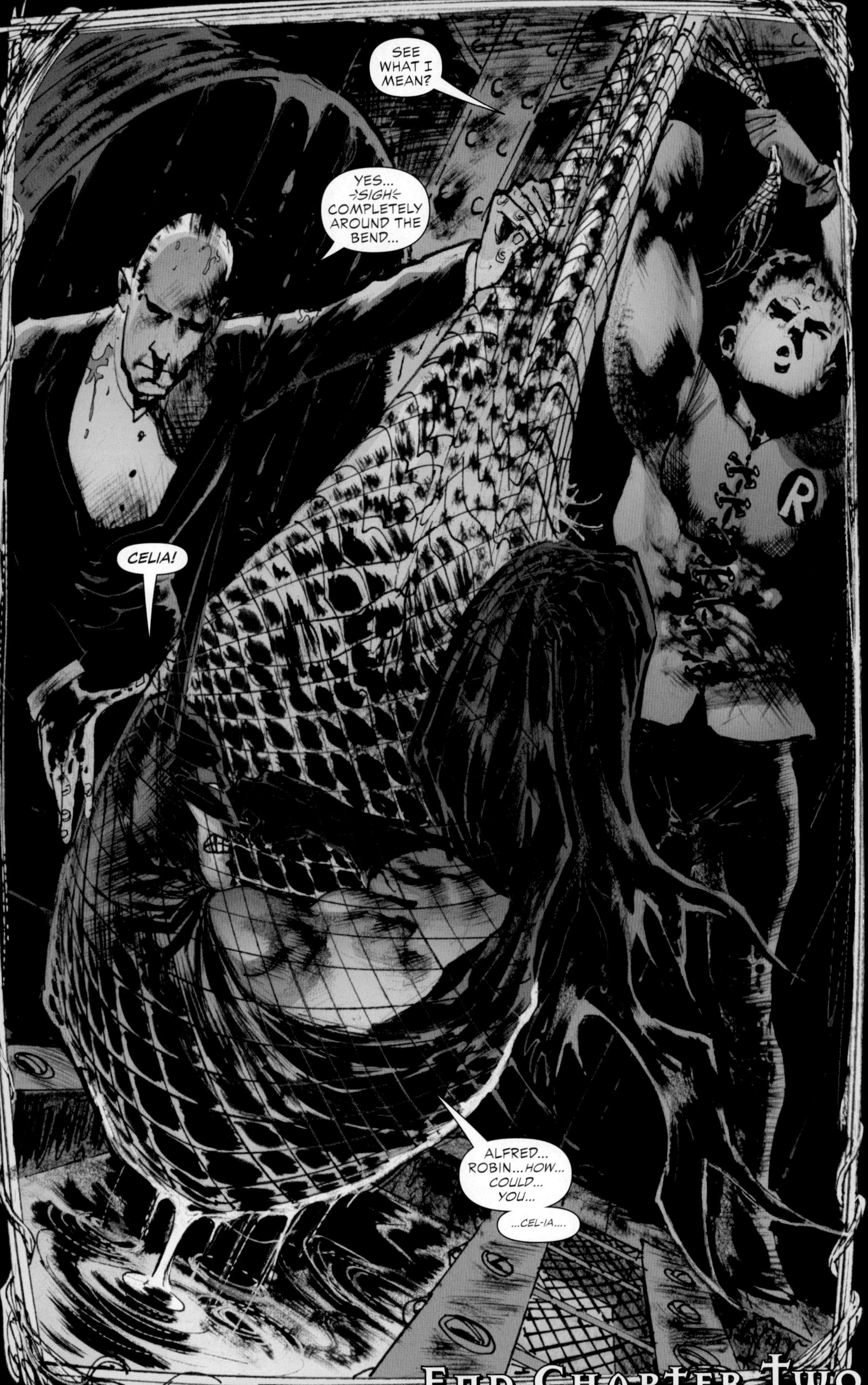

SEE WHAT I MEAN?
YES... ⇒SIGH⇐ COMPLETELY AROUND THE BEND...
CELIA!
ALFRED... ROBIN...HOW... COULD... YOU...
...CEL-IA....

END CHAPTER TWO

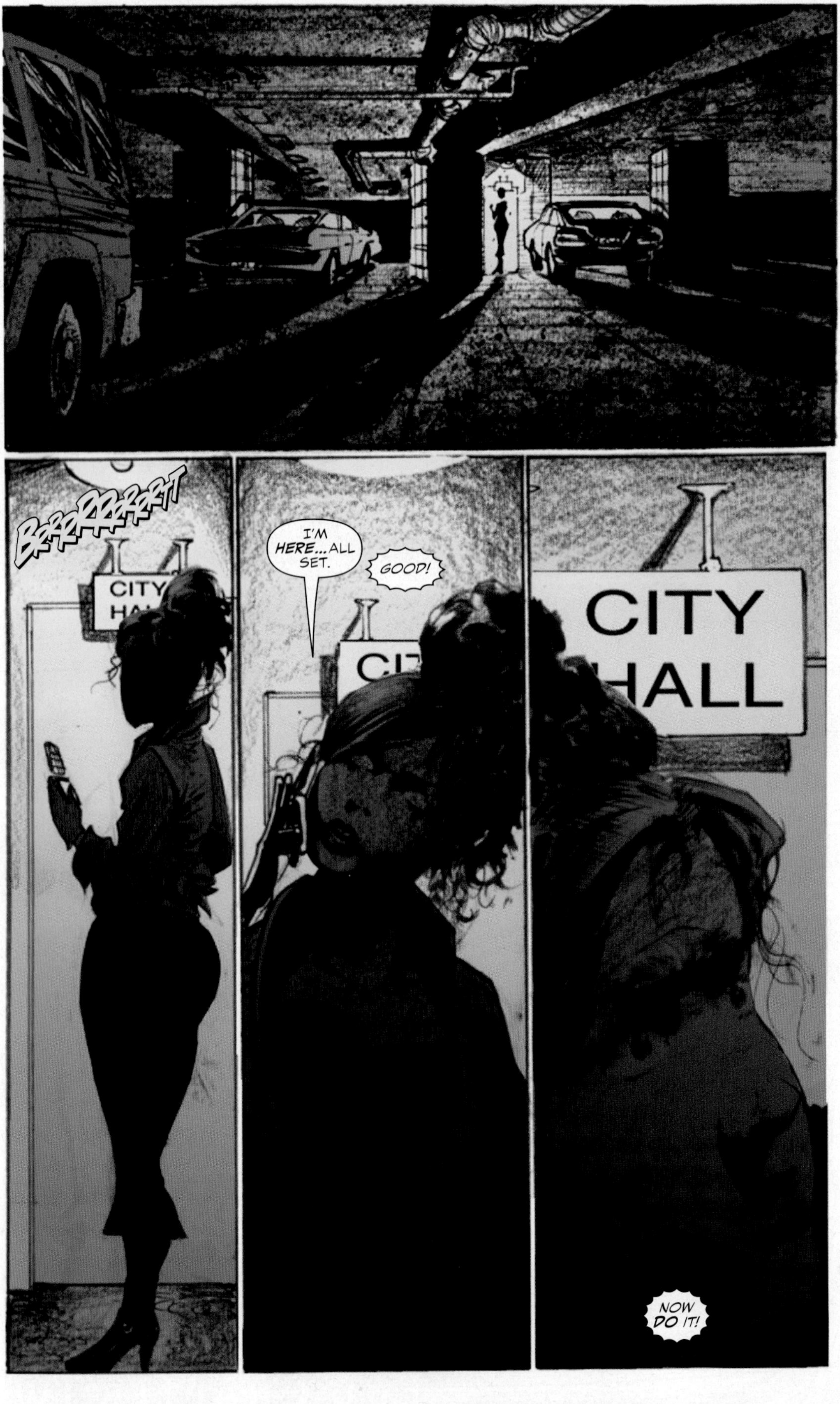
BRRRRRRRRT
CITY HALL
I'M HERE...ALL SET.
GOOD!
CITY HALL
NOW DO IT!

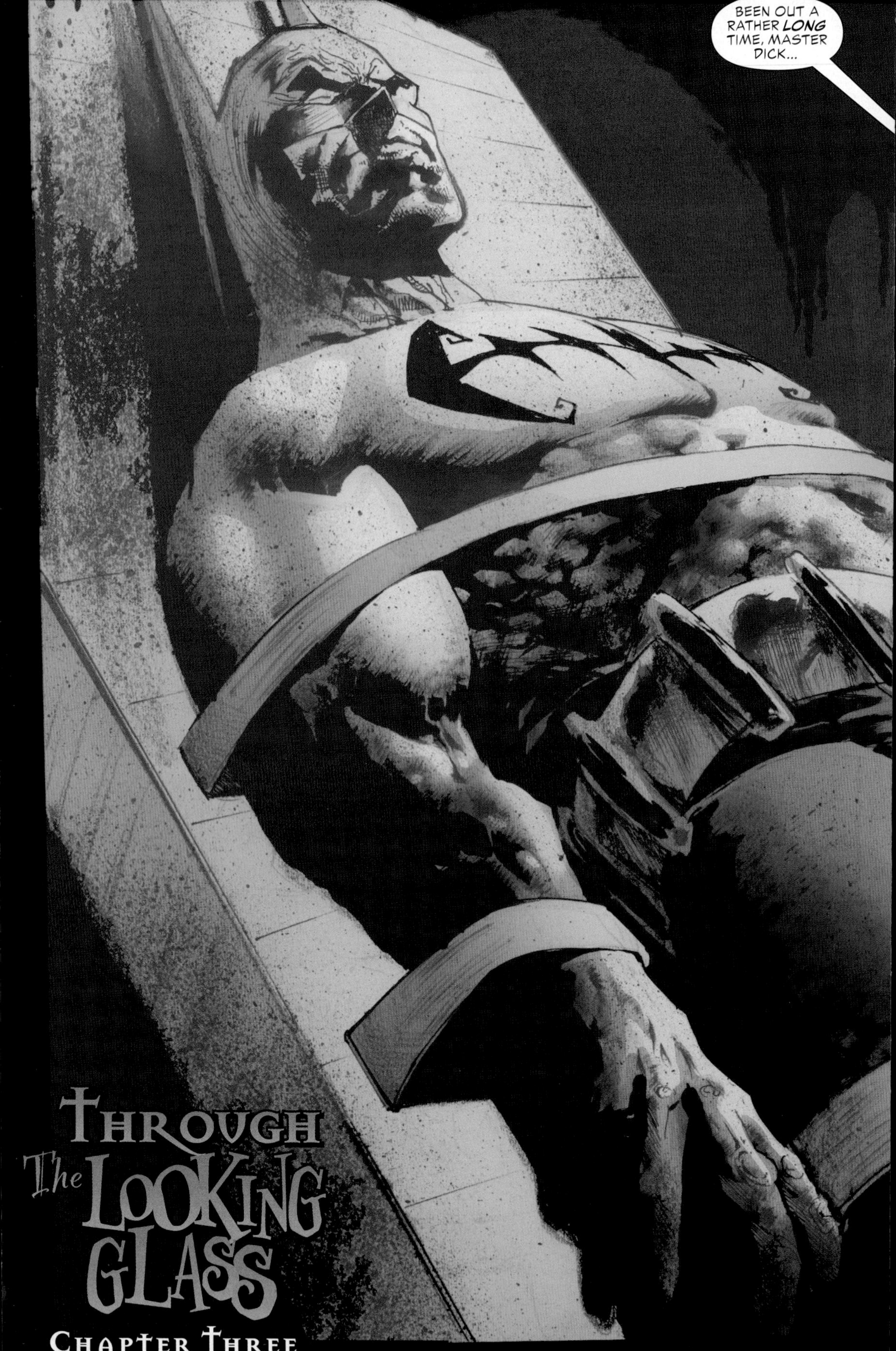
BEEN OUT A RATHER LONG TIME, MASTER DICK...
THROUGH The LOOKING GLASS
CHAPTER THREE

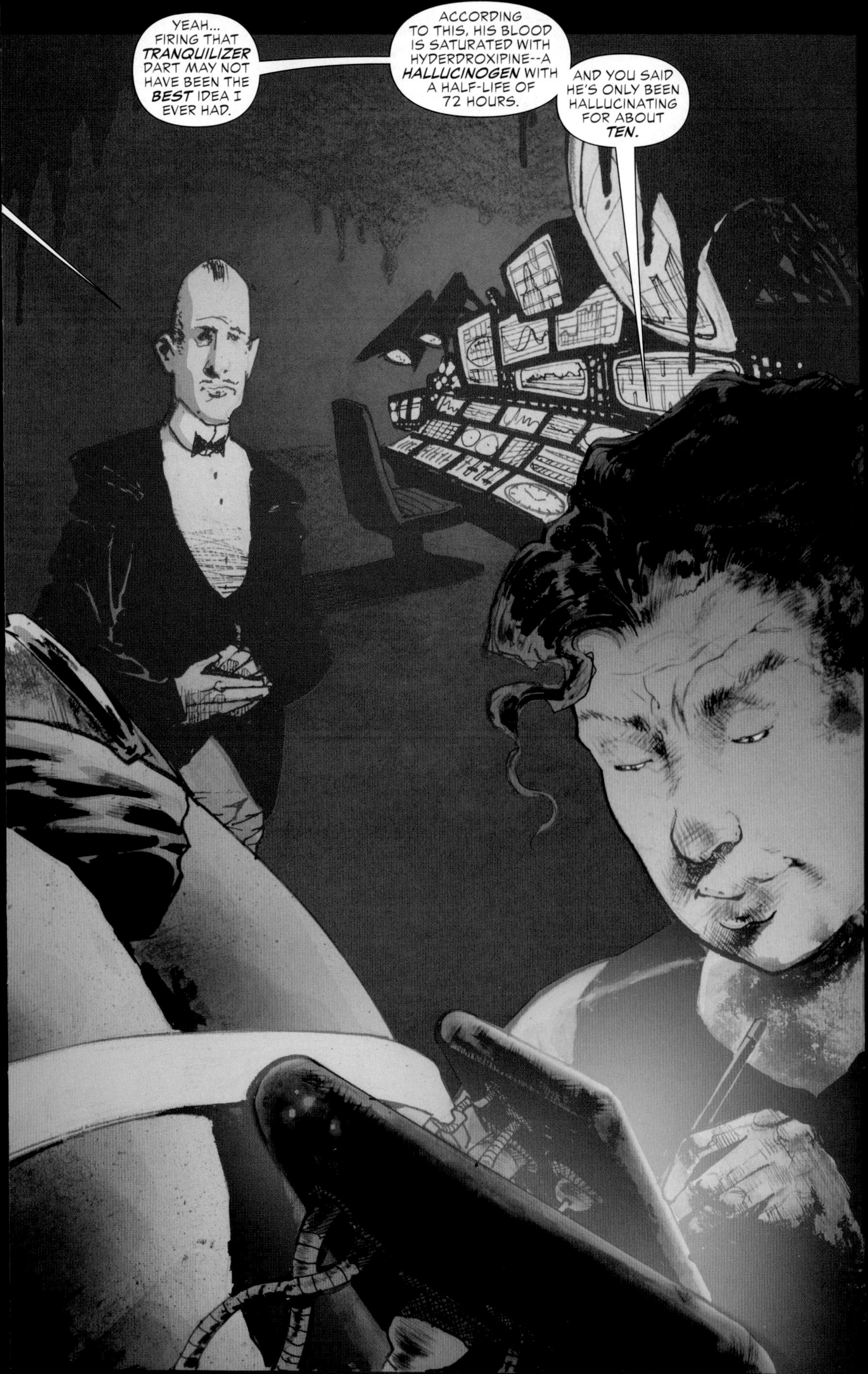
YEAH... FIRING THAT TRANQUILIZER DART MAY NOT HAVE BEEN THE BEST IDEA I EVER HAD.
ACCORDING TO THIS, HIS BLOOD IS SATURATED WITH HYDERDROXIPINE--A HALLUCINOGEN WITH A HALF-LIFE OF 72 HOURS.
AND YOU SAID HE'S ONLY BEEN HALLUCINATING FOR ABOUT TEN.

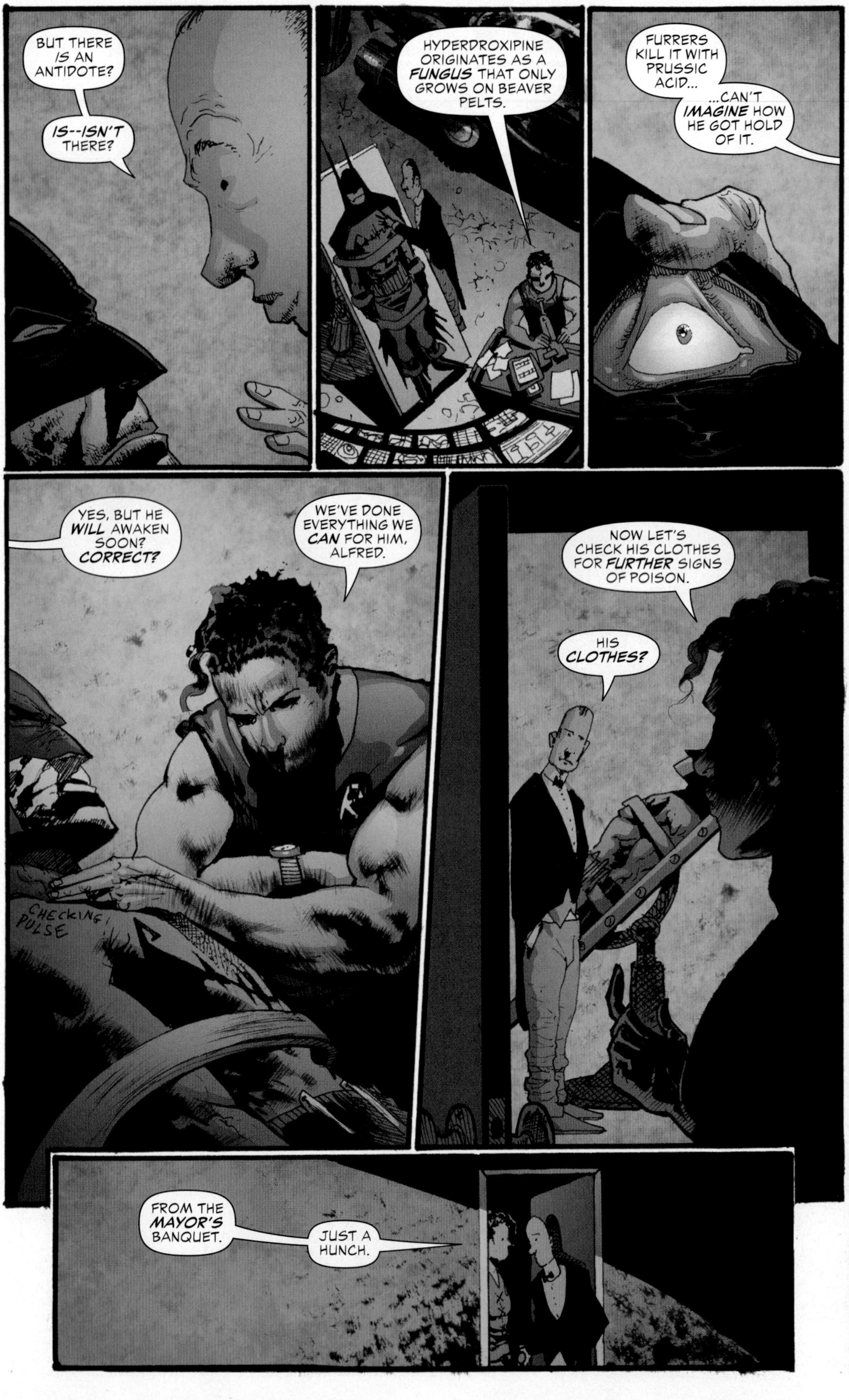
BUT THERE IS AN ANTIDOTE?
IS--ISN'T THERE?
HYDERDROXIPINE ORIGINATES AS A FUNGUS THAT ONLY GROWS ON BEAVER PELTS.
FURRERS KILL IT WITH PRUSSIC ACID...
...CAN'T IMAGINE HOW HE GOT HOLD OF IT.
YES, BUT HE WILL AWAKEN SOON? CORRECT?
WE'VE DONE EVERYTHING WE CAN FOR HIM, ALFRED.
CHECKING PULSE
NOW LET'S CHECK HIS CLOTHES FOR FURTHER SIGNS OF POISON.
HIS CLOTHES?
FROM THE MAYOR'S BANQUET.
JUST A HUNCH.

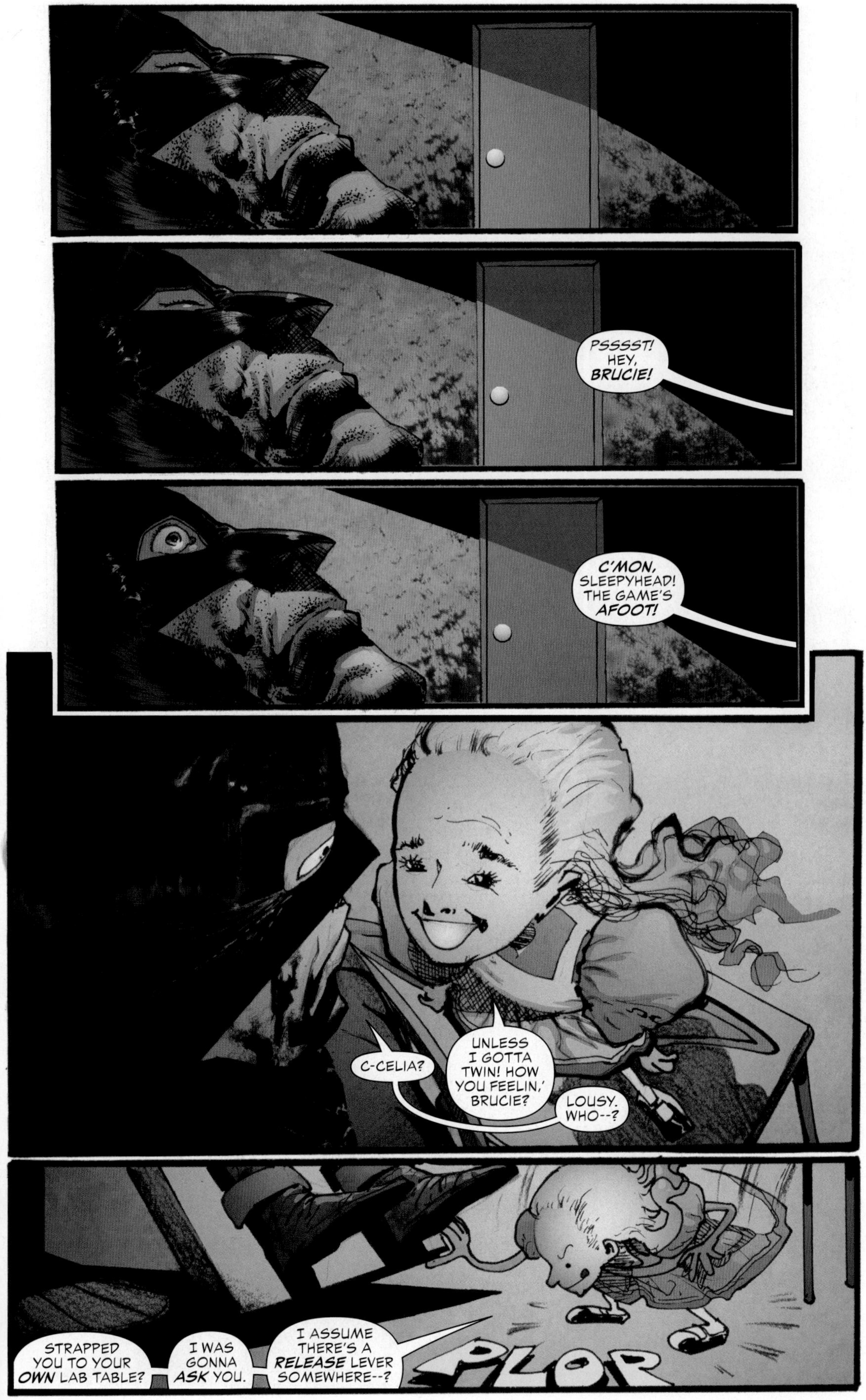
PSSSST! HEY, BRUCIE!
C'MON, SLEEPYHEAD! THE GAME'S AFOOT!
C-CELIA?
UNLESS I GOTTA TWIN! HOW YOU FEELIN,' BRUCIE?
LOUSY. WHO--?
STRAPPED YOU TO YOUR OWN LAB TABLE?
I WAS GONNA ASK YOU.
I ASSUME THERE'S A RELEASE LEVER SOMEWHERE--?
PLOP

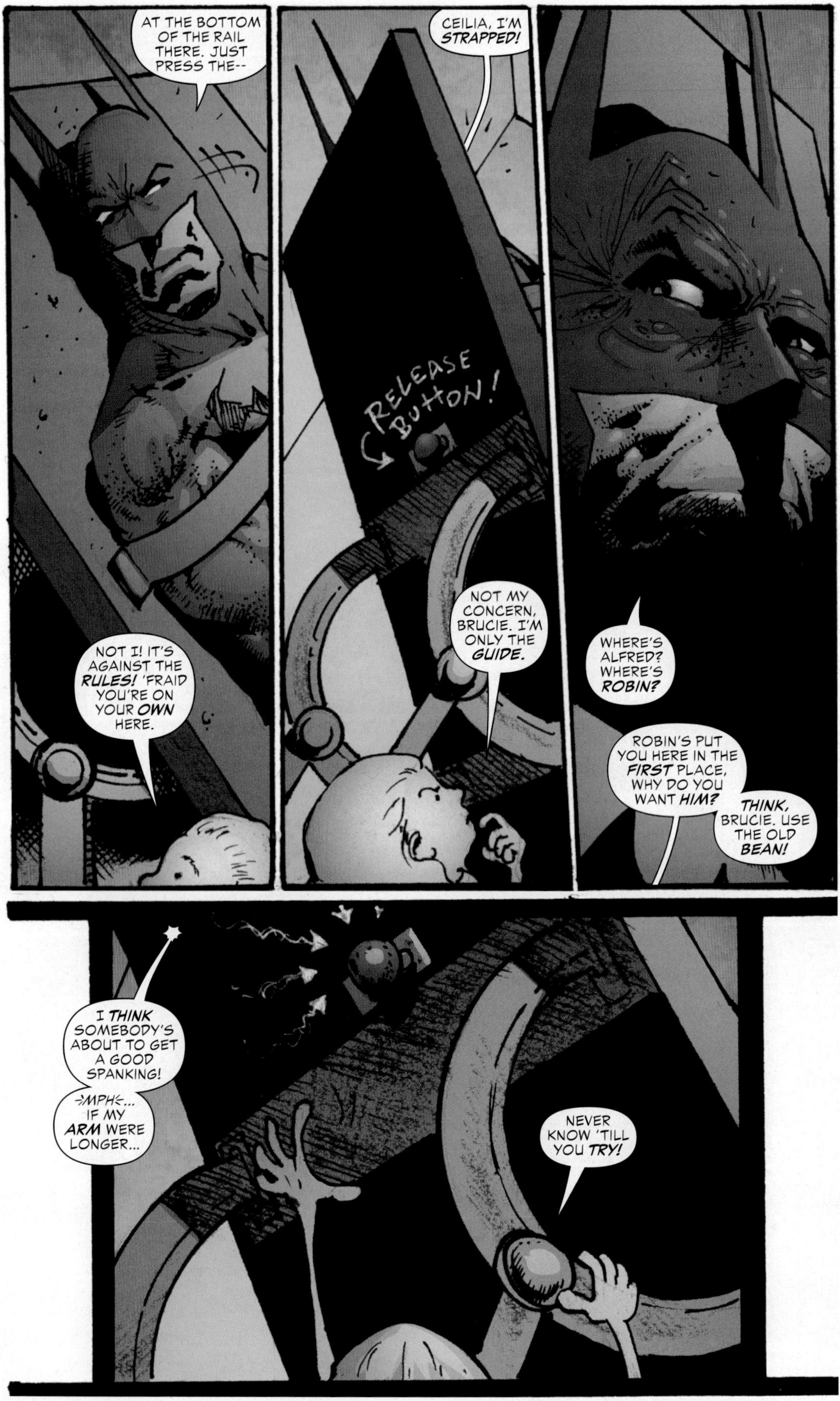
AT THE BOTTOM OF THE RAIL THERE. JUST PRESS THE--
NOT I! IT'S AGAINST THE RULES! 'FRAID YOU'RE ON YOUR OWN HERE.
CEILIA, I'M STRAPPED!
RELEASE BUTTON!
NOT MY CONCERN, BRUCIE. I'M ONLY THE GUIDE.
WHERE'S ALFRED? WHERE'S ROBIN?
ROBIN'S PUT YOU HERE IN THE FIRST PLACE, WHY DO YOU WANT HIM?
THINK, BRUCIE. USE THE OLD BEAN!
I THINK SOMEBODY'S ABOUT TO GET A GOOD SPANKING!
MPH... IF MY ARM WERE LONGER...
NEVER KNOW 'TILL YOU TRY!

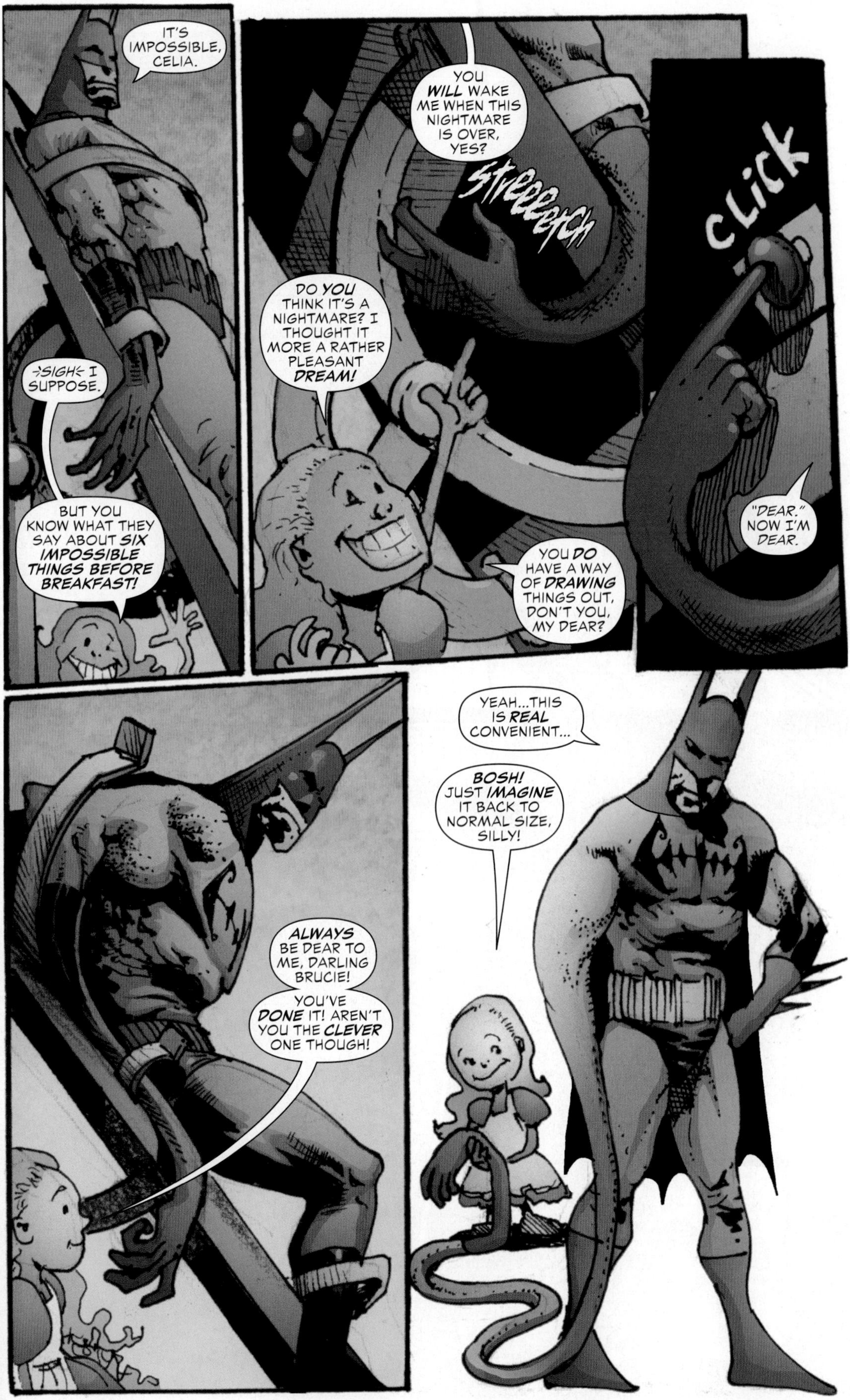

IT'S IMPOSSIBLE, CELIA.
YOU WILL WAKE ME WHEN THIS NIGHTMARE IS OVER, YES?
STREEETCH
CLICK
>SIGH< I SUPPOSE.
BUT YOU KNOW WHAT THEY SAY ABOUT SIX IMPOSSIBLE THINGS BEFORE BREAKFAST!
DO YOU THINK IT'S A NIGHTMARE? I THOUGHT IT MORE A RATHER PLEASANT DREAM!
YOU DO HAVE A WAY OF DRAWING THINGS OUT, DON'T YOU, MY DEAR?
"DEAR." NOW I'M DEAR.
ALWAYS BE DEAR TO ME, DARLING BRUCIE!
YOU'VE DONE IT! AREN'T YOU THE CLEVER ONE THOUGH!
YEAH...THIS IS REAL CONVENIENT...
BOSH! JUST IMAGINE IT BACK TO NORMAL SIZE, SILLY!

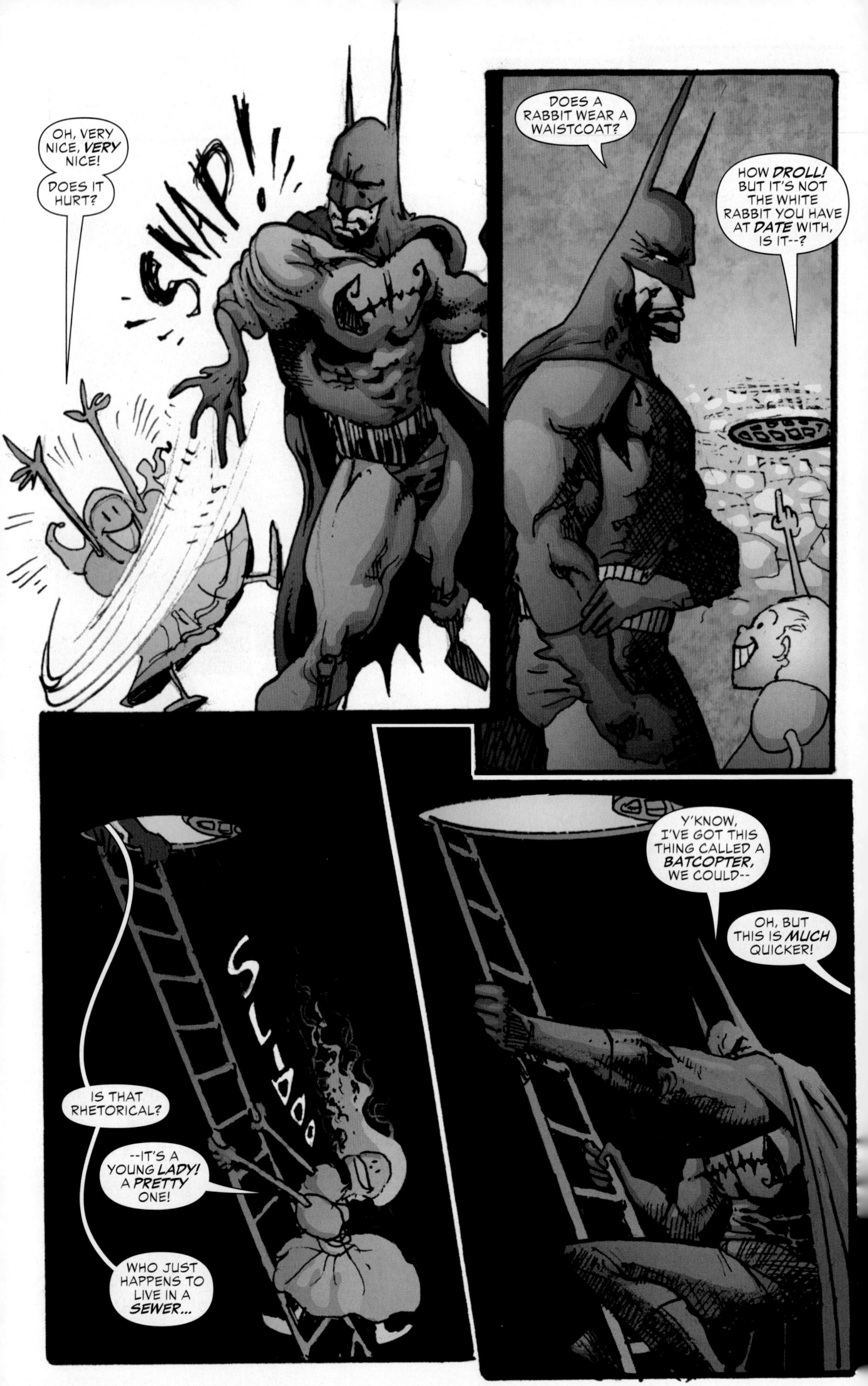
OH, VERY NICE, VERY NICE!
DOES IT HURT?
SNAP!
DOES A RABBIT WEAR A WAISTCOAT?
HOW DROLL! BUT IT'S NOT THE WHITE RABBIT YOU HAVE A DATE WITH, IS IT--?
IS THAT RHETORICAL?
--IT'S A YOUNG LADY! A PRETTY ONE!
WHO JUST HAPPENS TO LIVE IN A SEWER...
SLIDOO
Y'KNOW, I'VE GOT THIS THING CALLED A BATCOPTER, WE COULD--
OH, BUT THIS IS MUCH QUICKER!

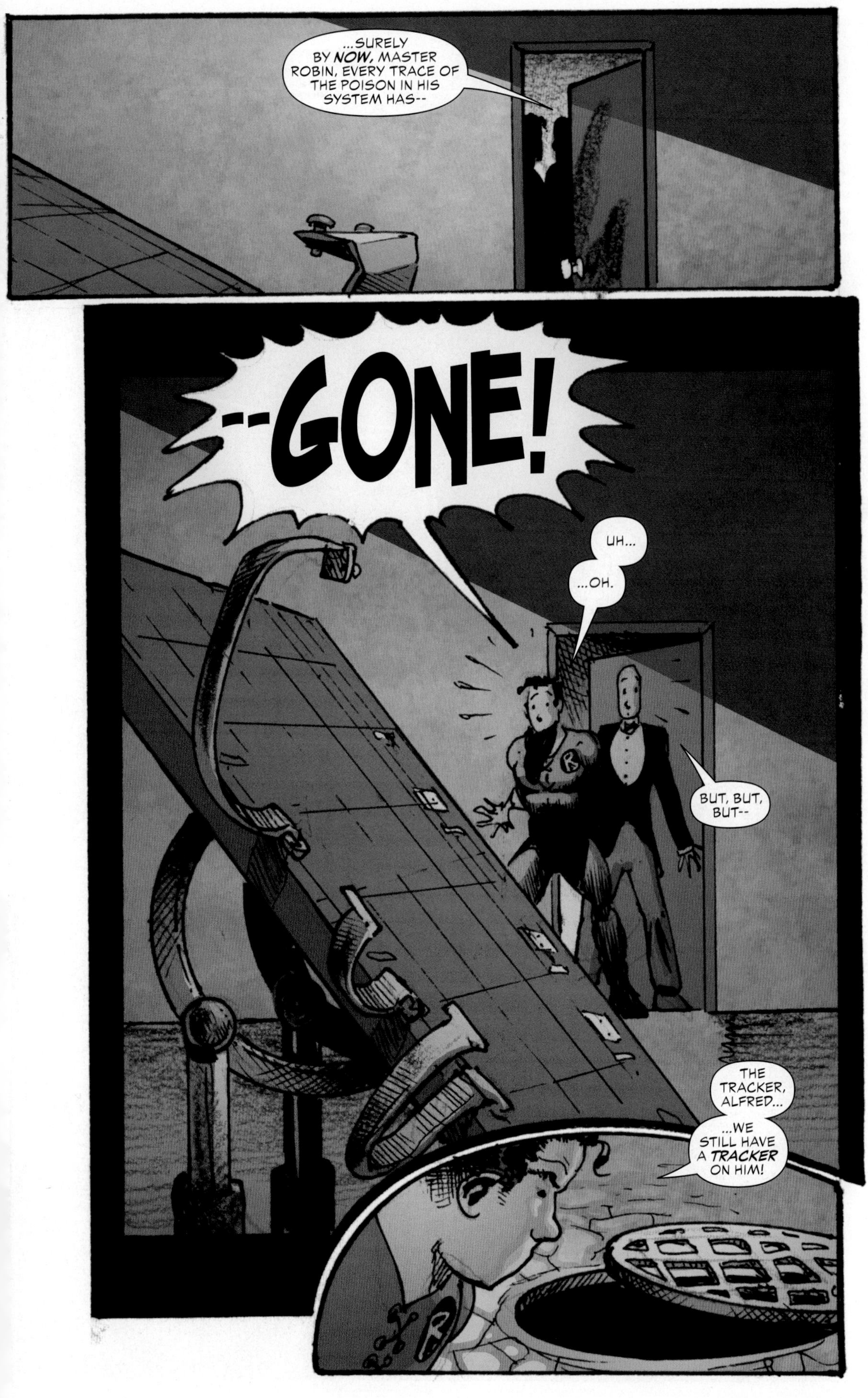
...SURELY BY NOW, MASTER ROBIN, EVERY TRACE OF THE POISON IN HIS SYSTEM HAS--
--GONE!
UH...
...OH.
BUT, BUT, BUT--
THE TRACKER, ALFRED...
...WE STILL HAVE A TRACKER ON HIM!

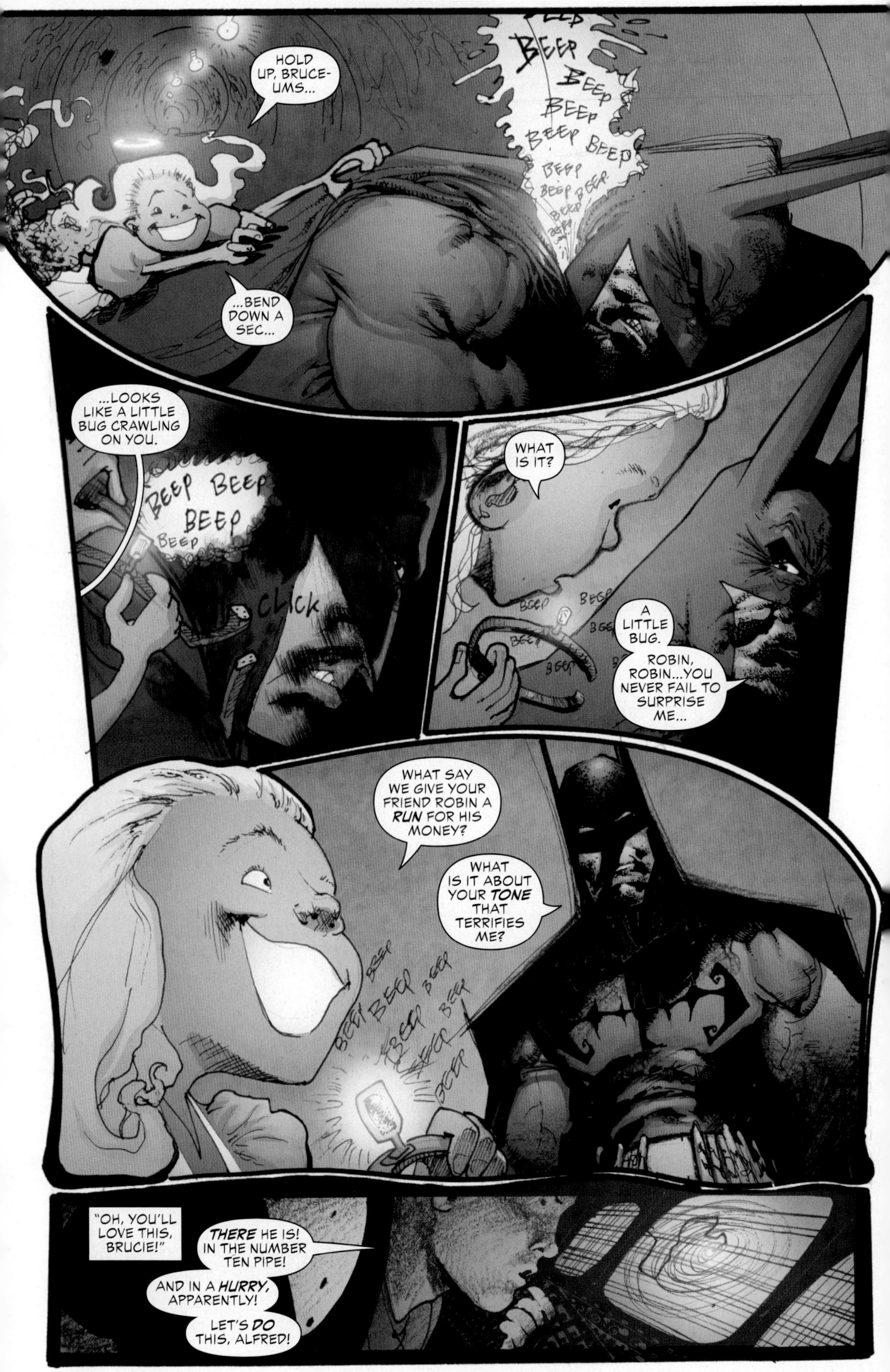
HOLD UP, BRUCE-UMS...
BEEP BEEP BEEP BEEP BEEP BEEP
...BEND DOWN A SEC...
...LOOKS LIKE A LITTLE BUG CRAWLING ON YOU.
BEEP BEEP BEEP BEEP
CLICK
WHAT IS IT?
A LITTLE BUG.
ROBIN, ROBIN...YOU NEVER FAIL TO SURPRISE ME...
WHAT SAY WE GIVE YOUR FRIEND ROBIN A RUN FOR HIS MONEY?
WHAT IS IT ABOUT YOUR TONE THAT TERRIFIES ME?
"OH, YOU'LL LOVE THIS, BRUCIE!"
THERE HE IS! IN THE NUMBER TEN PIPE!
AND IN A HURRY, APPARENTLY!
LET'S DO THIS, ALFRED!

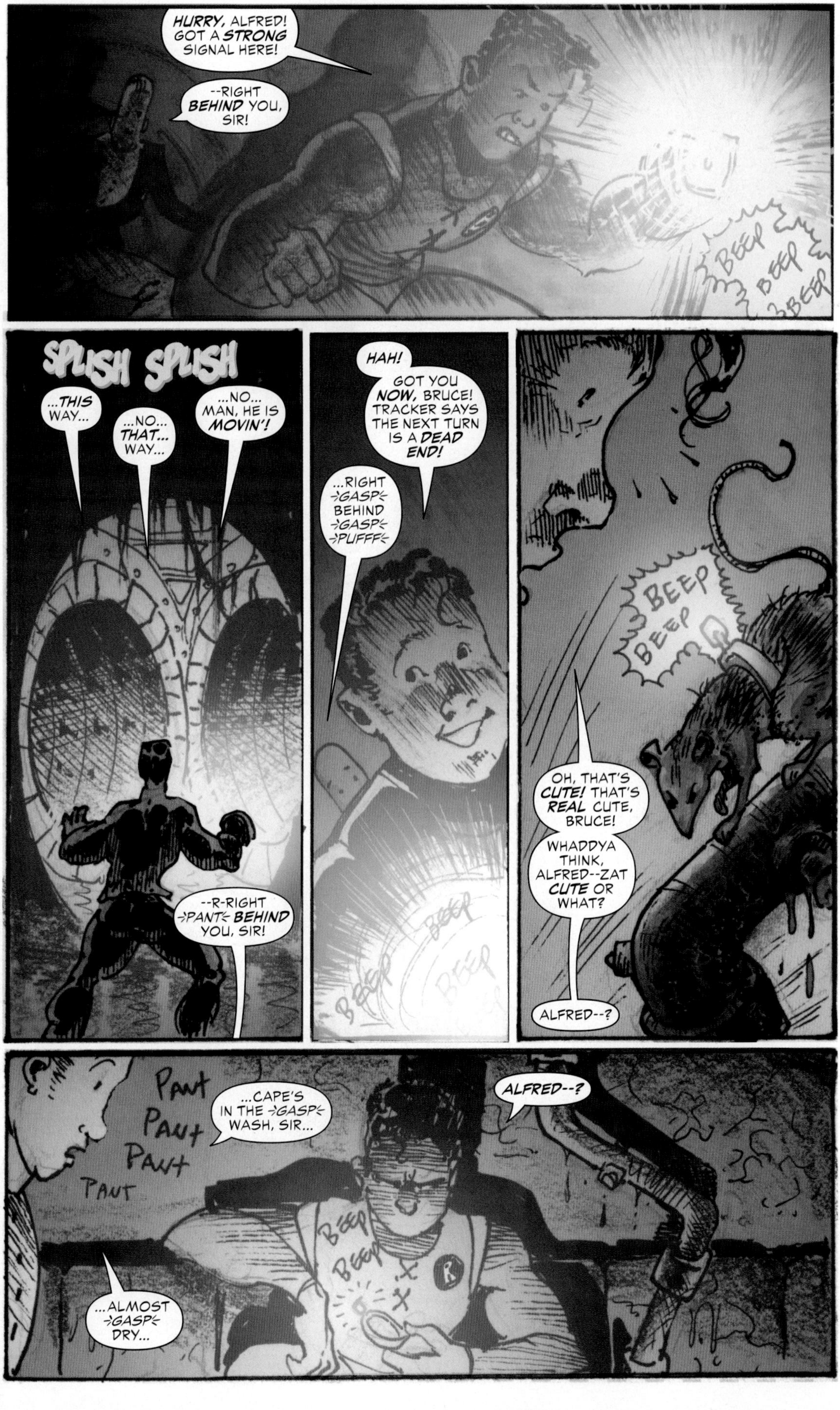
HURRY, ALFRED! GOT A STRONG SIGNAL HERE!
--RIGHT BEHIND YOU, SIR!
BEEP BEEP BEEP
SPLISH SPLISH
...THIS WAY...
...NO... THAT... WAY...
...NO... MAN, HE IS MOVIN'!
--R-RIGHT ›PANT‹ BEHIND YOU, SIR!
HAH!
GOT YOU NOW, BRUCE! TRACKER SAYS THE NEXT TURN IS A DEAD END!
...RIGHT ›GASP‹ BEHIND ›GASP‹ ›PUFFF‹
BEEP BEEP BEEP BEEP
BEEP BEEP
OH, THAT'S CUTE! THAT'S REAL CUTE, BRUCE!
WHADDYA THINK, ALFRED--ZAT CUTE OR WHAT?
ALFRED--?
PANT PANT PANT PANT
...CAPE'S IN THE ›GASP‹ WASH, SIR...
ALFRED--?
BEEP BEEP
...ALMOST ›GASP‹ DRY...

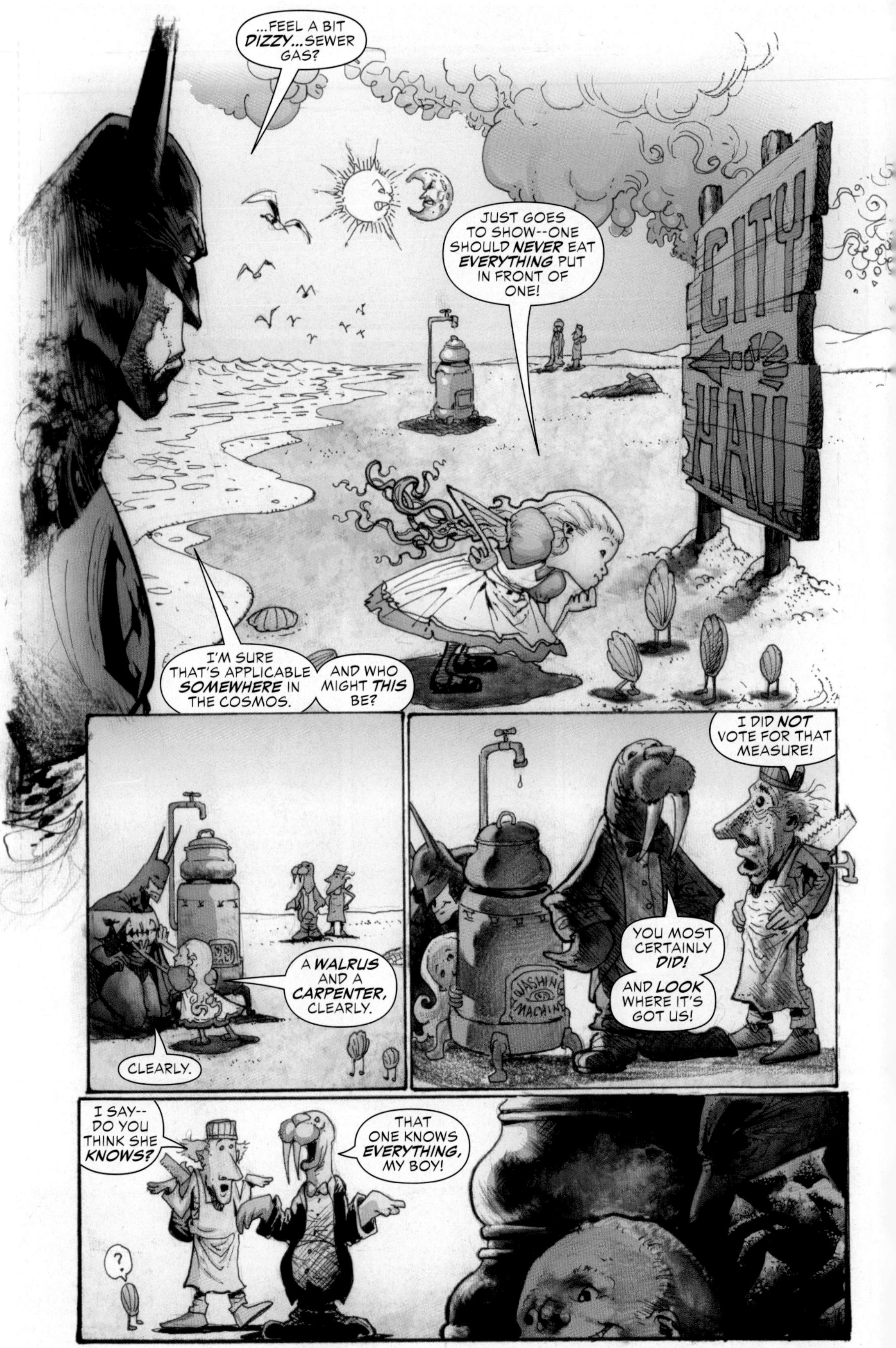
...FEEL A BIT DIZZY...SEWER GAS?
JUST GOES TO SHOW--ONE SHOULD NEVER EAT EVERYTHING PUT IN FRONT OF ONE!
CITY HALL
I'M SURE THAT'S APPLICABLE SOMEWHERE IN THE COSMOS.
AND WHO MIGHT THIS BE?
A WALRUS AND A CARPENTER, CLEARLY.
CLEARLY.
I DID NOT VOTE FOR THAT MEASURE!
YOU MOST CERTAINLY DID!
AND LOOK WHERE IT'S GOT US!
WASHING MACHINE
I SAY-- DO YOU THINK SHE KNOWS?
THAT ONE KNOWS EVERYTHING, MY BOY!
?

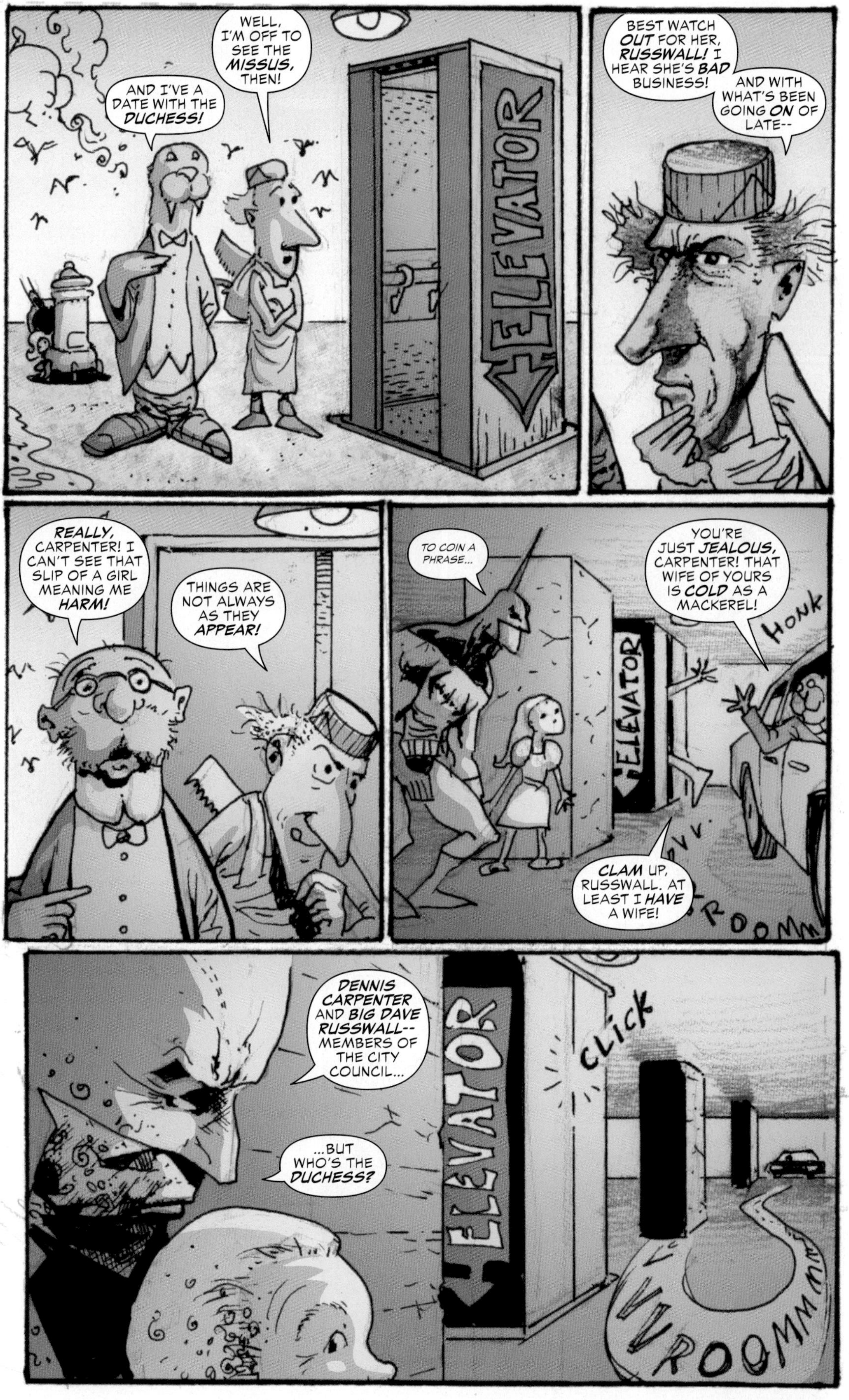
WELL, I'M OFF TO SEE THE MISSUS, THEN!
AND I'VE A DATE WITH THE DUCHESS!
ELEVATOR
BEST WATCH OUT FOR HER, RUSSWALL! I HEAR SHE'S BAD BUSINESS!
AND WITH WHAT'S BEEN GOING ON OF LATE--
REALLY, CARPENTER! I CAN'T SEE THAT SLIP OF A GIRL MEANING ME HARM!
THINGS ARE NOT ALWAYS AS THEY APPEAR!
TO COIN A PHRASE...
YOU'RE JUST JEALOUS, CARPENTER! THAT WIFE OF YOURS IS COLD AS A MACKEREL!
HONK
ELEVATOR
CLAM UP, RUSSWALL. AT LEAST I HAVE A WIFE!
VROOMM
DENNIS CARPENTER AND BIG DAVE RUSSWALL-- MEMBERS OF THE CITY COUNCIL...
...BUT WHO'S THE DUCHESS?
ELEVATOR
CLICK
VVROOMMMM

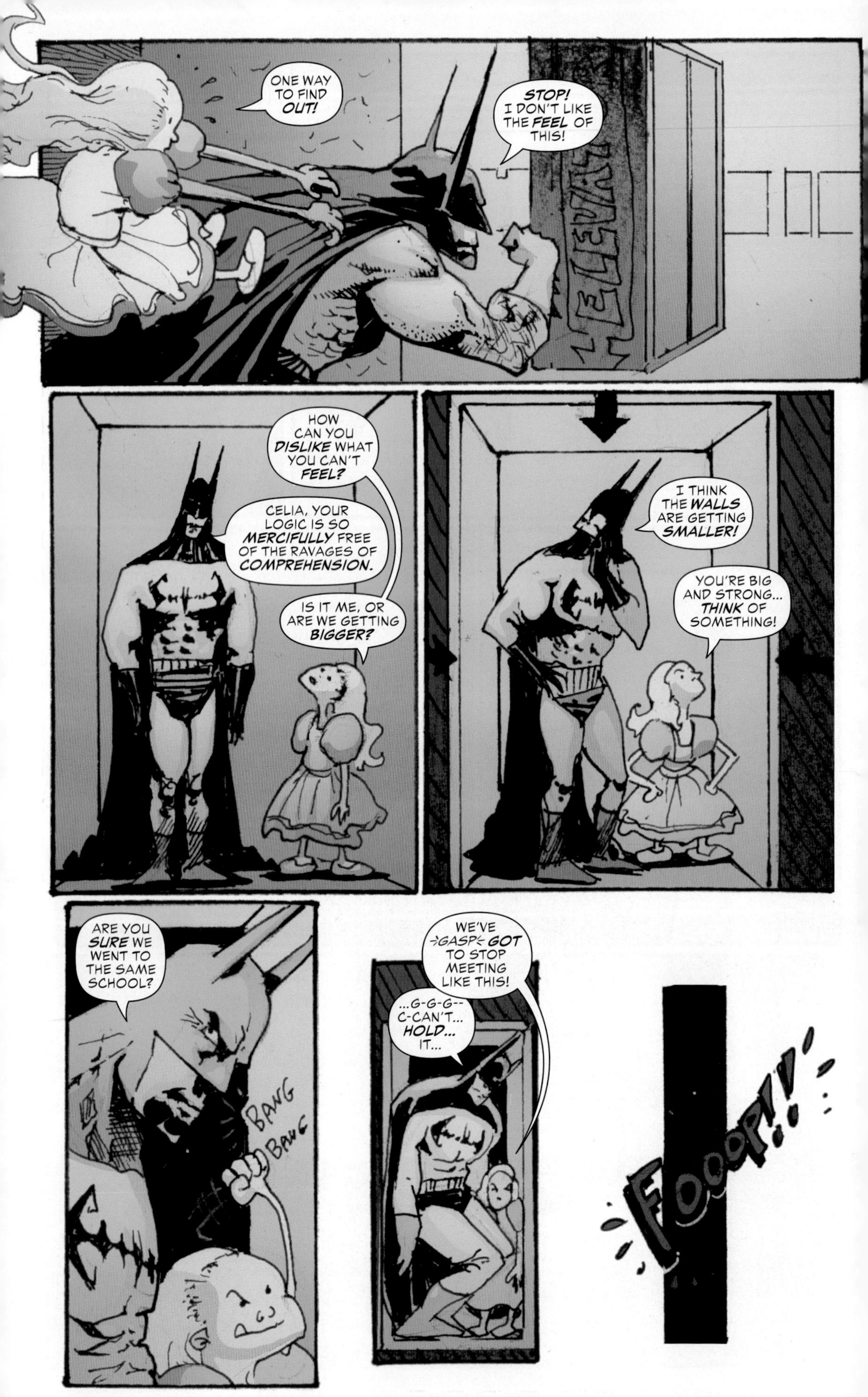
ONE WAY TO FIND OUT!
STOP! I DON'T LIKE THE FEEL OF THIS!
HOW CAN YOU DISLIKE WHAT YOU CAN'T FEEL?
CELIA, YOUR LOGIC IS SO MERCIFULLY FREE OF THE RAVAGES OF COMPREHENSION.
IS IT ME, OR ARE WE GETTING BIGGER?
I THINK THE WALLS ARE GETTING SMALLER!
YOU'RE BIG AND STRONG... THINK OF SOMETHING!
ARE YOU SURE WE WENT TO THE SAME SCHOOL?
BANG
BANG
WE'VE ⇒GASP⇐ GOT TO STOP MEETING LIKE THIS!
...G-G-G-- C-CAN'T... HOLD... IT...
FOOOPT!!

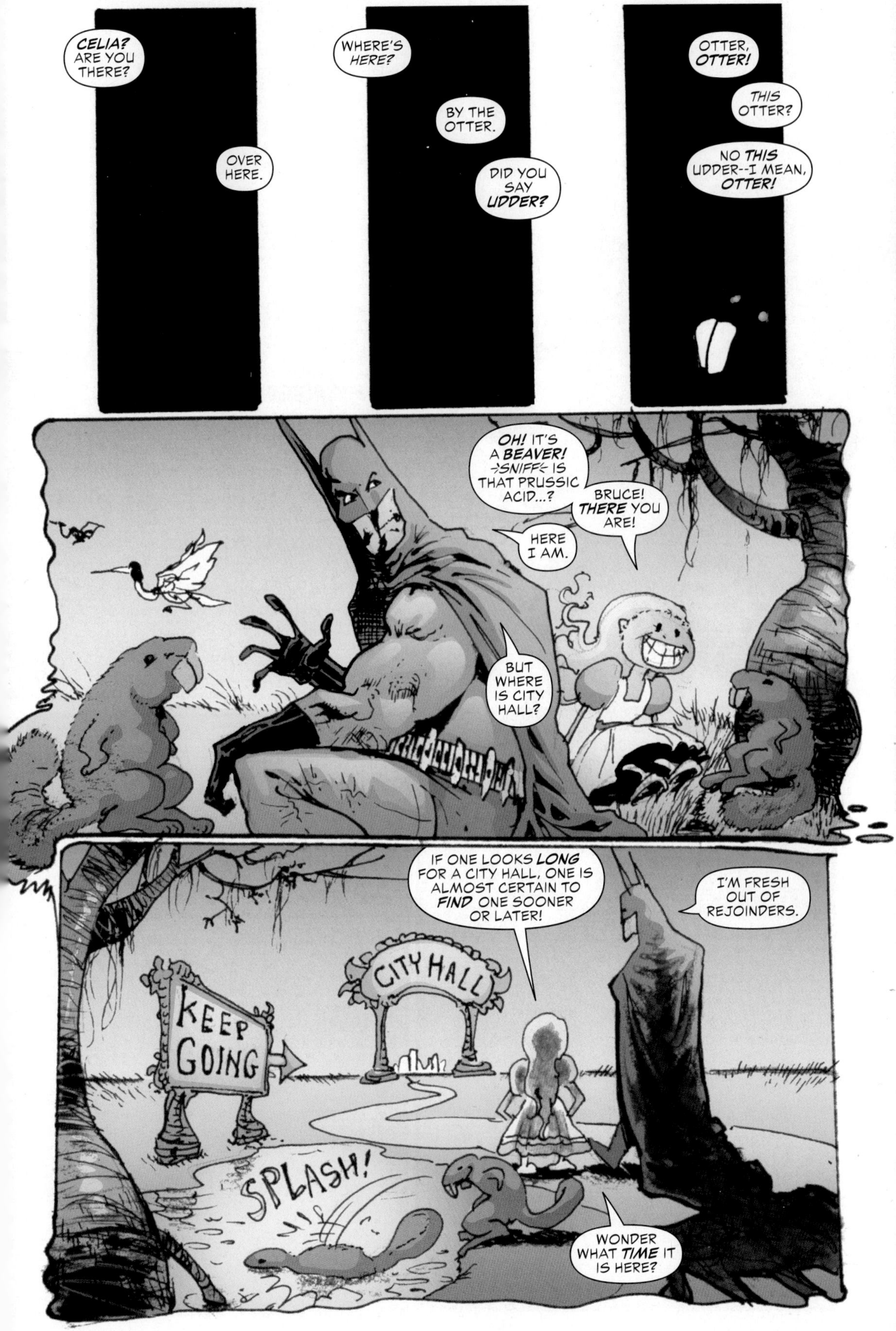
CELIA? ARE YOU THERE?
OVER HERE.
WHERE'S HERE?
BY THE OTTER.
DID YOU SAY UDDER?
OTTER, OTTER!
THIS OTTER?
NO THIS UDDER--I MEAN, OTTER!
OH! IT'S A BEAVER! SNIFF IS THAT PRUSSIC ACID...?
BRUCE! THERE YOU ARE!
HERE I AM.
BUT WHERE IS CITY HALL?
IF ONE LOOKS LONG FOR A CITY HALL, ONE IS ALMOST CERTAIN TO FIND ONE SOONER OR LATER!
I'M FRESH OUT OF REJOINDERS.
CITY HALL
KEEP GOING
SPLASH!
WONDER WHAT TIME IT IS HERE?

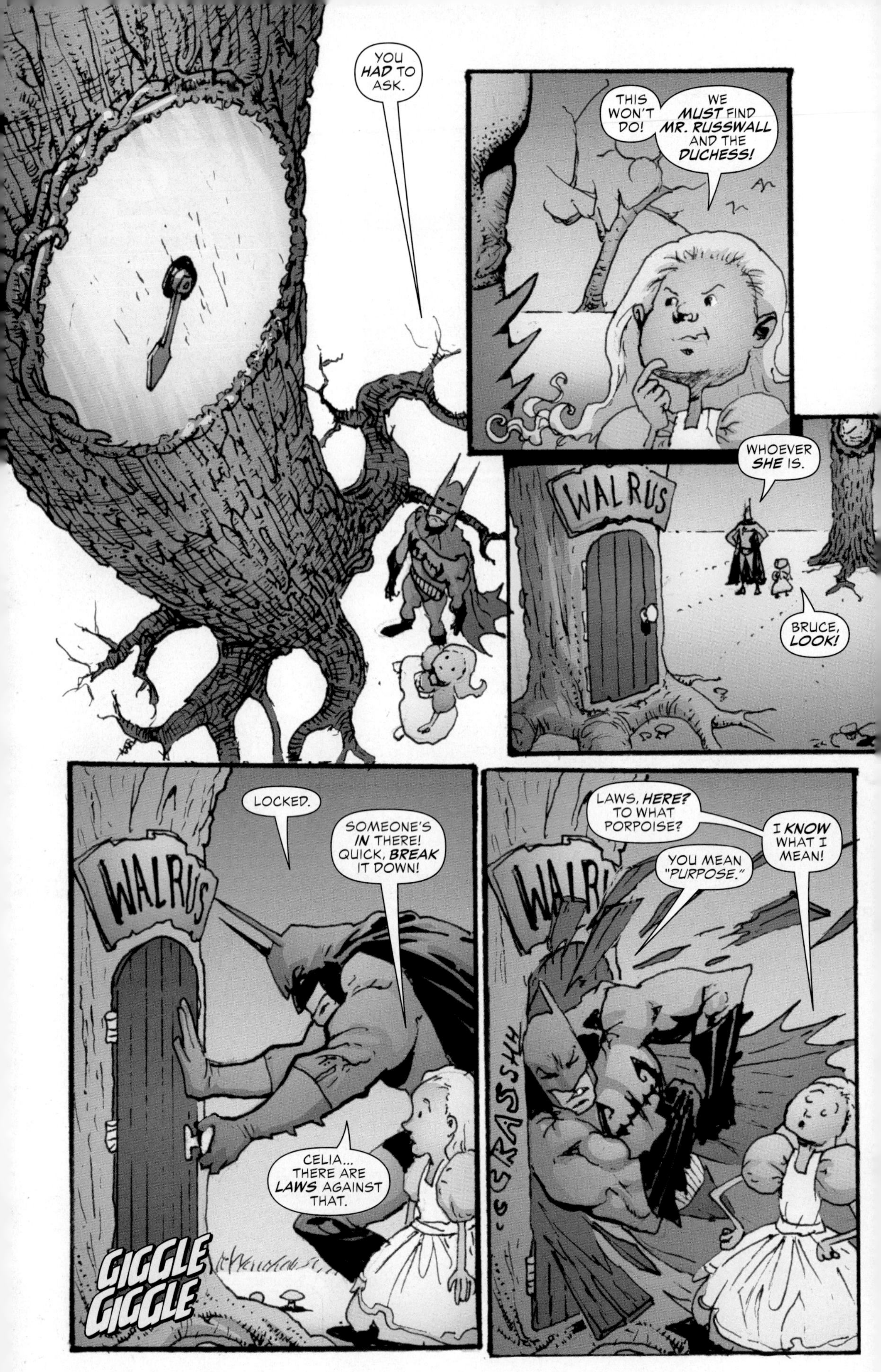
YOU HAD TO ASK.
THIS WON'T DO!
WE MUST FIND MR. RUSSWALL AND THE DUCHESS!
WALRUS
WHOEVER SHE IS.
BRUCE, LOOK!
WALRUS
LOCKED.
SOMEONE'S IN THERE! QUICK, BREAK IT DOWN!
CELIA... THERE ARE LAWS AGAINST THAT.
GIGGLE GIGGLE
WALRUS
LAWS, HERE? TO WHAT PORPOISE?
YOU MEAN "PURPOSE."
I KNOW WHAT I MEAN!
CRASSHH

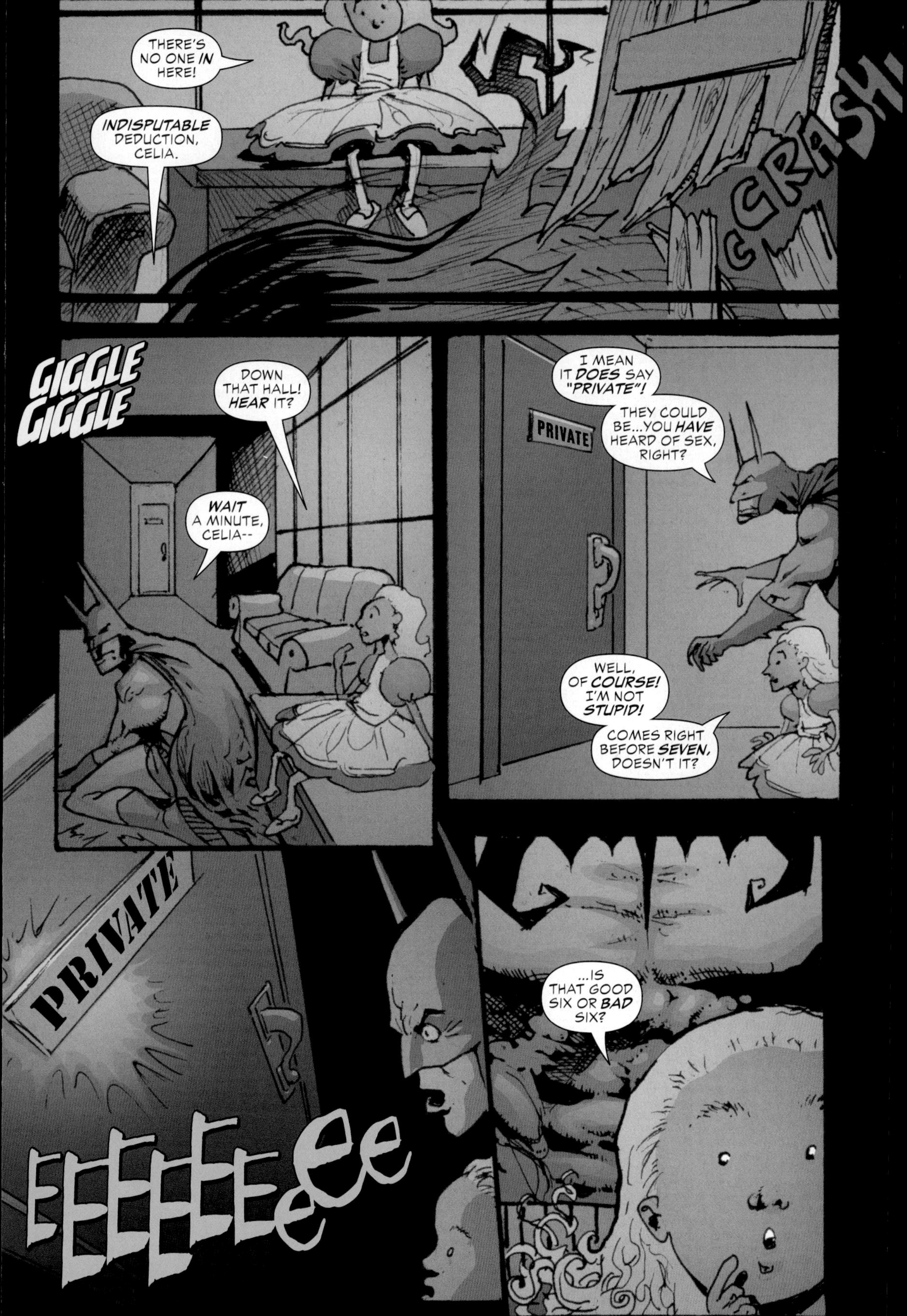
THERE'S NO ONE *IN* HERE!
INDISPUTABLE DEDUCTION, CELIA.
CRASH!
GIGGLE GIGGLE
DOWN THAT HALL! *HEAR* IT?
WAIT A MINUTE, CELIA--
PRIVATE
I MEAN IT *DOES* SAY *"PRIVATE"*!
THEY COULD BE...YOU *HAVE* HEARD OF SEX, RIGHT?
WELL, OF *COURSE!* I'M NOT *STUPID!*
COMES RIGHT BEFORE *SEVEN,* DOESN'T IT?
PRIVATE
EEEEEEEeee
...IS THAT GOOD SIX OR *BAD* SIX?

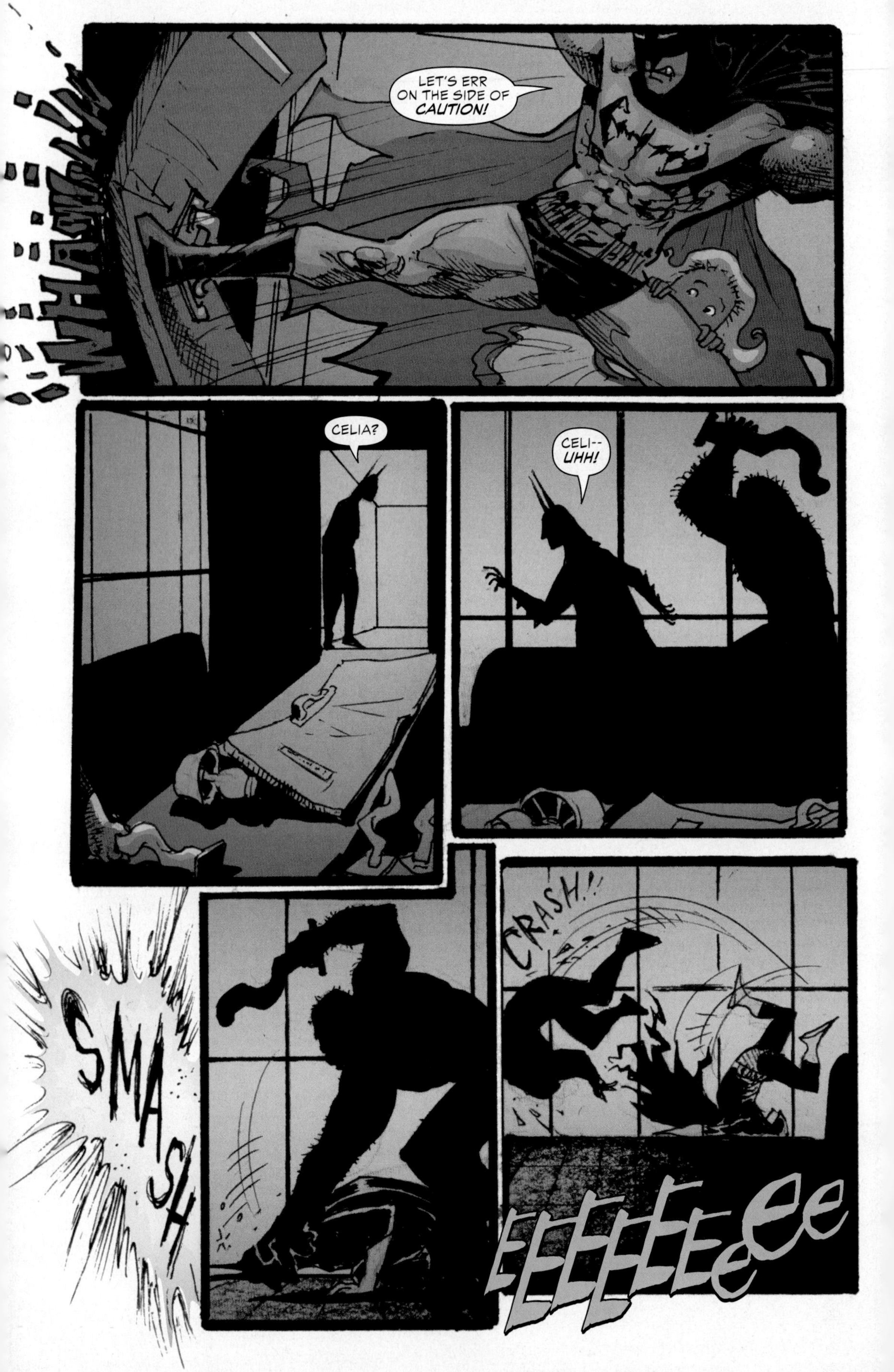
WHAAAM!!
LET'S ERR ON THE SIDE OF CAUTION!
CELIA?
CELI-- UHH!
SMASH
CRASH!!
EEEEEEEeee

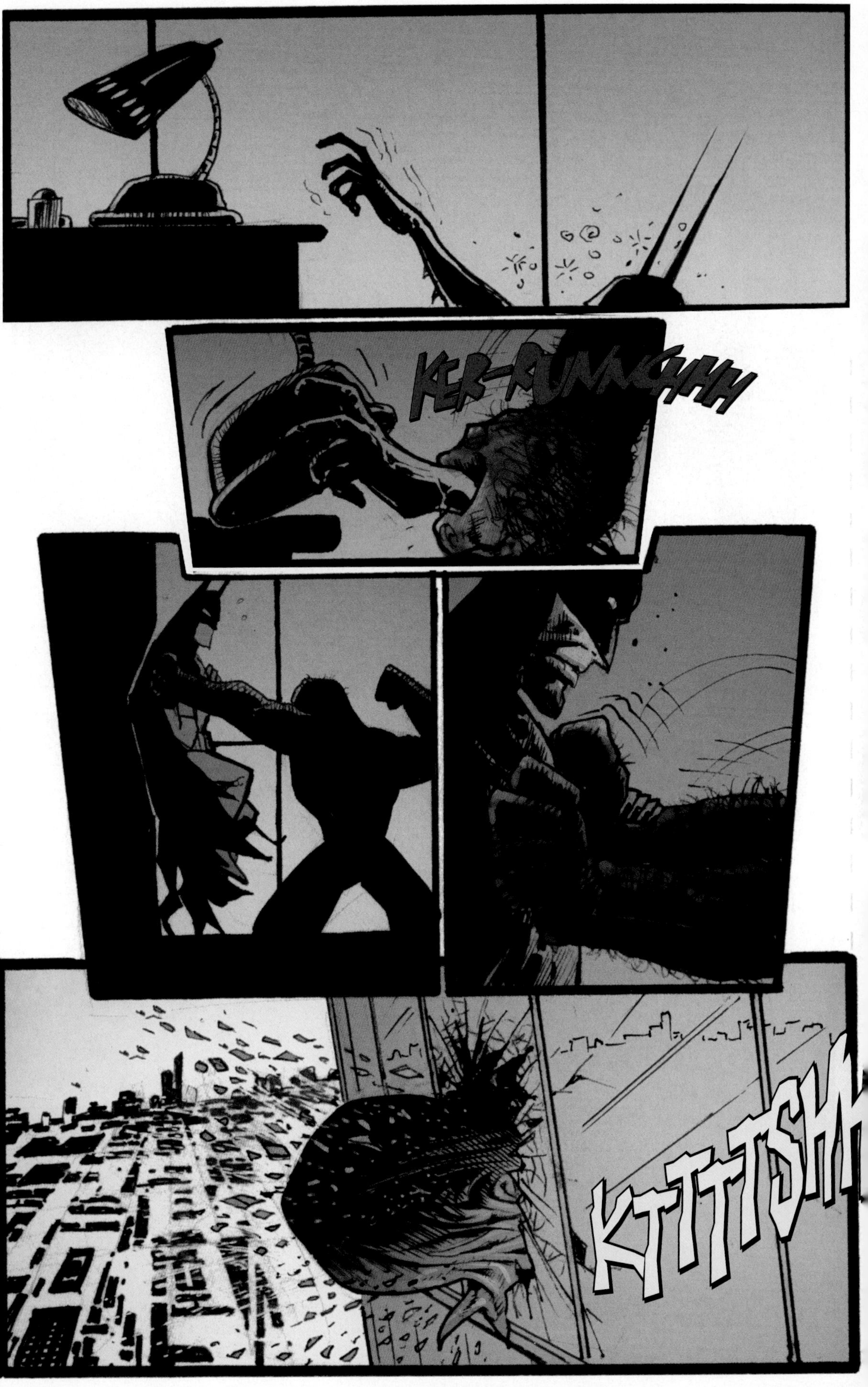
KER-RUNNCHHH
KTTTSHH

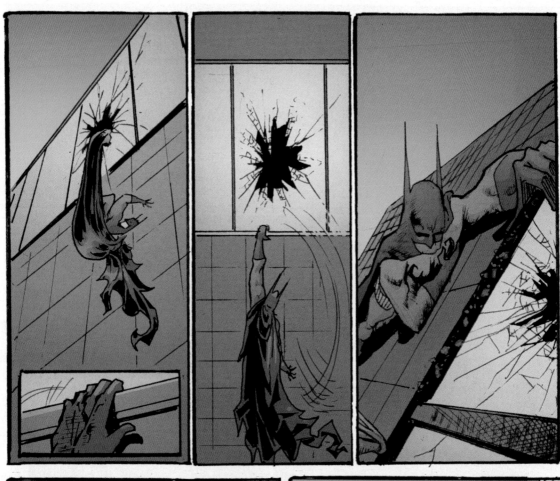

--RUSSWALL!

WELL, WELL...

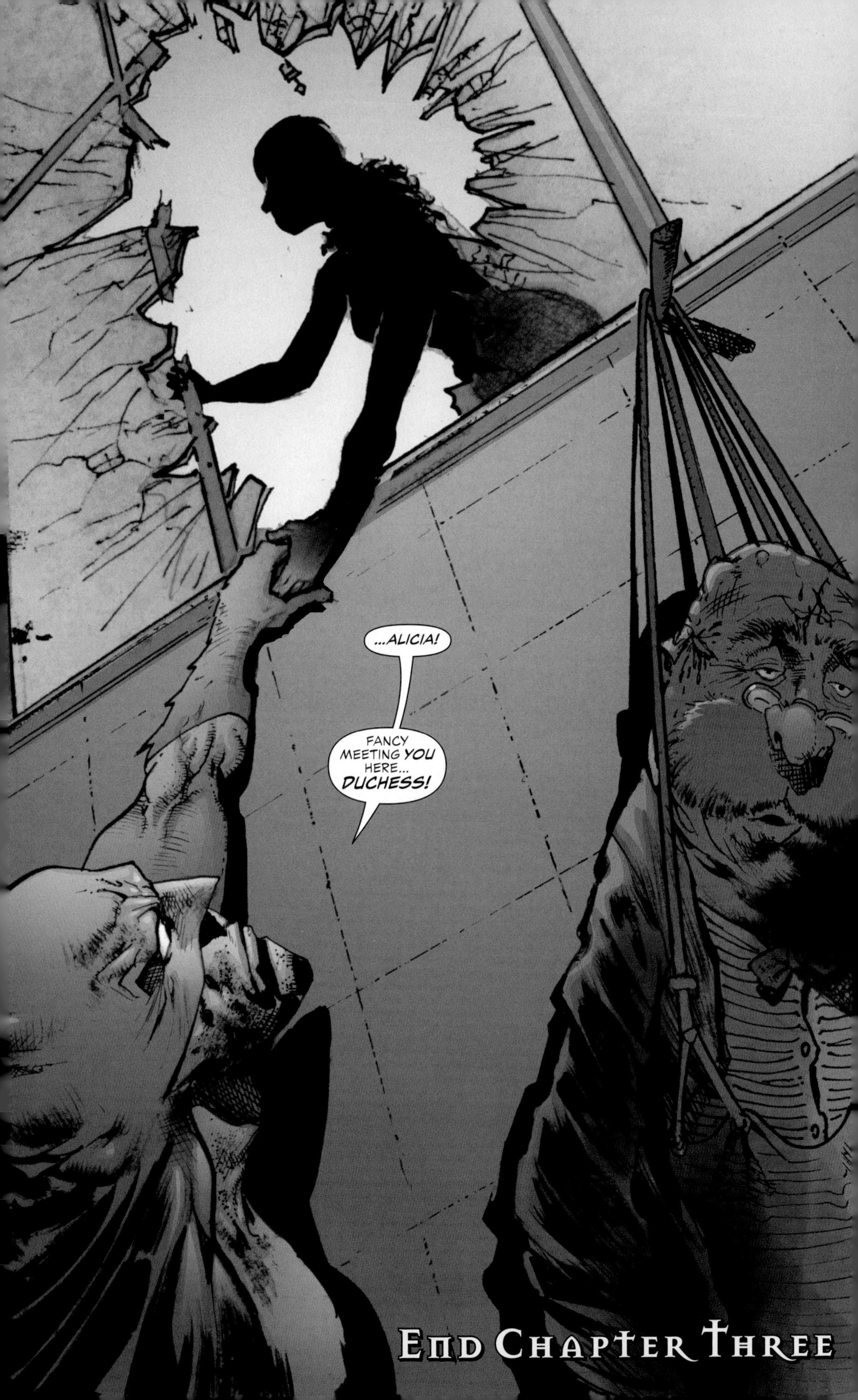
...ALICIA!
FANCY MEETING YOU HERE... DUCHESS!
END CHAPTER THREE

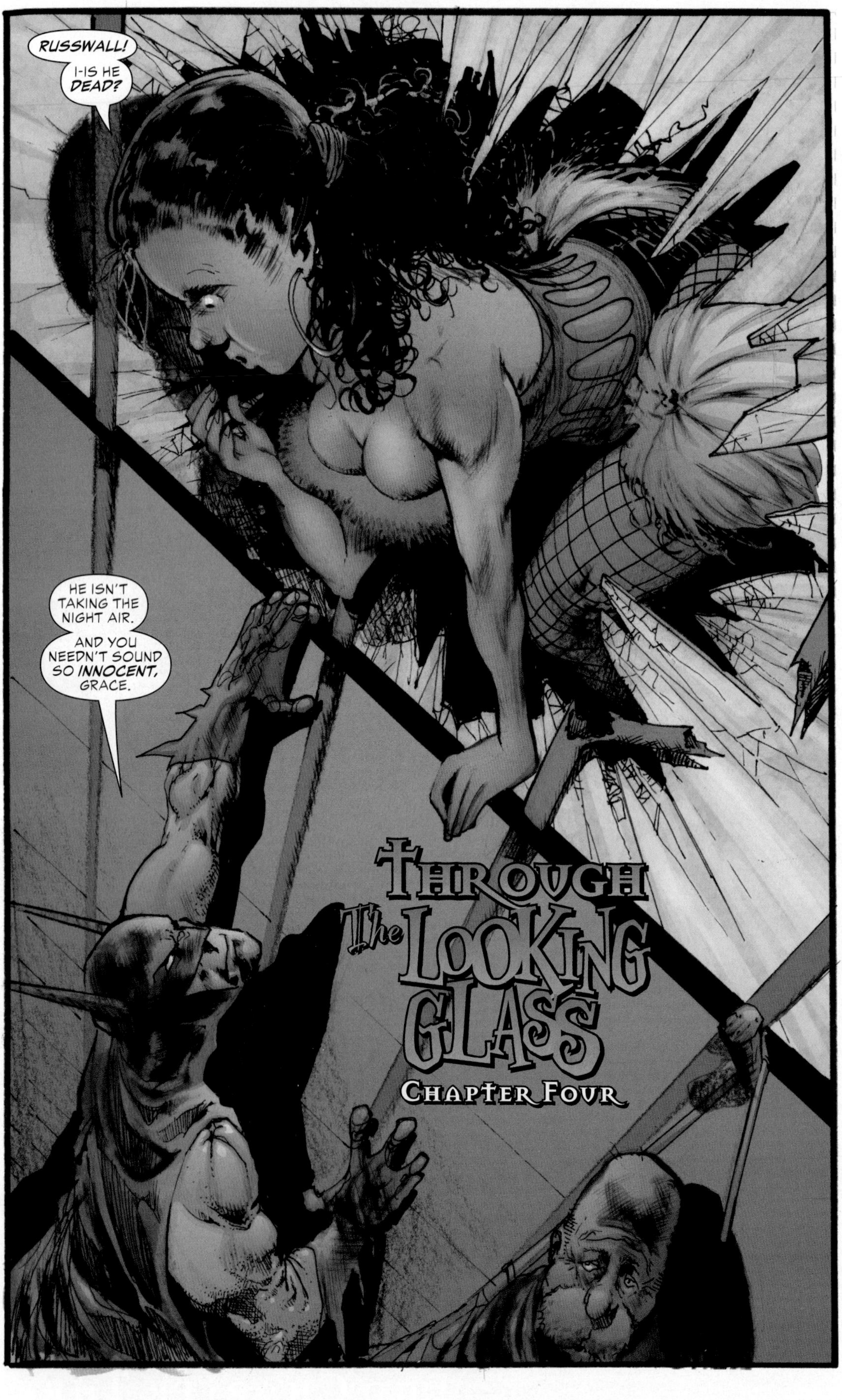
RUSSWALL! I-IS HE DEAD?
HE ISN'T TAKING THE NIGHT AIR.
AND YOU NEEDN'T SOUND SO INNOCENT, GRACE.
THROUGH THE LOOKING GLASS
CHAPTER FOUR

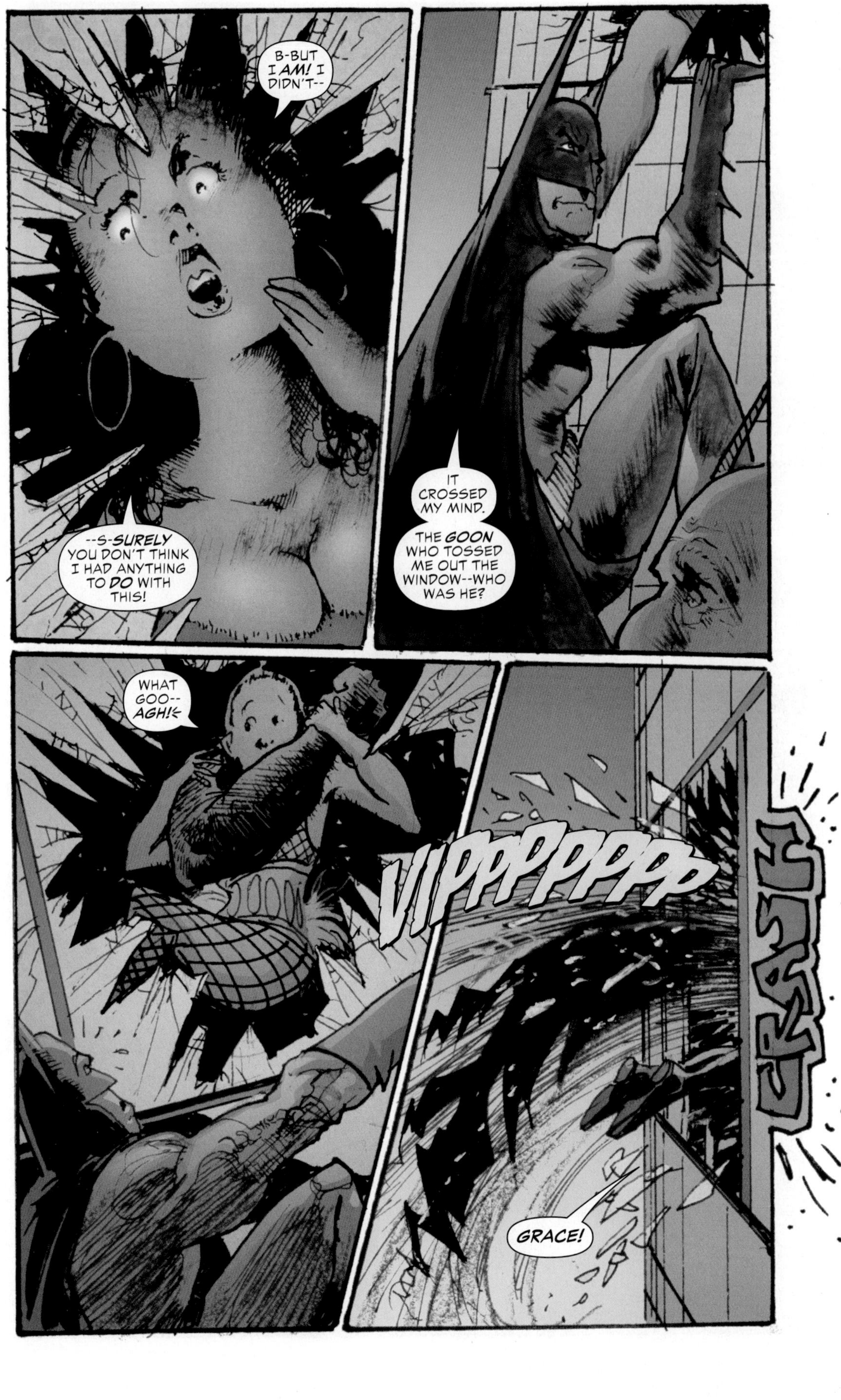
B-BUT I AM! I DIDN'T--
--S-SURELY YOU DON'T THINK I HAD ANYTHING TO DO WITH THIS!
IT CROSSED MY MIND.
THE GOON WHO TOSSED ME OUT THE WINDOW--WHO WAS HE?
WHAT GOO--AGH!
VIPPPPPPPP
CRASH
GRACE!

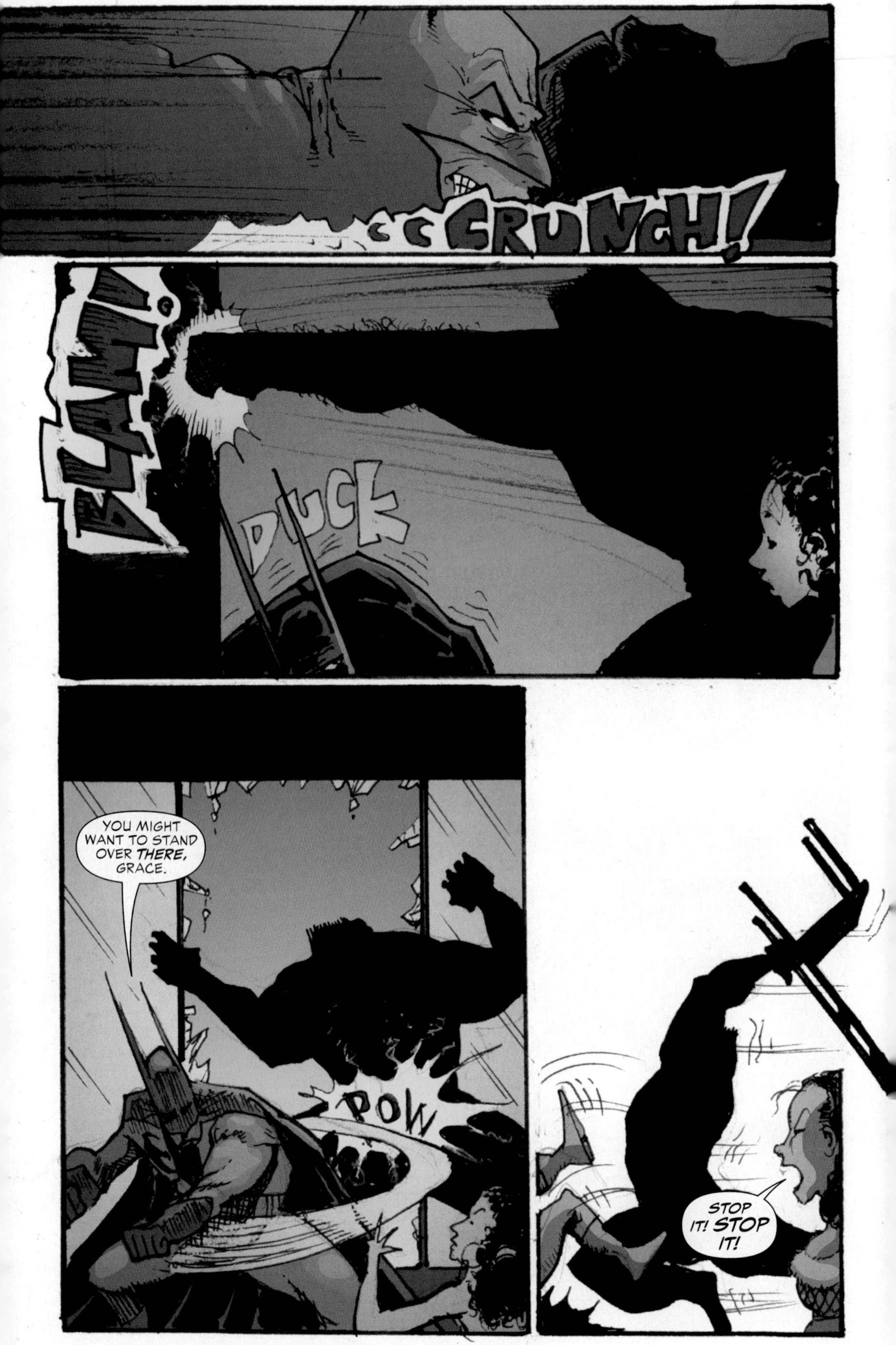
CCCRUNCH!
BLAMM!
DUCK
YOU MIGHT WANT TO STAND OVER THERE, GRACE.
POW
STOP IT! STOP IT!

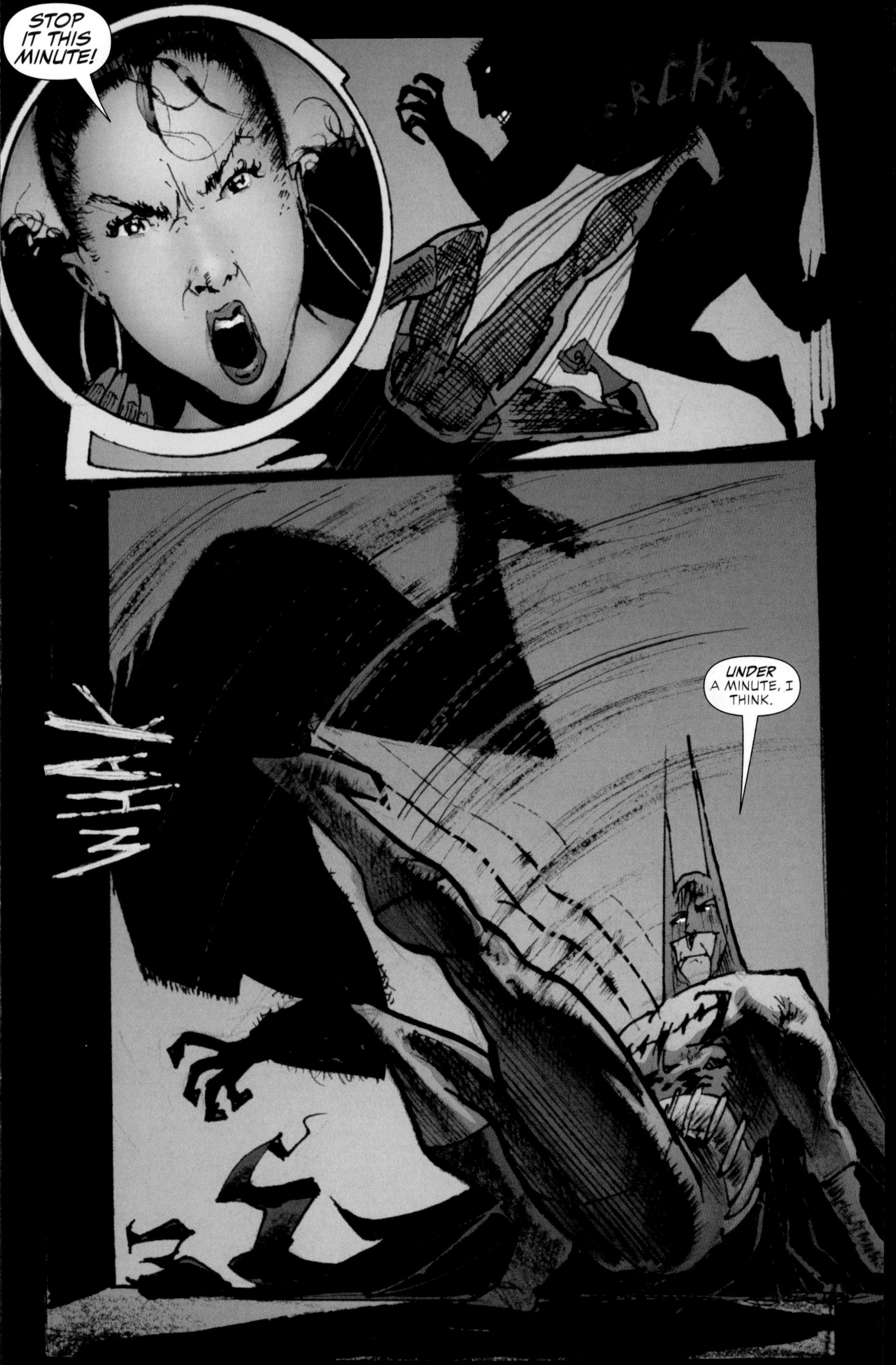
STOP IT THIS MINUTE!
WHAM
UNDER A MINUTE, I THINK.

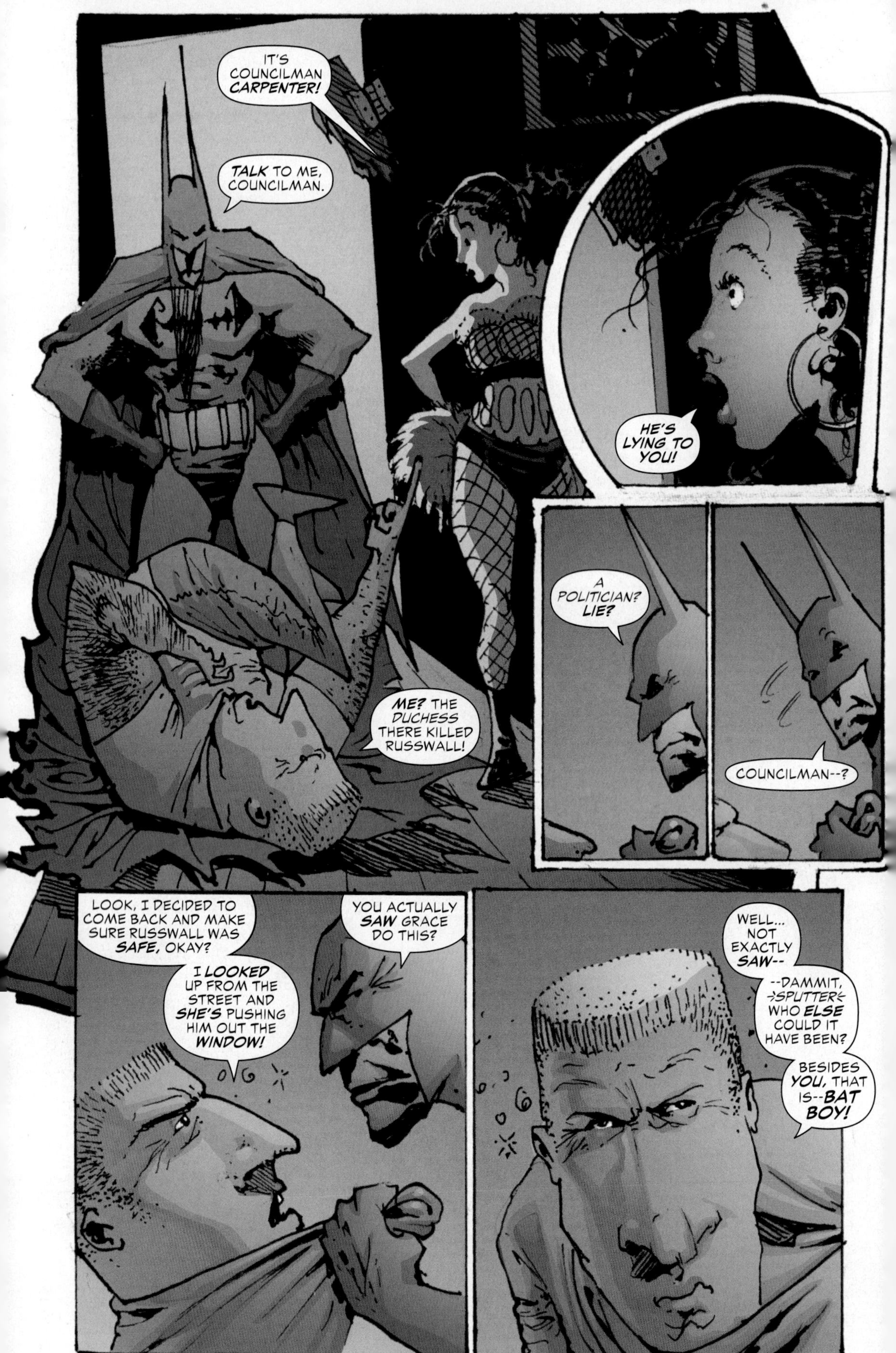
IT'S COUNCILMAN CARPENTER!
TALK TO ME, COUNCILMAN.
HE'S LYING TO YOU!
ME? THE DUCHESS THERE KILLED RUSSWALL!
A POLITICIAN? LIE?
COUNCILMAN--?
LOOK, I DECIDED TO COME BACK AND MAKE SURE RUSSWALL WAS SAFE, OKAY?
I LOOKED UP FROM THE STREET AND SHE'S PUSHING HIM OUT THE WINDOW!
YOU ACTUALLY SAW GRACE DO THIS?
WELL... NOT EXACTLY SAW--
--DAMMIT, ›SPUTTER‹ WHO ELSE COULD IT HAVE BEEN?
BESIDES YOU, THAT IS--BAT BOY!

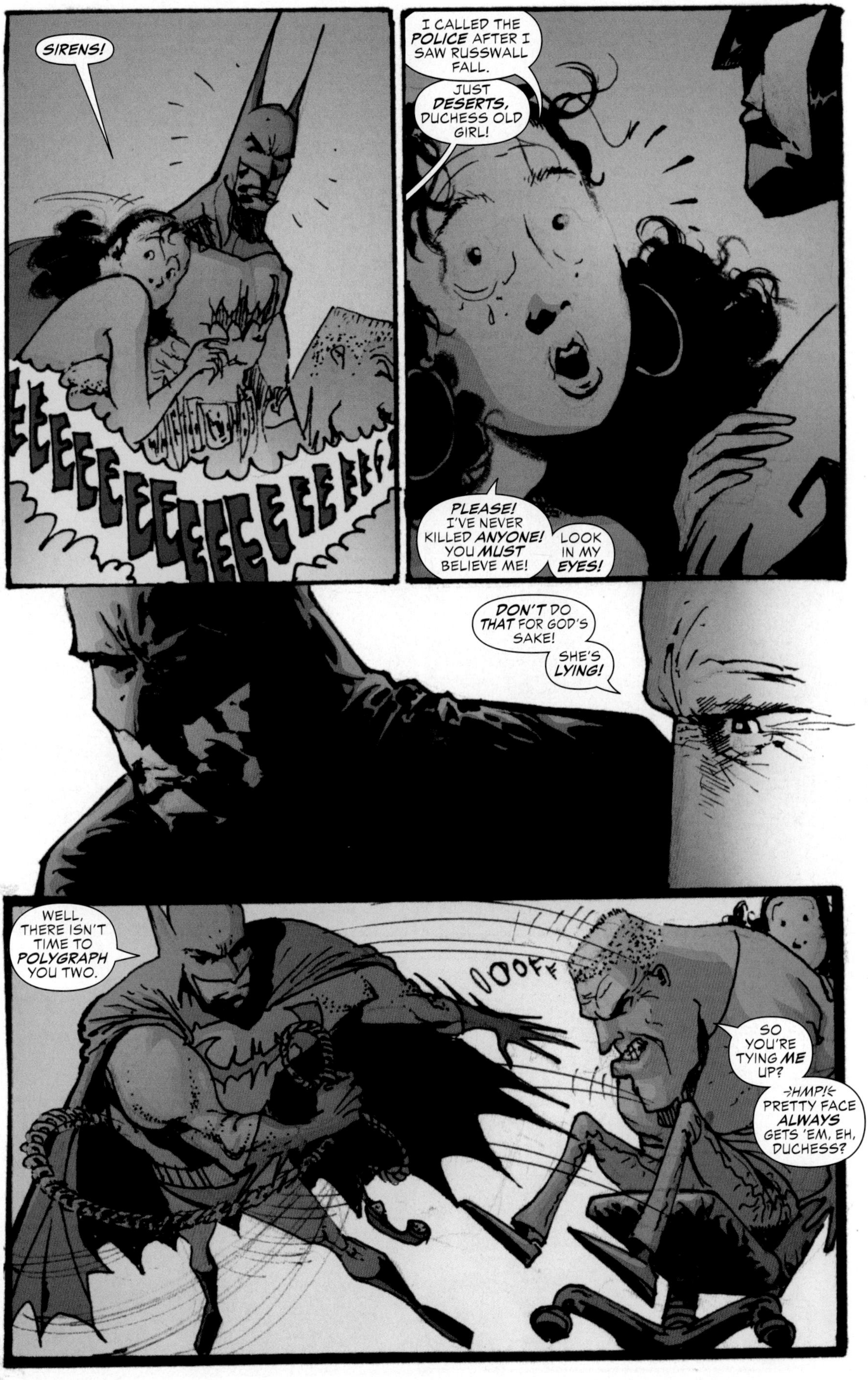
SIRENS!
EEEEEEEEEEEEEEEEEEEEE
I CALLED THE POLICE AFTER I SAW RUSSWALL FALL.
JUST DESERTS, DUCHESS OLD GIRL!
PLEASE! I'VE NEVER KILLED ANYONE! YOU MUST BELIEVE ME!
LOOK IN MY EYES!
DON'T DO THAT FOR GOD'S SAKE!
SHE'S LYING!
WELL, THERE ISN'T TIME TO POLYGRAPH YOU TWO.
OOOF
SO YOU'RE TYING ME UP?
HMP! PRETTY FACE ALWAYS GETS 'EM, EH, DUCHESS?

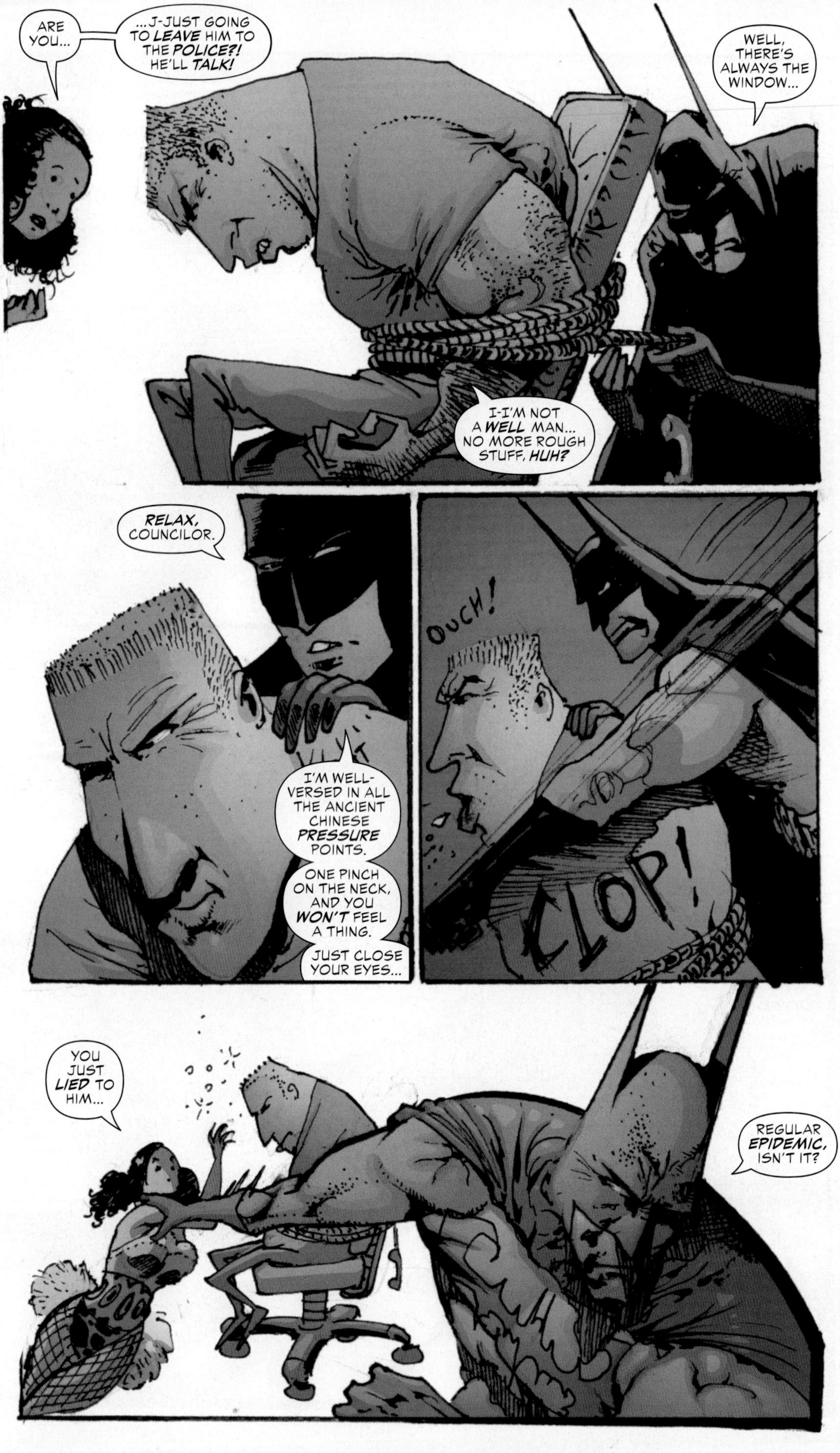
ARE YOU...
...J-JUST GOING TO LEAVE HIM TO THE POLICE?! HE'LL TALK!
WELL, THERE'S ALWAYS THE WINDOW...
I-I'M NOT A WELL MAN... NO MORE ROUGH STUFF, HUH?
RELAX, COUNCILOR.
I'M WELL-VERSED IN ALL THE ANCIENT CHINESE PRESSURE POINTS.
ONE PINCH ON THE NECK, AND YOU WON'T FEEL A THING.
JUST CLOSE YOUR EYES...
OUCH!
CLOP!
YOU JUST LIED TO HIM...
REGULAR EPIDEMIC, ISN'T IT?

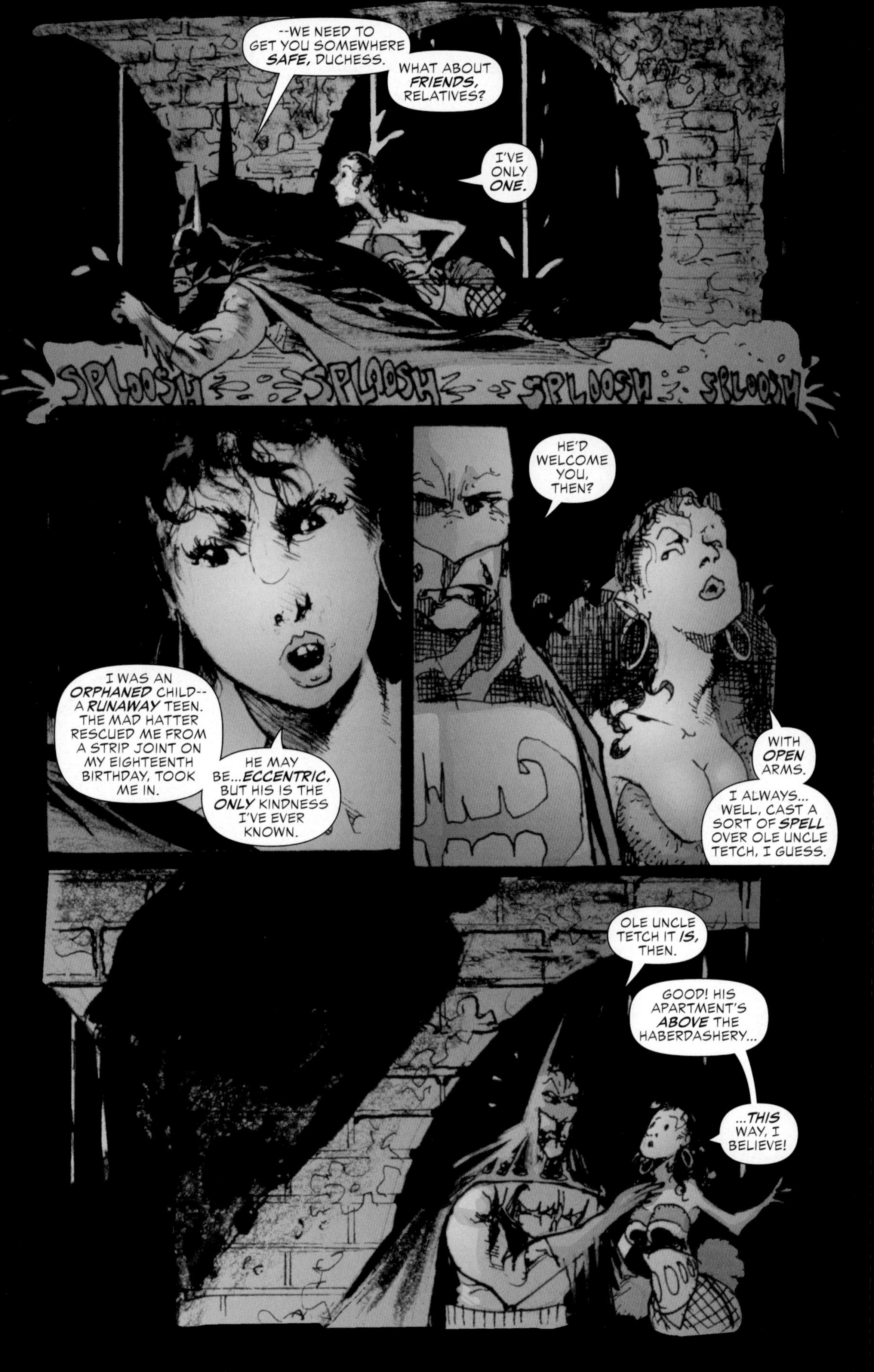
--WE NEED TO GET YOU SOMEWHERE SAFE, DUCHESS.
WHAT ABOUT FRIENDS, RELATIVES?
I'VE ONLY ONE.
SPLOOSH SPLOOSH SPLOOSH SPLOOSH
I WAS AN ORPHANED CHILD-- A RUNAWAY TEEN. THE MAD HATTER RESCUED ME FROM A STRIP JOINT ON MY EIGHTEENTH BIRTHDAY, TOOK ME IN.
HE MAY BE...ECCENTRIC, BUT HIS IS THE ONLY KINDNESS I'VE EVER KNOWN.
HE'D WELCOME YOU, THEN?
WITH OPEN ARMS.
I ALWAYS... WELL, CAST A SORT OF SPELL OVER OLE UNCLE TETCH, I GUESS.
OLE UNCLE TETCH IT IS, THEN.
GOOD! HIS APARTMENT'S ABOVE THE HABERDASHERY...
...THIS WAY, I BELIEVE!

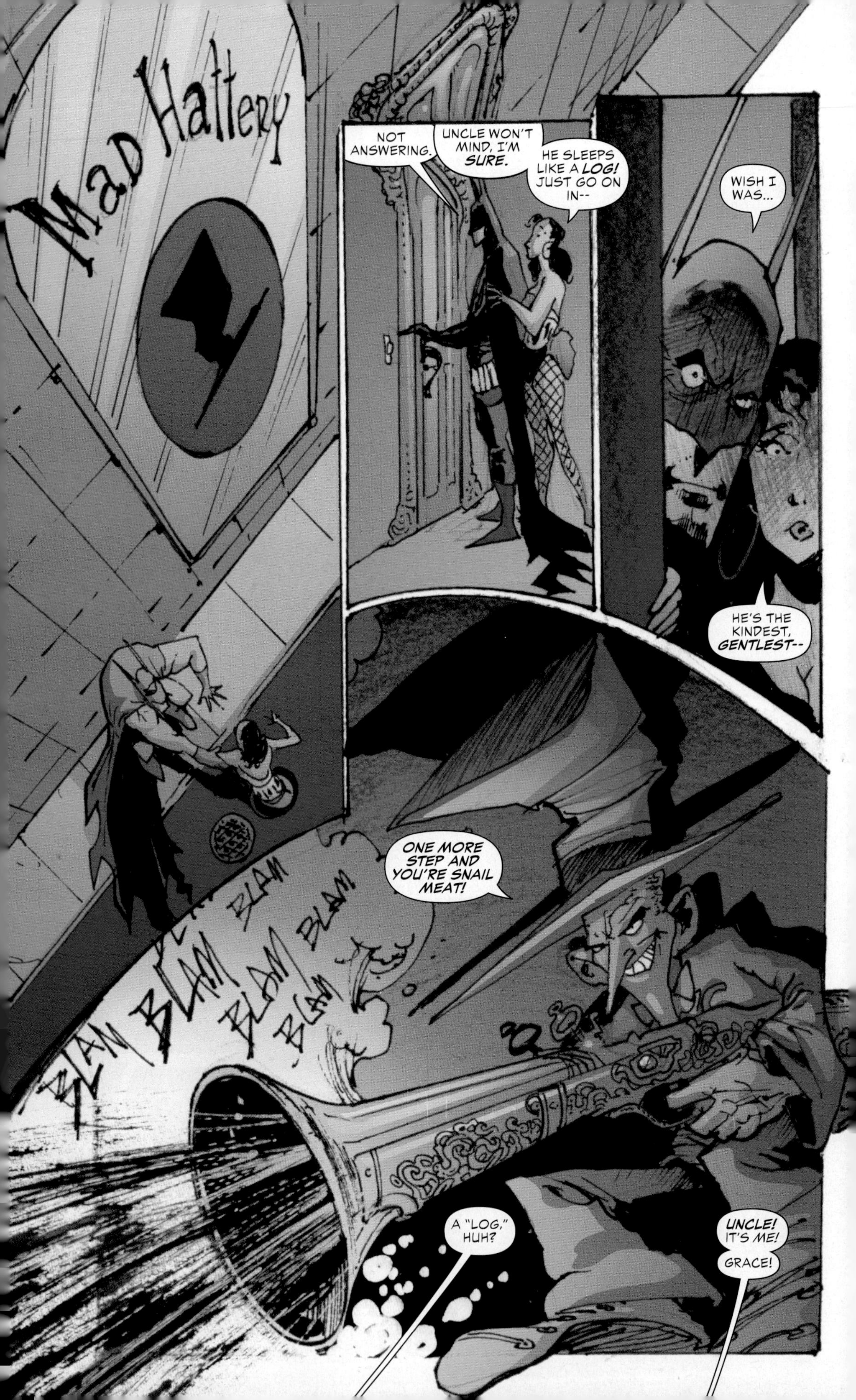
Mad Hattery
NOT ANSWERING.
UNCLE WON'T MIND, I'M SURE.
HE SLEEPS LIKE A LOG! JUST GO ON IN--
WISH I WAS...
HE'S THE KINDEST, GENTLEST--
ONE MORE STEP AND YOU'RE SNAIL MEAT!
BLAM BLAM BLAM BLAM BLAM BLAM BLAM
A "LOG," HUH?
UNCLE! IT'S ME!
GRACE!

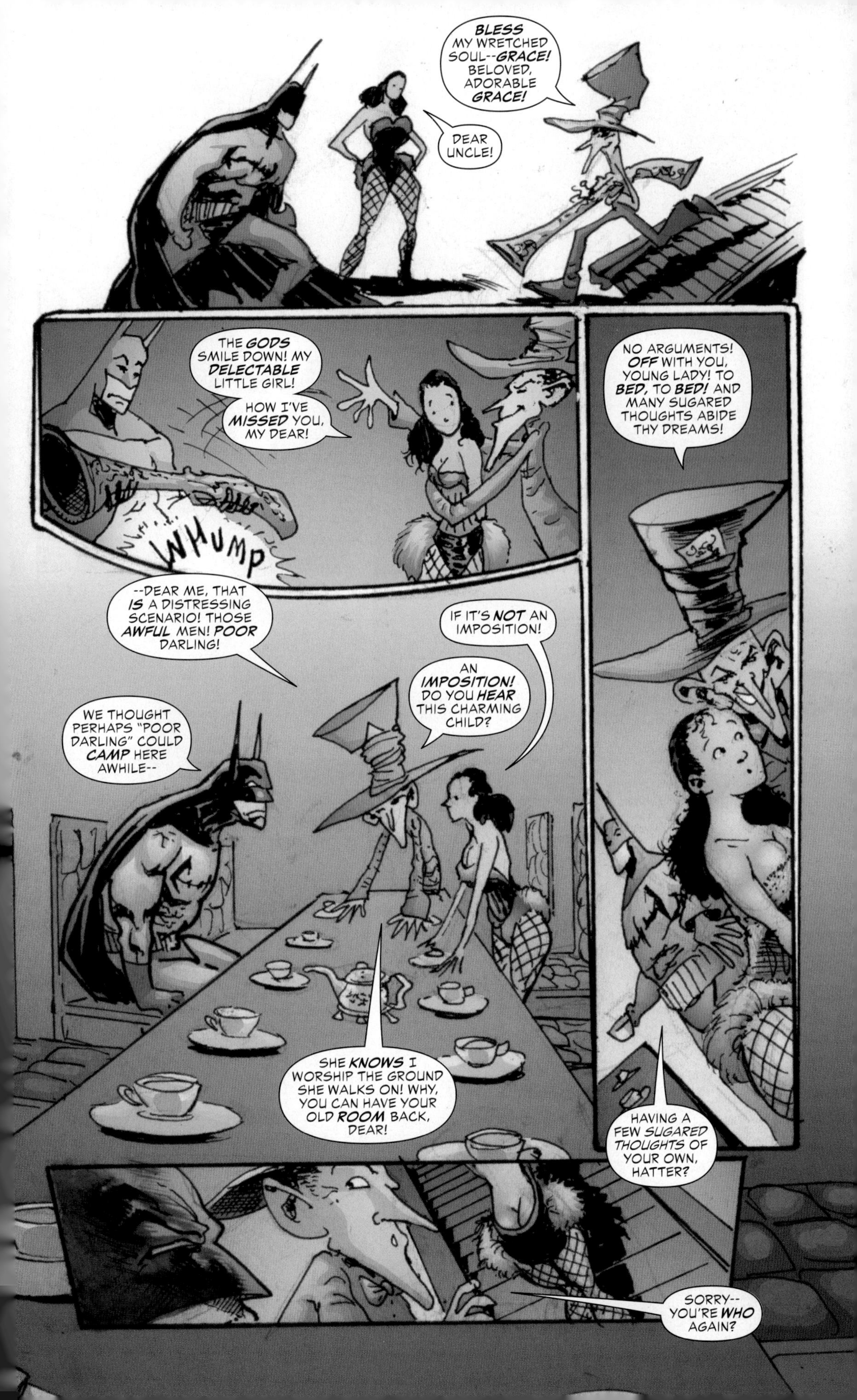
BLESS MY WRETCHED SOUL--GRACE! BELOVED, ADORABLE GRACE!
DEAR UNCLE!
THE GODS SMILE DOWN! MY DELECTABLE LITTLE GIRL!
HOW I'VE MISSED YOU, MY DEAR!
WHUMP
NO ARGUMENTS! OFF WITH YOU, YOUNG LADY! TO BED, TO BED! AND MANY SUGARED THOUGHTS ABIDE THY DREAMS!
--DEAR ME, THAT IS A DISTRESSING SCENARIO! THOSE AWFUL MEN! POOR DARLING!
WE THOUGHT PERHAPS "POOR DARLING" COULD CAMP HERE AWHILE--
IF IT'S NOT AN IMPOSITION!
AN IMPOSITION! DO YOU HEAR THIS CHARMING CHILD?
SHE KNOWS I WORSHIP THE GROUND SHE WALKS ON! WHY, YOU CAN HAVE YOUR OLD ROOM BACK, DEAR!
HAVING A FEW SUGARED THOUGHTS OF YOUR OWN, HATTER?
SORRY-- YOU'RE WHO AGAIN?

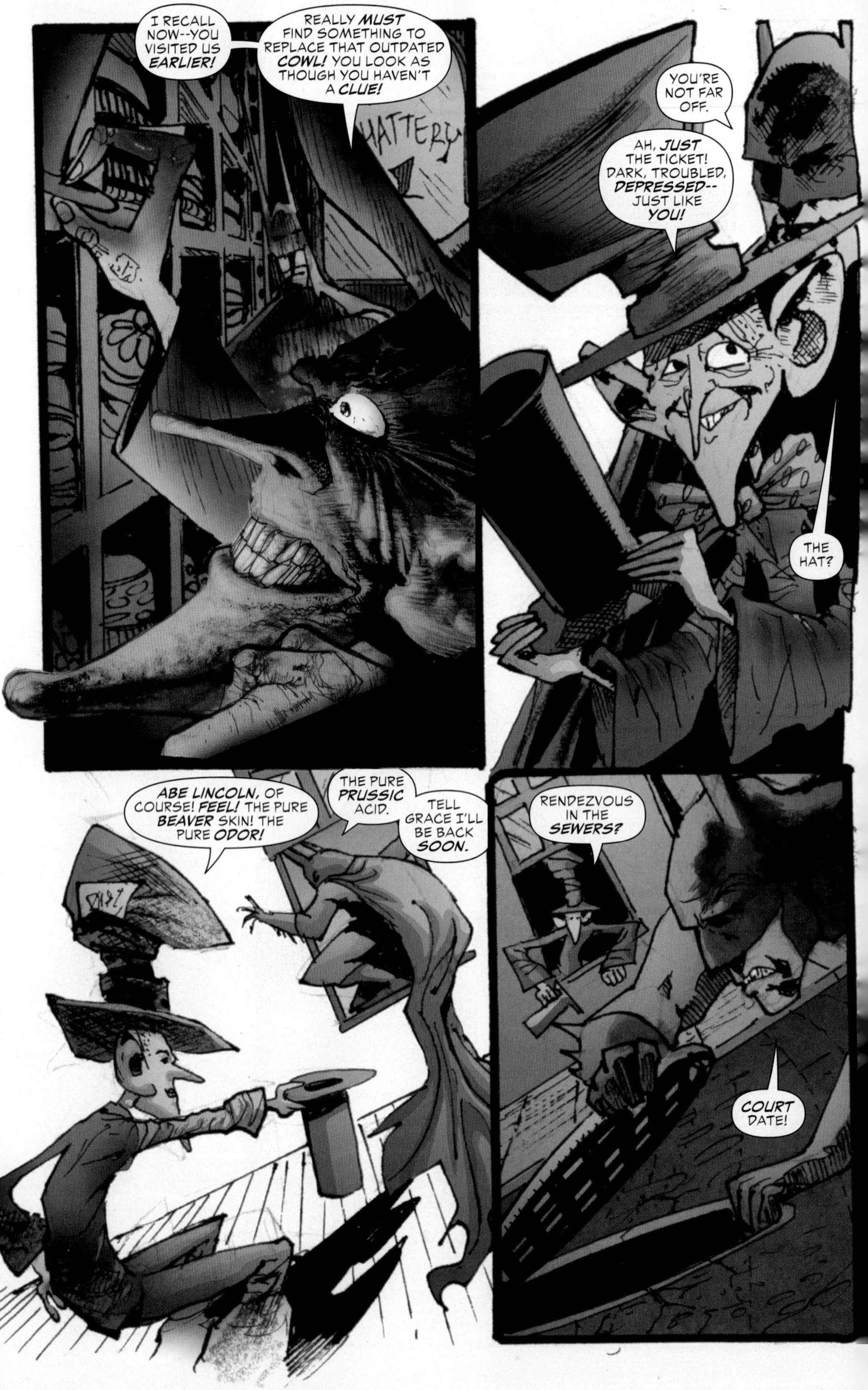
I RECALL NOW--YOU VISITED US EARLIER!
REALLY MUST FIND SOMETHING TO REPLACE THAT OUTDATED COWL! YOU LOOK AS THOUGH YOU HAVEN'T A CLUE!
HATTERY
YOU'RE NOT FAR OFF.
AH, JUST THE TICKET! DARK, TROUBLED, DEPRESSED-- JUST LIKE YOU!
THE HAT?
ABE LINCOLN, OF COURSE! FEEL! THE PURE BEAVER SKIN! THE PURE ODOR!
THE PURE PRUSSIC ACID.
TELL GRACE I'LL BE BACK SOON.
RENDEZVOUS IN THE SEWERS?
COURT DATE!

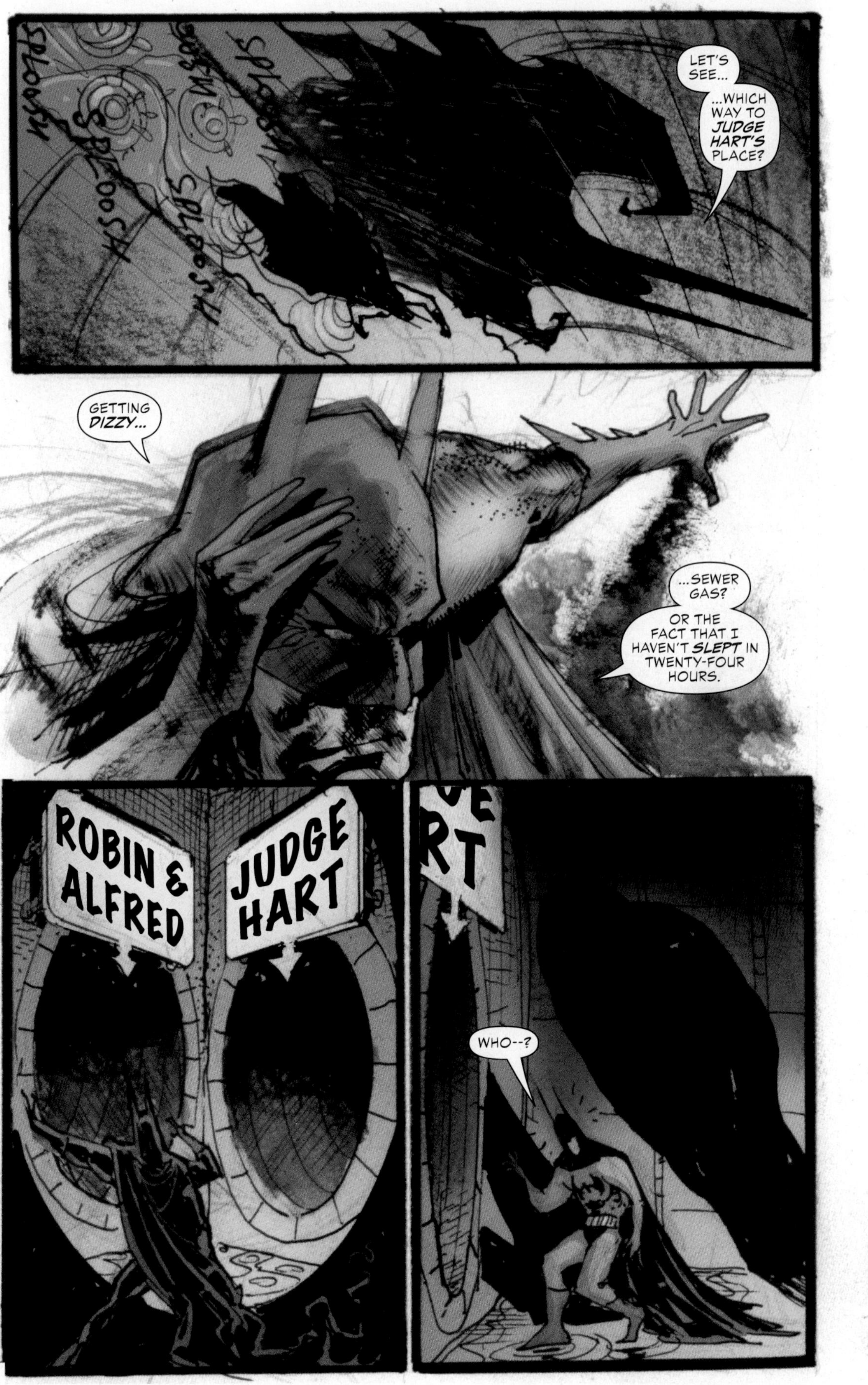
SPLOOSH
SPLOOSH
SPLOOSH
SPLOOSH
SPLOOSH
LET'S SEE...
...WHICH WAY TO JUDGE HART'S PLACE?
GETTING DIZZY...
...SEWER GAS?
OR THE FACT THAT I HAVEN'T SLEPT IN TWENTY-FOUR HOURS.
ROBIN & ALFRED
JUDGE HART
WHO--?

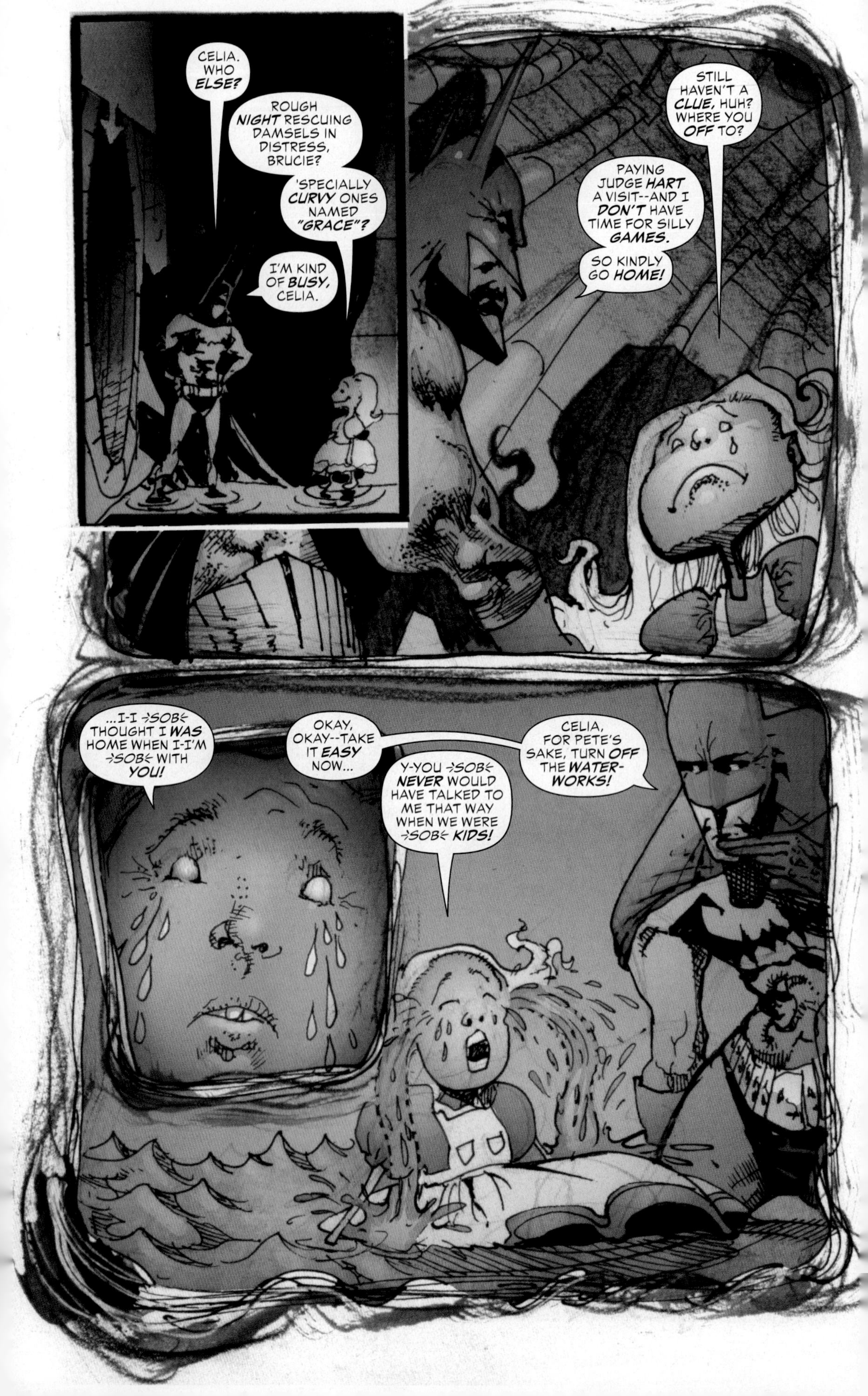
CELIA. WHO ELSE?
ROUGH NIGHT RESCUING DAMSELS IN DISTRESS, BRUCIE?
'SPECIALLY CURVY ONES NAMED "GRACE"?
I'M KIND OF BUSY, CELIA.
STILL HAVEN'T A CLUE, HUH? WHERE YOU OFF TO?
PAYING JUDGE HART A VISIT--AND I DON'T HAVE TIME FOR SILLY GAMES.
SO KINDLY GO HOME!
...I-I →SOB← THOUGHT I WAS HOME WHEN I-I'M →SOB← WITH YOU!
OKAY, OKAY--TAKE IT EASY NOW...
CELIA, FOR PETE'S SAKE, TURN OFF THE WATER-WORKS!
Y-YOU →SOB← NEVER WOULD HAVE TALKED TO ME THAT WAY WHEN WE WERE →SOB← KIDS!

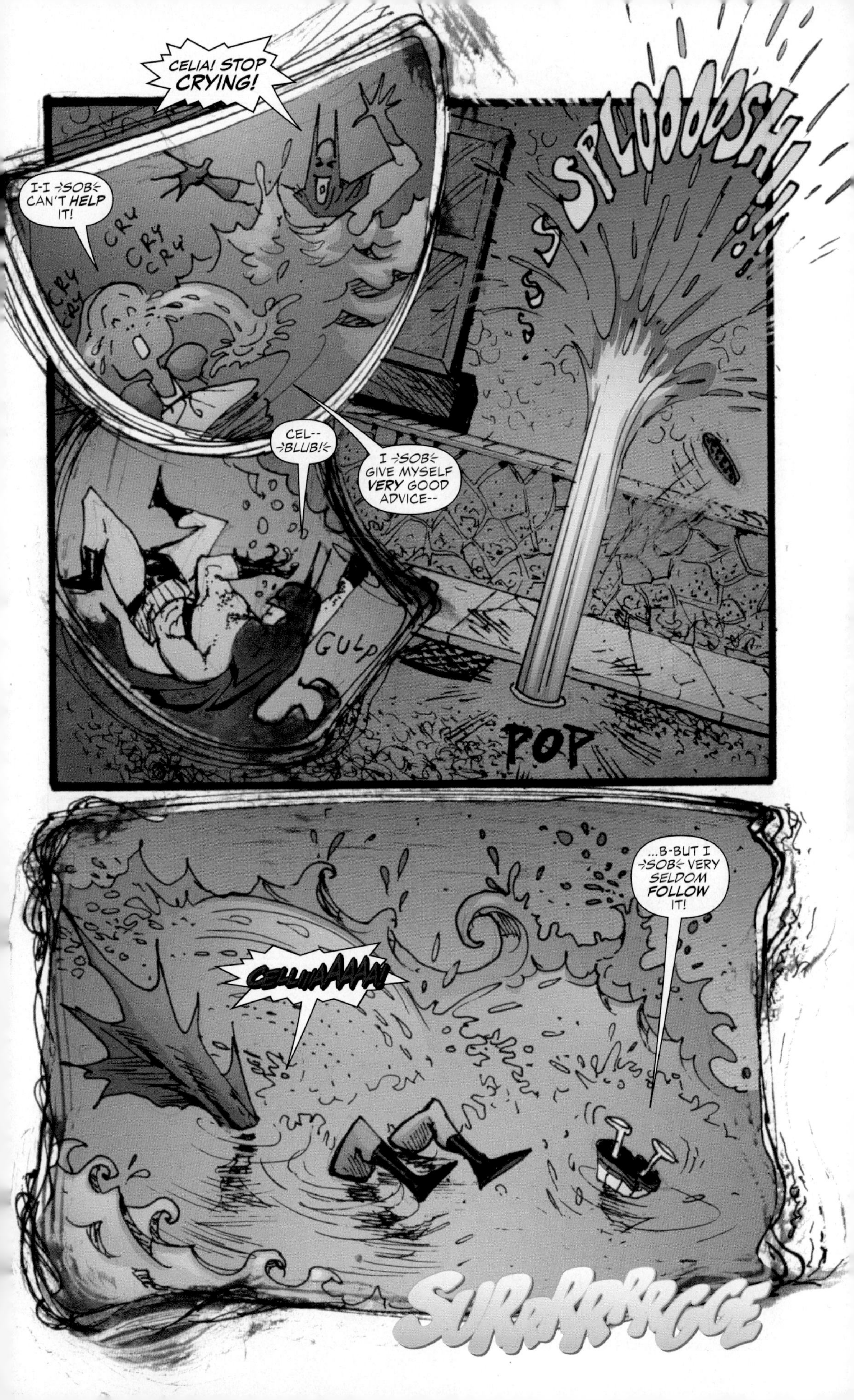
CELIA! STOP CRYING!
I-I ≻SOB≺ CAN'T HELP IT!
CRY CRY CRY CRY
CRY CRY
SPLOOOOSH!!
S S S
CEL-- ≻BLUB!≺
I ≻SOB≺ GIVE MYSELF VERY GOOD ADVICE--
GULP
POP
...B-BUT I ≻SOB≺ VERY SELDOM FOLLOW IT!
CELLIIIAAAAA!
SURRRRRGGE

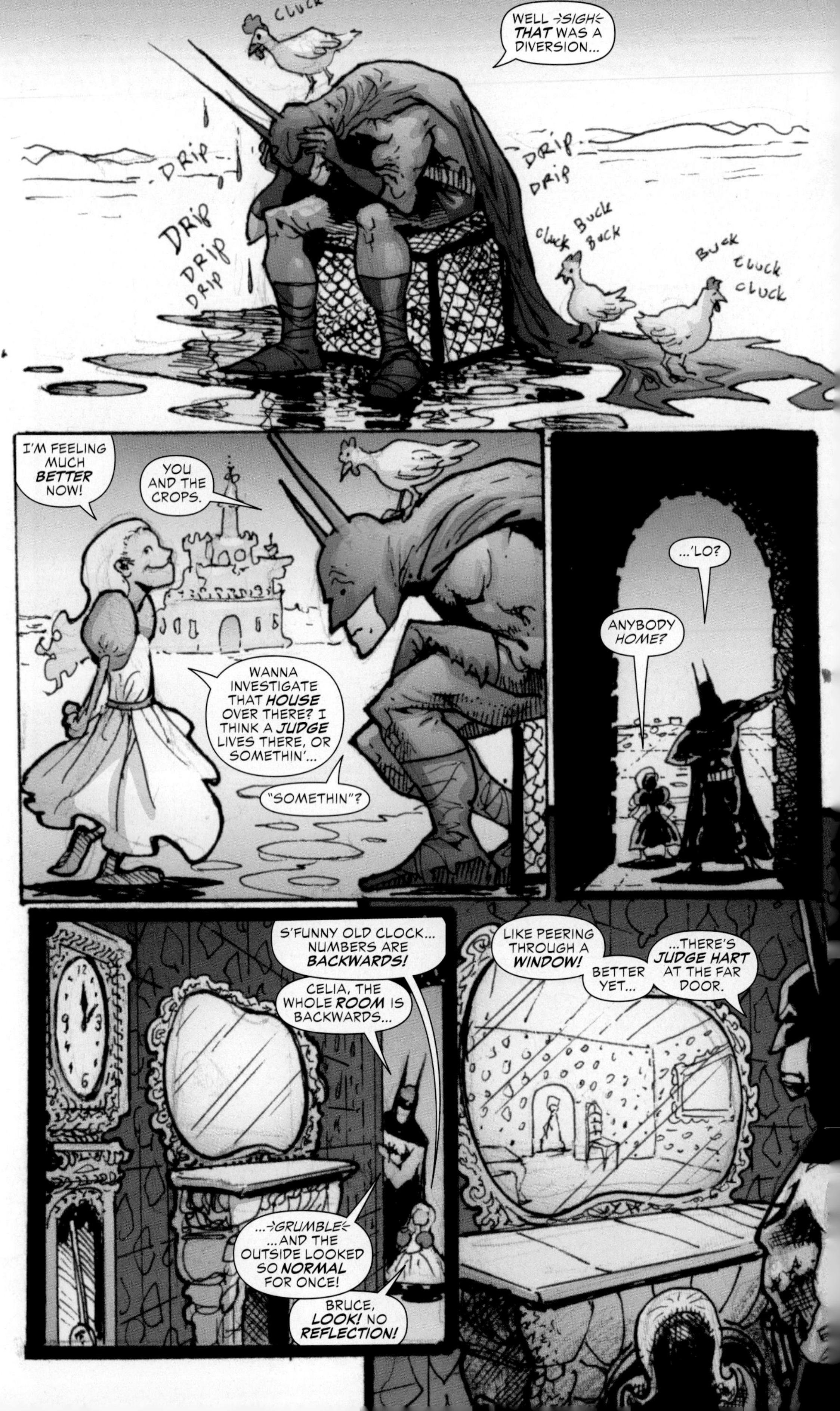
CLUCK
WELL →SIGH← THAT WAS A DIVERSION...
DRIP
DRIP
DRIP
DRIP DRIP
DRIP DRIP
CLUCK BUCK BUCK
BUCK CLUCK CLUCK
I'M FEELING MUCH BETTER NOW!
YOU AND THE CROPS.
WANNA INVESTIGATE THAT HOUSE OVER THERE? I THINK A JUDGE LIVES THERE, OR SOMETHIN'...
"SOMETHIN"?
...'LO?
ANYBODY HOME?
S'FUNNY OLD CLOCK... NUMBERS ARE BACKWARDS!
CELIA, THE WHOLE ROOM IS BACKWARDS...
...→GRUMBLE← ...AND THE OUTSIDE LOOKED SO NORMAL FOR ONCE!
BRUCE, LOOK! NO REFLECTION!
LIKE PEERING THROUGH A WINDOW!
BETTER YET...
...THERE'S JUDGE HART AT THE FAR DOOR.

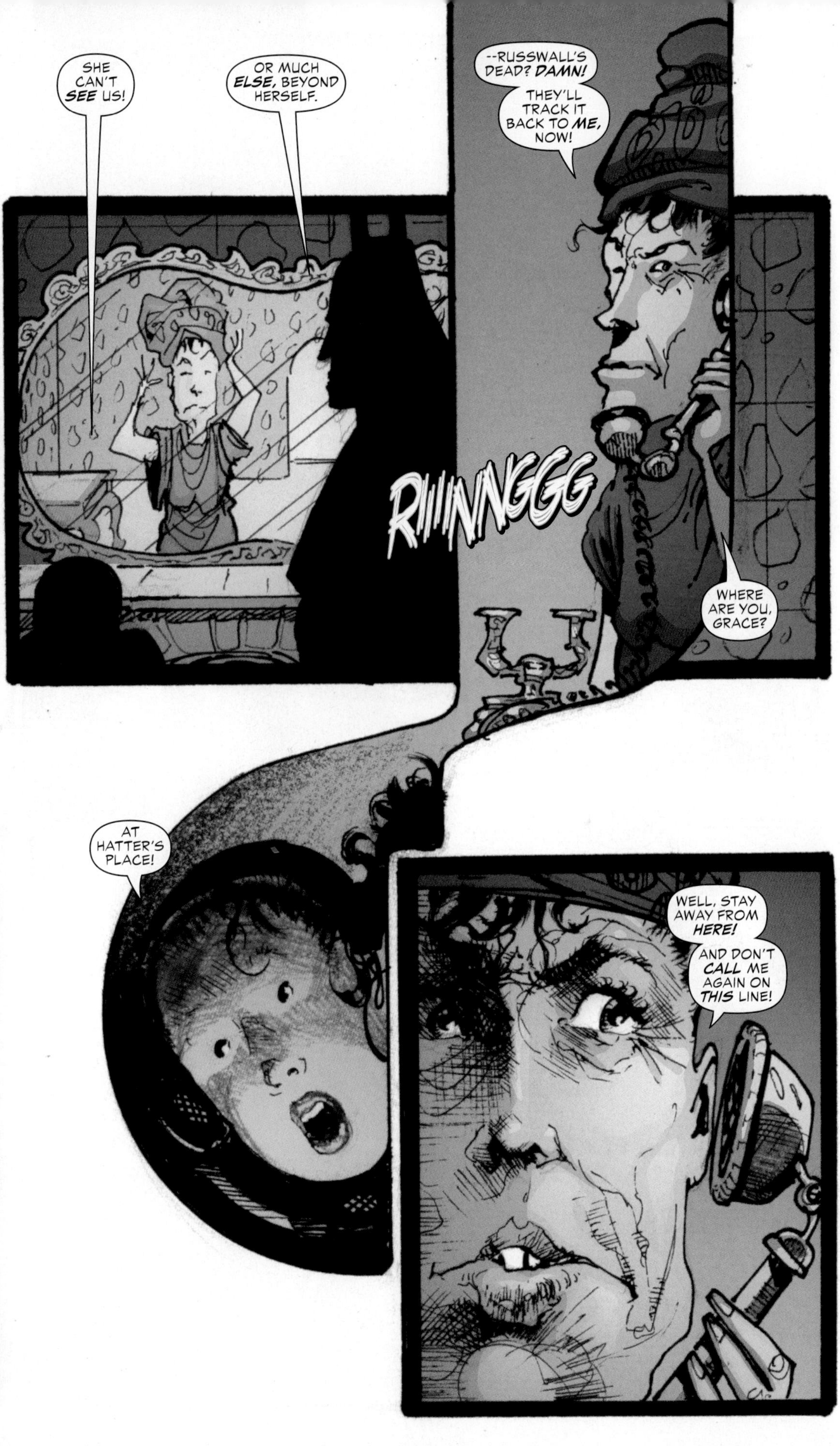
SHE CAN'T SEE US!
OR MUCH ELSE, BEYOND HERSELF.
--RUSSWALL'S DEAD? DAMN!
THEY'LL TRACK IT BACK TO ME, NOW!
RIIINNGGG
WHERE ARE YOU, GRACE?
AT HATTER'S PLACE!
WELL, STAY AWAY FROM HERE!
AND DON'T CALL ME AGAIN ON THIS LINE!

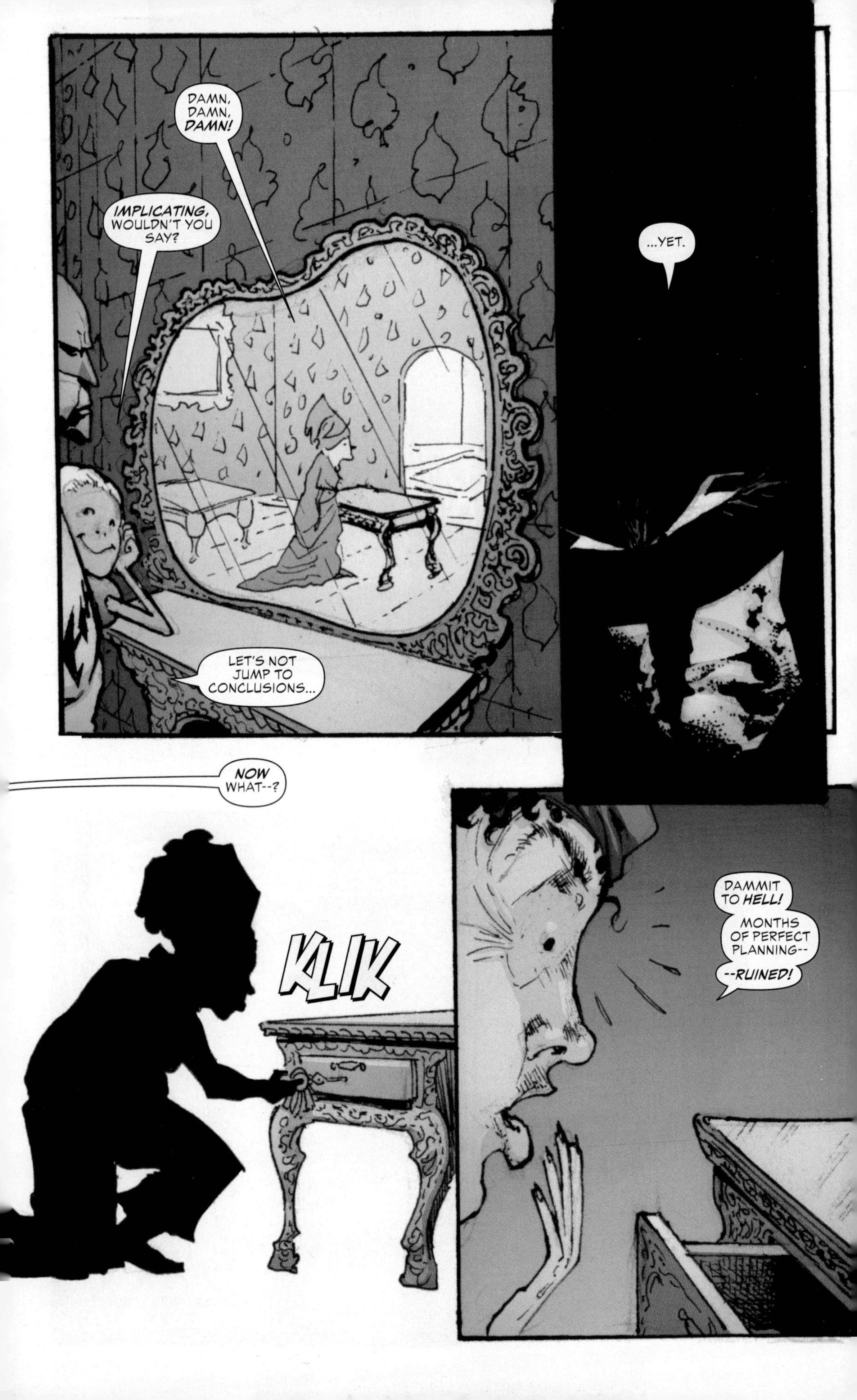

DAMN, DAMN, DAMN!
IMPLICATING, WOULDN'T YOU SAY?
LET'S NOT JUMP TO CONCLUSIONS...
...YET.
NOW WHAT--?
KLIK
DAMMIT TO HELL!
MONTHS OF PERFECT PLANNING--
--RUINED!

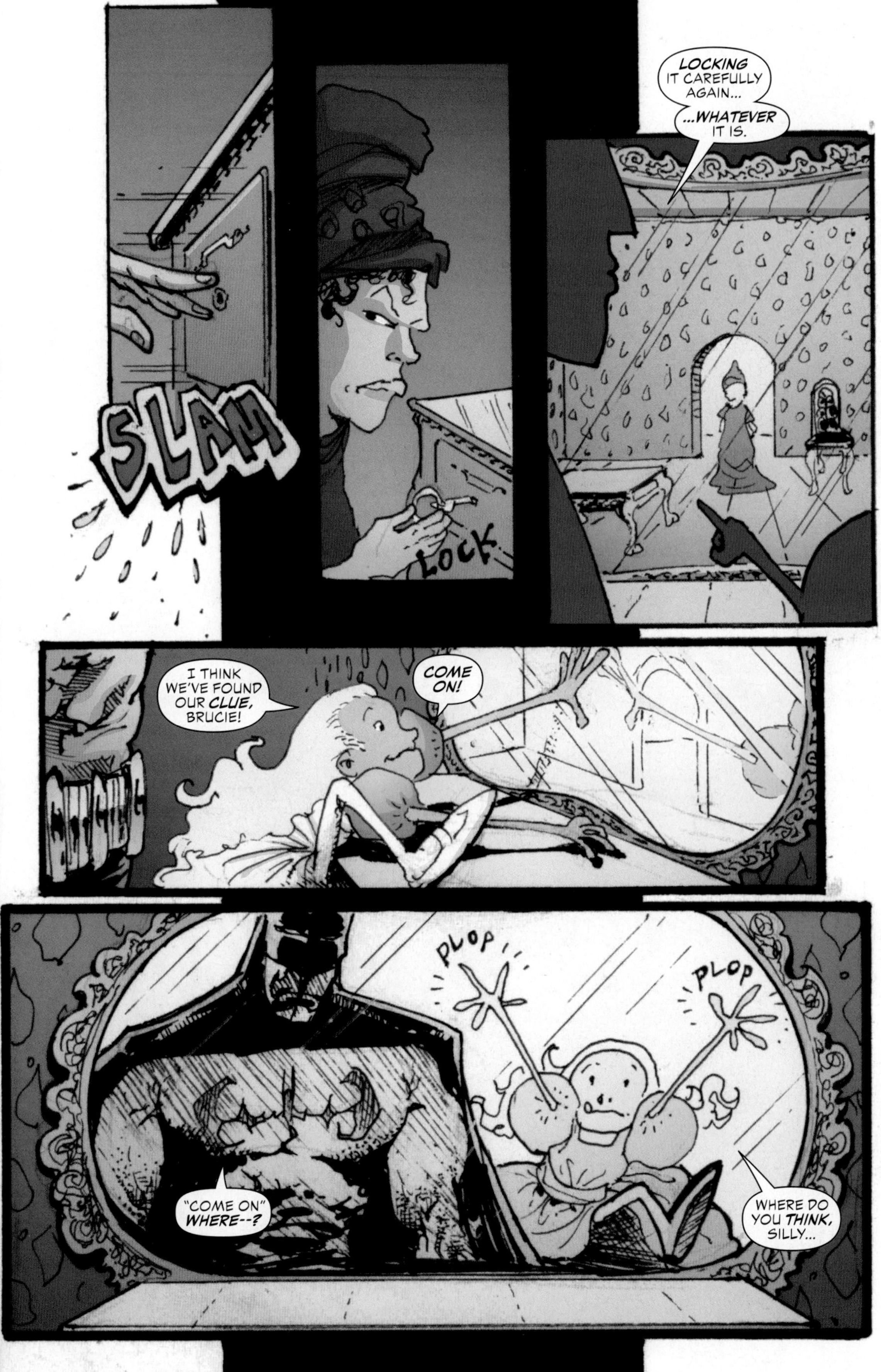
SLAM
LOCK
LOCKING IT CAREFULLY AGAIN...
...WHATEVER IT IS.
I THINK WE'VE FOUND OUR CLUE, BRUCIE!
COME ON!
PLOP
PLOP
"COME ON" WHERE--?
WHERE DO YOU THINK, SILLY...

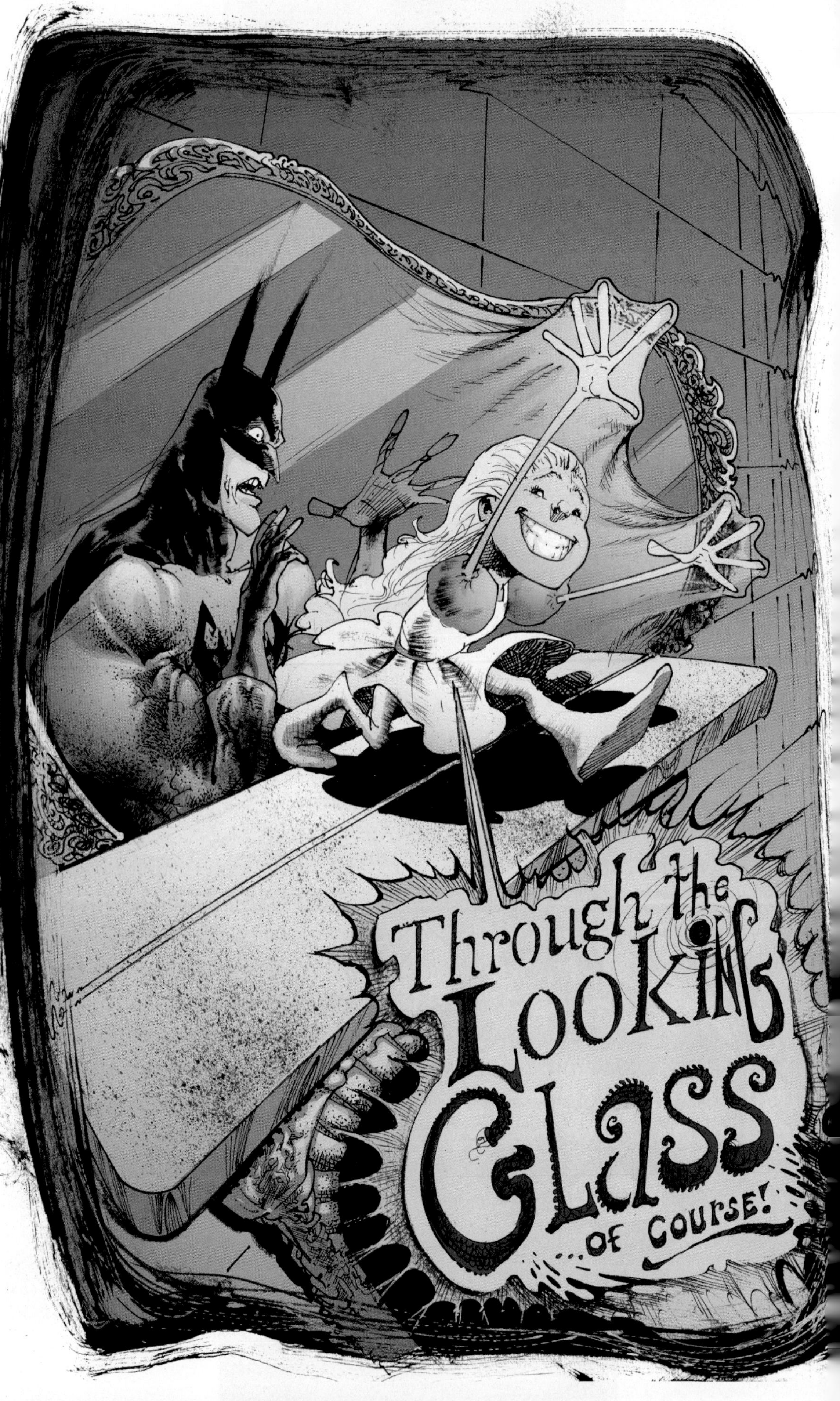
Through the LOOKING GLASS
...OF COURSE!

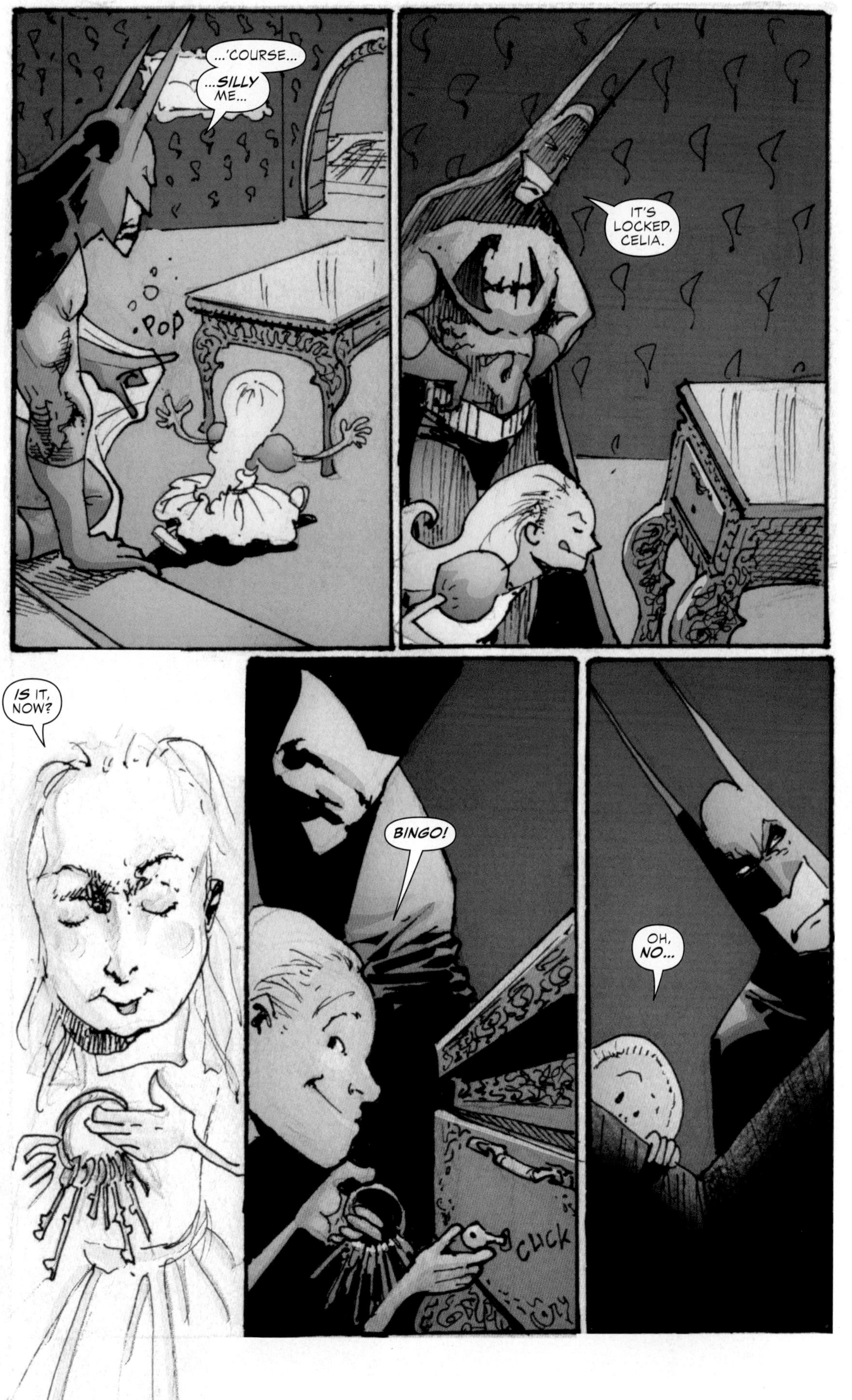
...'COURSE...
...SILLY ME...
POP
IT'S LOCKED, CELIA.
IS IT, NOW?
BINGO!
CLICK
OH, NO...

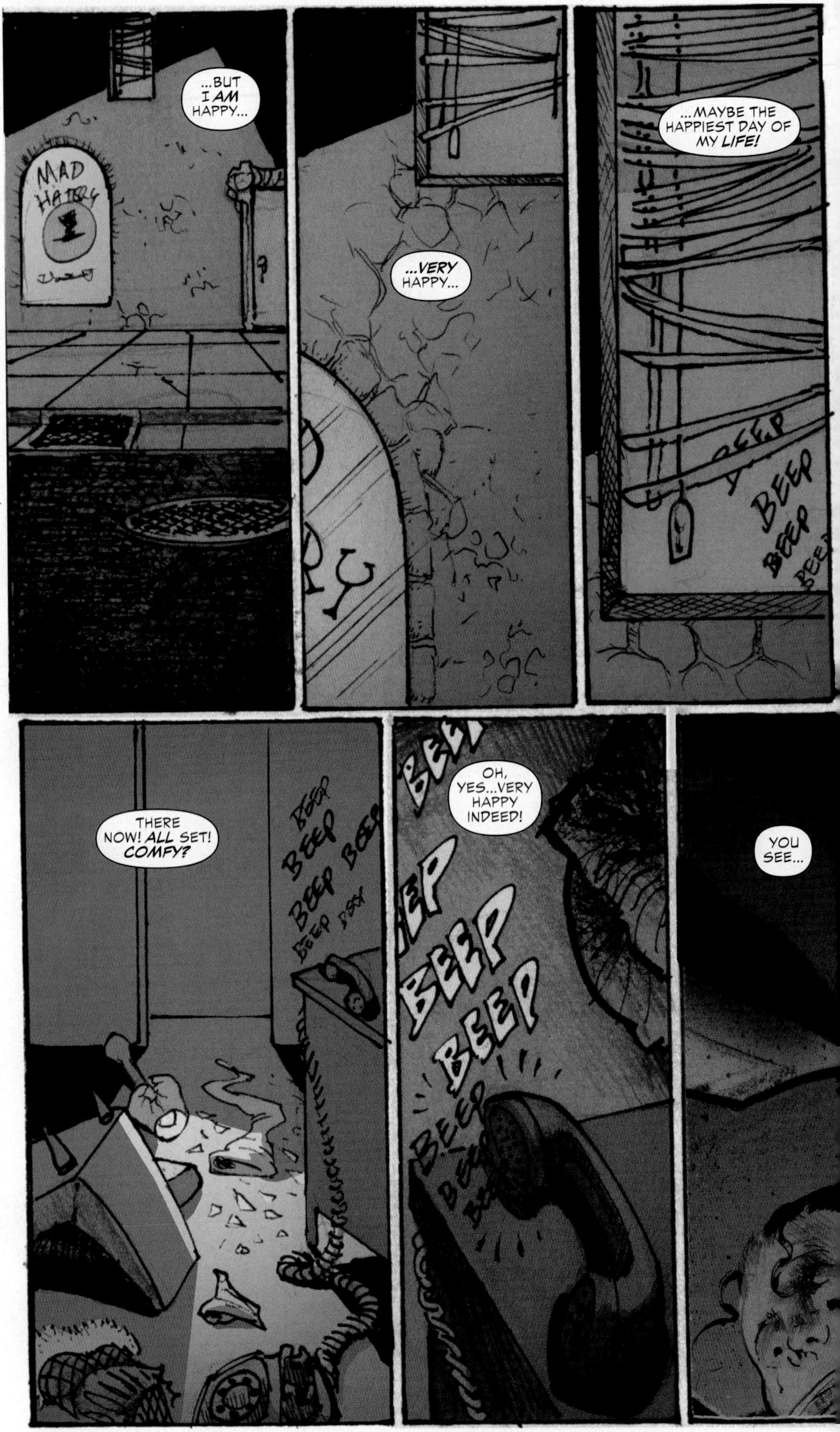
...BUT I AM HAPPY...
MAD HATTER
...VERY HAPPY...
...MAYBE THE HAPPIEST DAY OF MY LIFE!
BEEP BEEP BEEP
THERE NOW! ALL SET! COMFY?
BEEP BEEP BEEP BEEP BEEP
OH, YES...VERY HAPPY INDEED!
BEEP BEEP BEEP BEEP
YOU SEE...

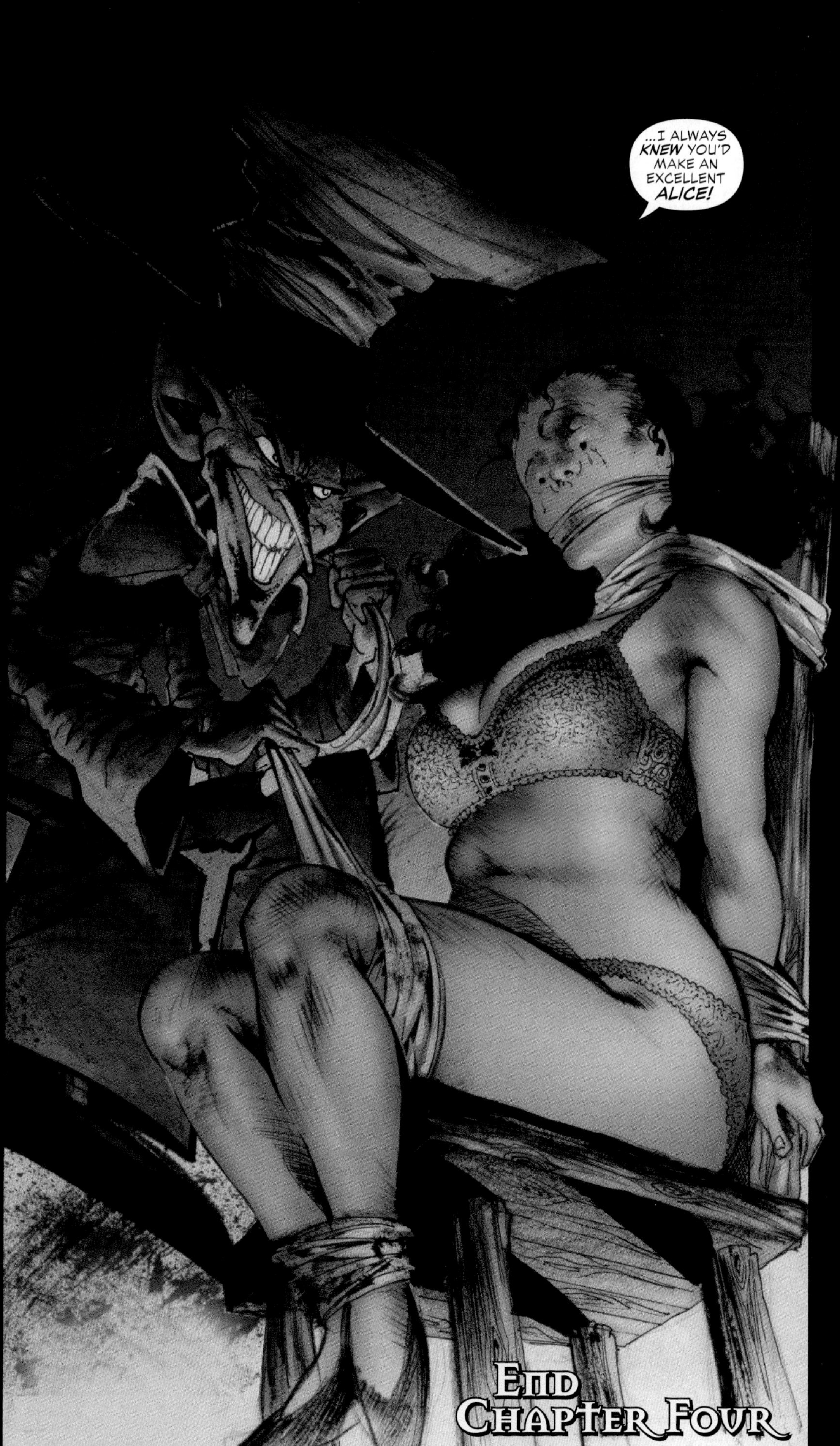
...I ALWAYS KNEW YOU'D MAKE AN EXCELLENT ALICE!
END CHAPTER FOUR

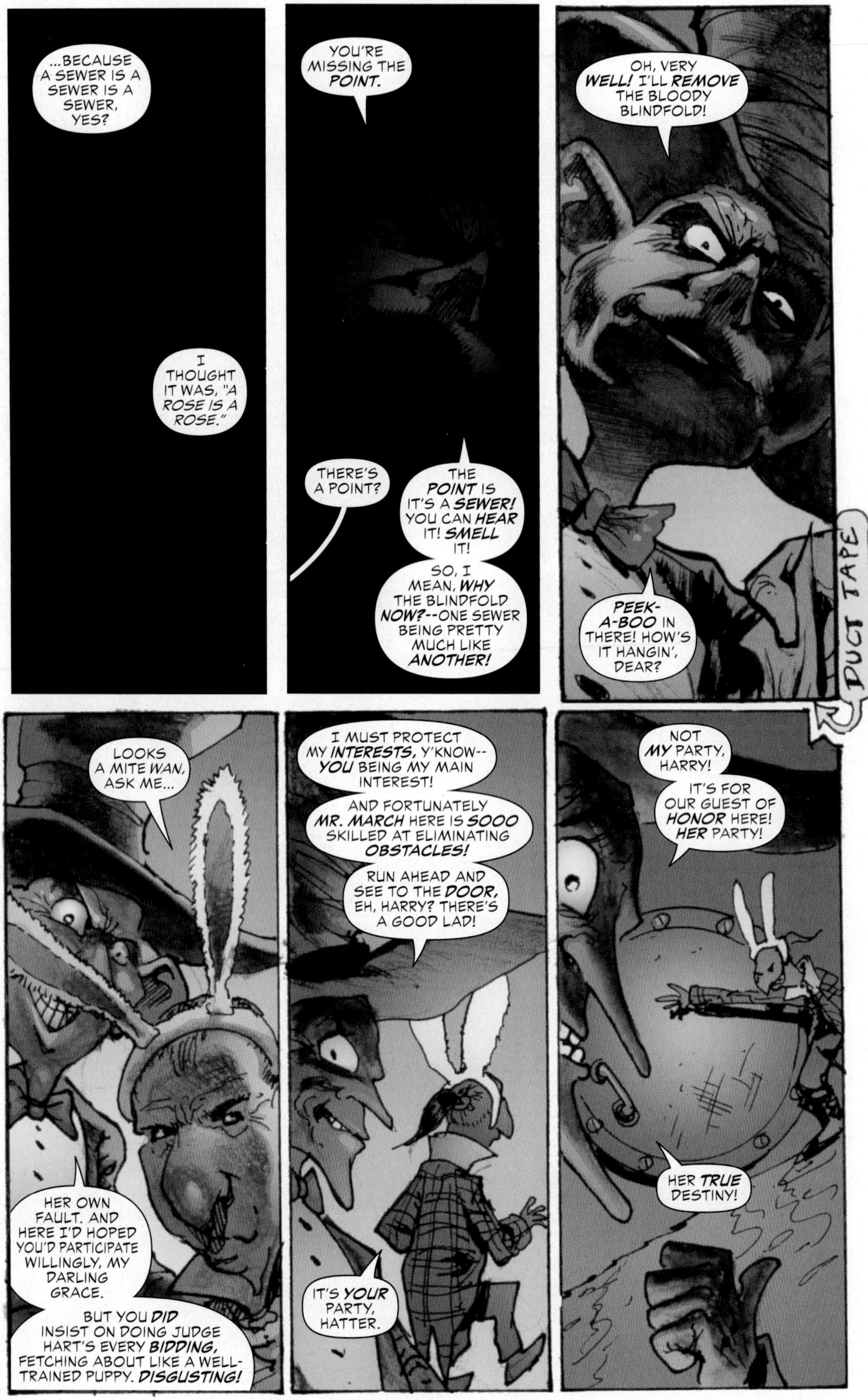
...BECAUSE A SEWER IS A SEWER IS A SEWER, YES?
I THOUGHT IT WAS, "A ROSE IS A ROSE."
YOU'RE MISSING THE POINT.
THERE'S A POINT?
THE POINT IS IT'S A SEWER! YOU CAN HEAR IT! SMELL IT!
SO, I MEAN, WHY THE BLINDFOLD NOW?--ONE SEWER BEING PRETTY MUCH LIKE ANOTHER!
OH, VERY WELL! I'LL REMOVE THE BLOODY BLINDFOLD!
PEEK-A-BOO IN THERE! HOW'S IT HANGIN', DEAR?
DUCT TAPE
LOOKS A MITE WAN, ASK ME...
HER OWN FAULT. AND HERE I'D HOPED YOU'D PARTICIPATE WILLINGLY, MY DARLING GRACE.
BUT YOU DID INSIST ON DOING JUDGE HART'S EVERY BIDDING, FETCHING ABOUT LIKE A WELL-TRAINED PUPPY. DISGUSTING!
I MUST PROTECT MY INTERESTS, Y'KNOW--YOU BEING MY MAIN INTEREST!
AND FORTUNATELY MR. MARCH HERE IS SOOO SKILLED AT ELIMINATING OBSTACLES!
RUN AHEAD AND SEE TO THE DOOR, EH, HARRY? THERE'S A GOOD LAD!
IT'S YOUR PARTY, HATTER.
NOT MY PARTY, HARRY!
IT'S FOR OUR GUEST OF HONOR HERE! HER PARTY!
HER TRUE DESTINY!

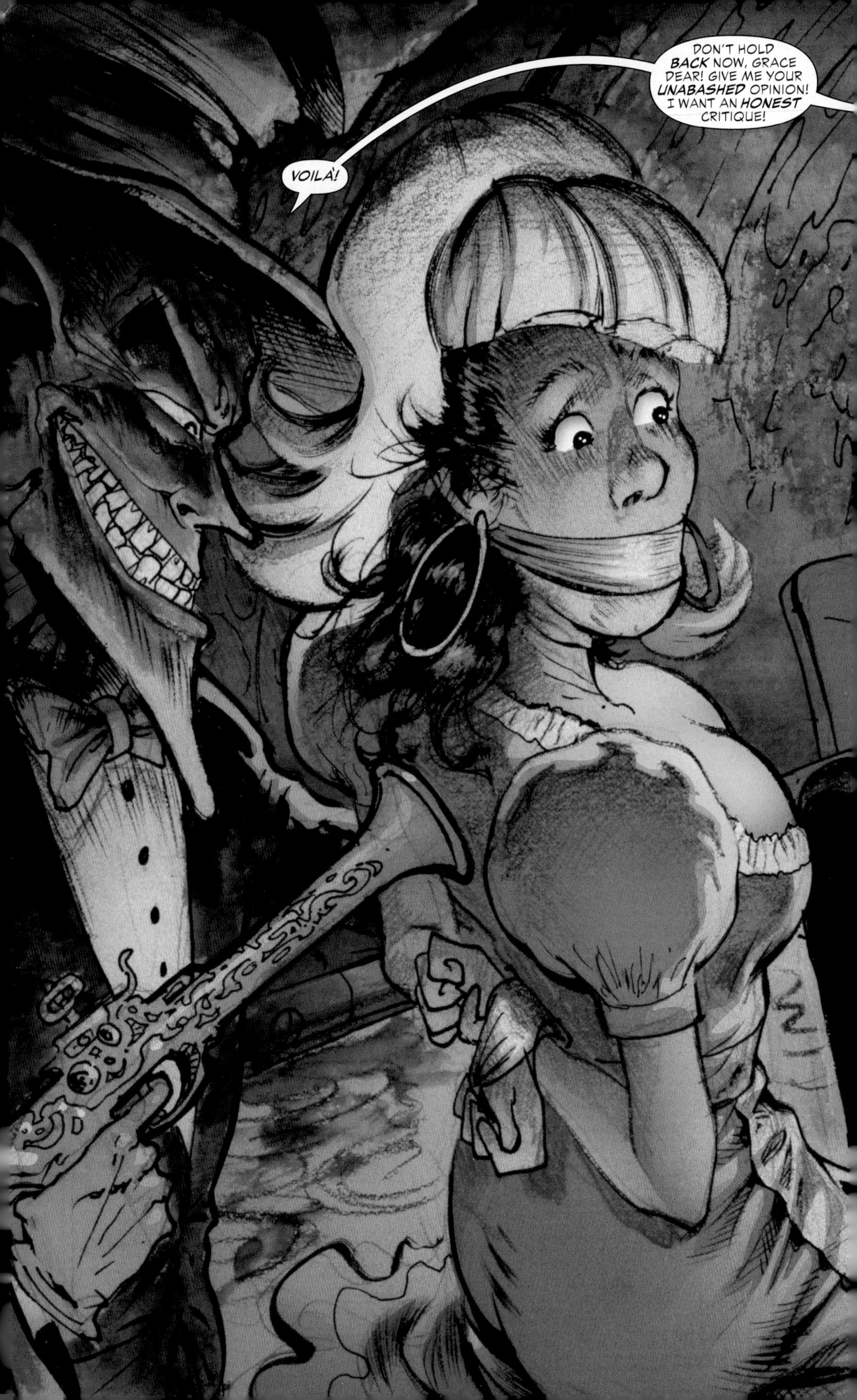
VOILÀ!
DON'T HOLD BACK NOW, GRACE DEAR! GIVE ME YOUR UNABASHED OPINION! I WANT AN HONEST CRITIQUE!

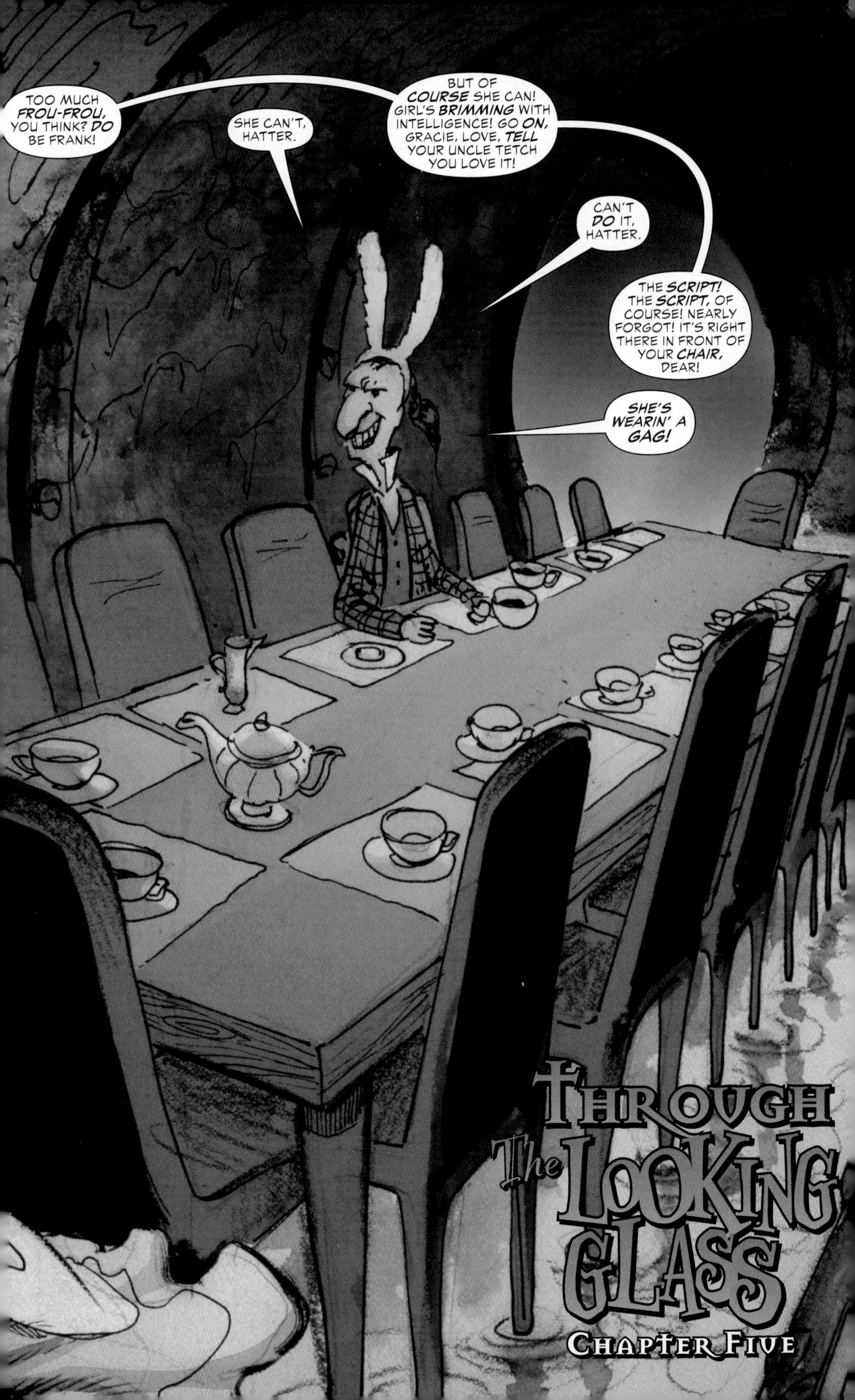
TOO MUCH FROU-FROU, YOU THINK? DO BE FRANK!
SHE CAN'T, HATTER.
BUT OF COURSE SHE CAN! GIRL'S BRIMMING WITH INTELLIGENCE! GO ON, GRACIE, LOVE, TELL YOUR UNCLE TETCH YOU LOVE IT!
CAN'T DO IT, HATTER.
THE SCRIPT! THE SCRIPT, OF COURSE! NEARLY FORGOT! IT'S RIGHT THERE IN FRONT OF YOUR CHAIR, DEAR!
SHE'S WEARIN' A GAG!
THROUGH THE LOOKING GLASS
CHAPTER FIVE

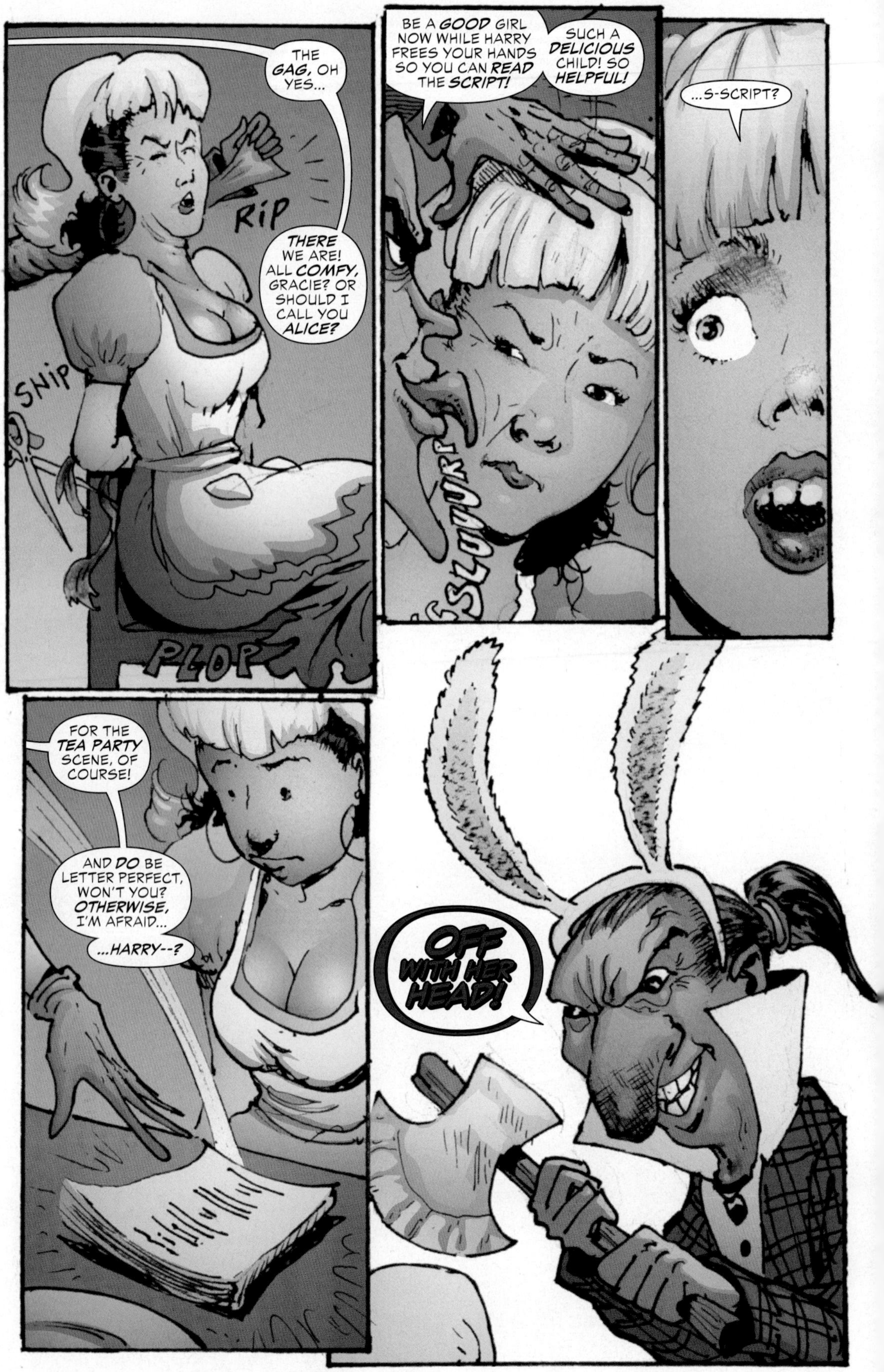
THE GAG, OH YES...
RIP
THERE WE ARE! ALL COMFY, GRACIE? OR SHOULD I CALL YOU ALICE?
SNIP
PLOP
BE A GOOD GIRL NOW WHILE HARRY FREES YOUR HANDS SO YOU CAN READ THE SCRIPT!
SUCH A DELICIOUS CHILD! SO HELPFUL!
SSLUUURP
...S-SCRIPT?
FOR THE TEA PARTY SCENE, OF COURSE!
AND DO BE LETTER PERFECT, WON'T YOU? OTHERWISE, I'M AFRAID...
...HARRY--?
OFF WITH HER HEAD!

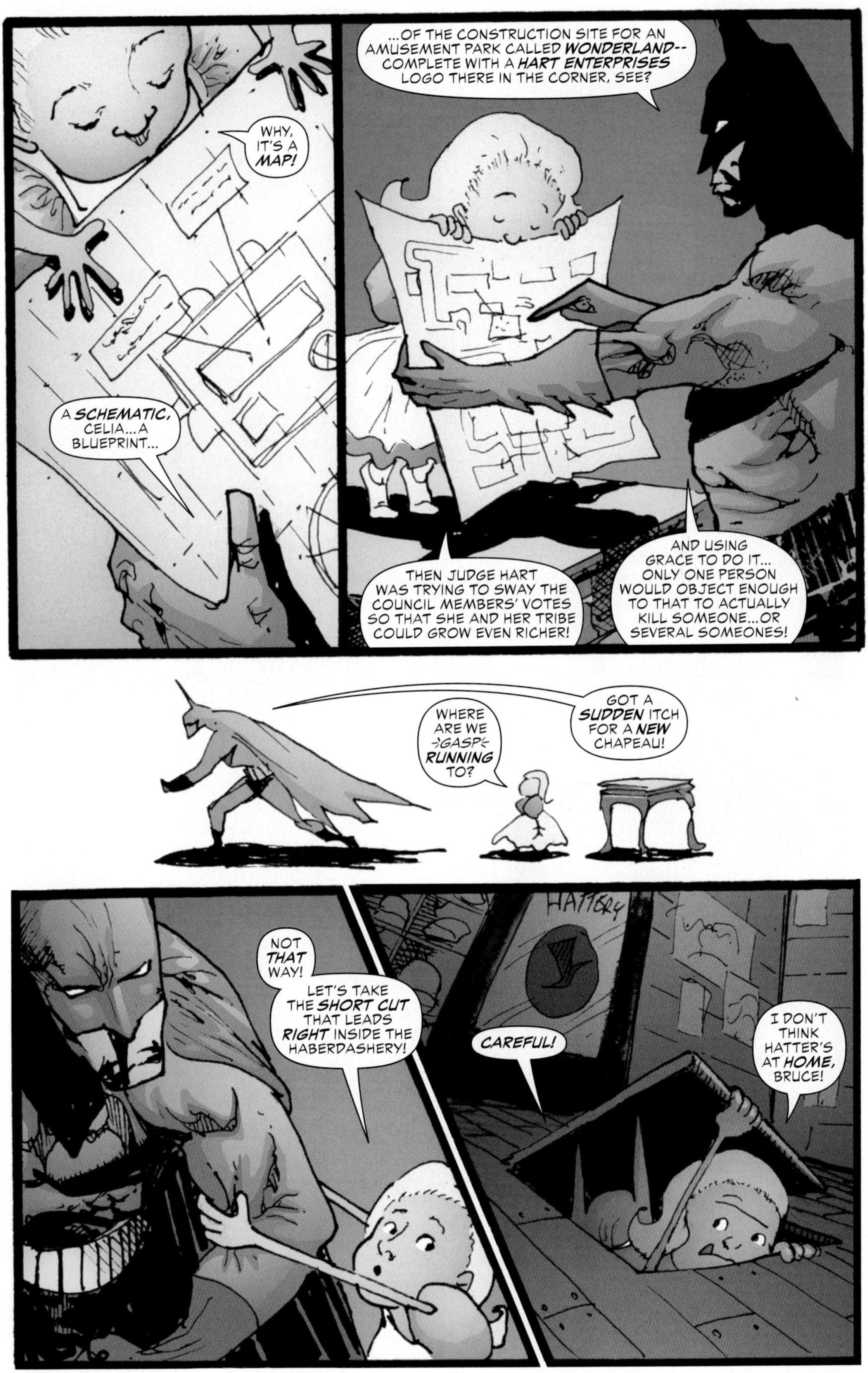
WHY, IT'S A MAP!
A SCHEMATIC, CELIA...A BLUEPRINT...
...OF THE CONSTRUCTION SITE FOR AN AMUSEMENT PARK CALLED WONDERLAND-- COMPLETE WITH A HART ENTERPRISES LOGO THERE IN THE CORNER, SEE?
THEN JUDGE HART WAS TRYING TO SWAY THE COUNCIL MEMBERS' VOTES SO THAT SHE AND HER TRIBE COULD GROW EVEN RICHER!
AND USING GRACE TO DO IT... ONLY ONE PERSON WOULD OBJECT ENOUGH TO THAT TO ACTUALLY KILL SOMEONE...OR SEVERAL SOMEONES!
GOT A SUDDEN ITCH FOR A NEW CHAPEAU!
WHERE ARE WE -GASP- RUNNING TO?
NOT THAT WAY!
LET'S TAKE THE SHORT CUT THAT LEADS RIGHT INSIDE THE HABERDASHERY!
HATTERY
CAREFUL!
I DON'T THINK HATTER'S AT HOME, BRUCE!

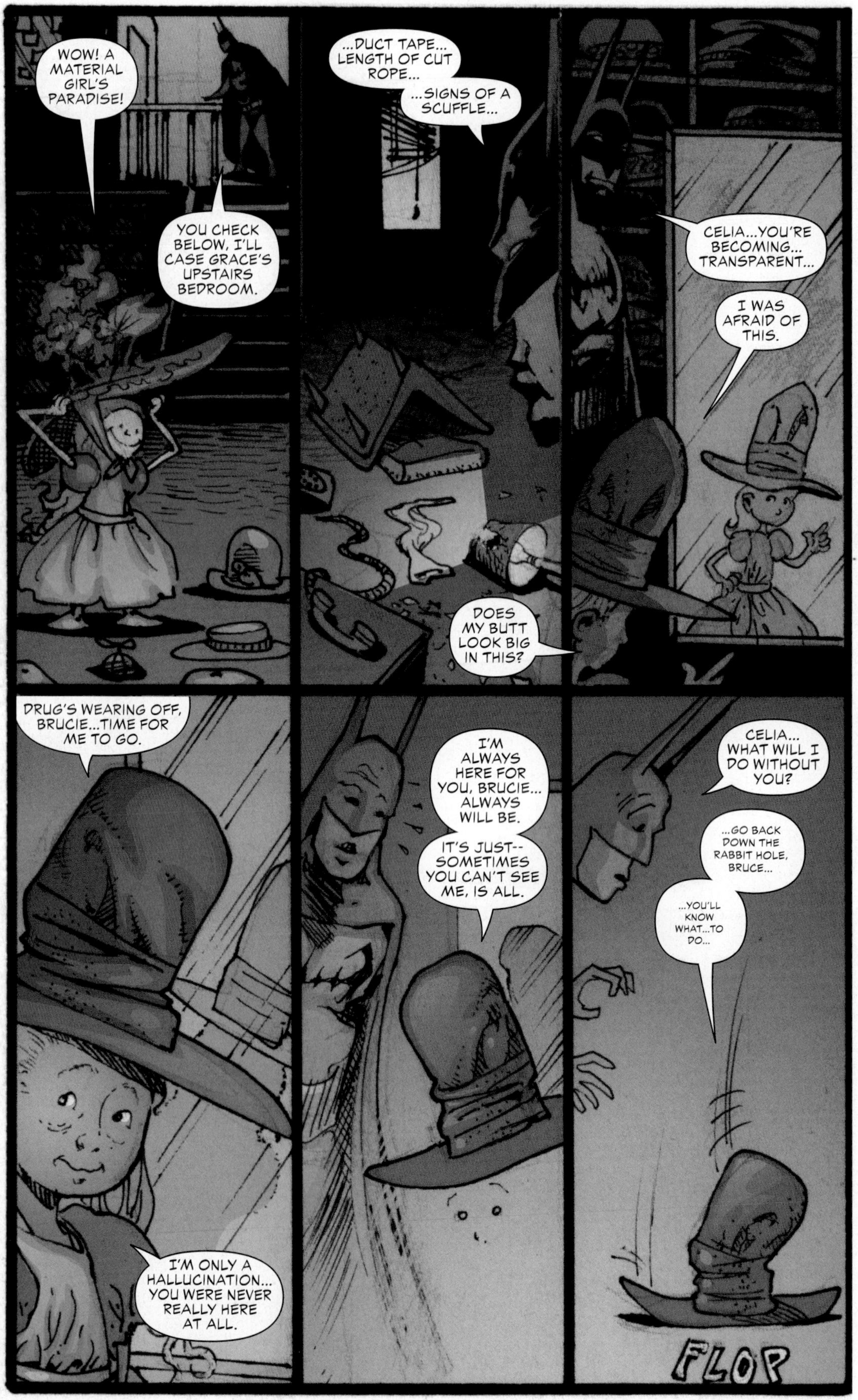
WOW! A MATERIAL GIRL'S PARADISE!
YOU CHECK BELOW, I'LL CASE GRACE'S UPSTAIRS BEDROOM.
...DUCT TAPE... LENGTH OF CUT ROPE...
...SIGNS OF A SCUFFLE...
CELIA...YOU'RE BECOMING... TRANSPARENT...
I WAS AFRAID OF THIS.
DOES MY BUTT LOOK BIG IN THIS?
DRUG'S WEARING OFF, BRUCIE...TIME FOR ME TO GO.
I'M ONLY A HALLUCINATION... YOU WERE NEVER REALLY HERE AT ALL.
I'M ALWAYS HERE FOR YOU, BRUCIE... ALWAYS WILL BE.
IT'S JUST-- SOMETIMES YOU CAN'T SEE ME, IS ALL.
CELIA... WHAT WILL I DO WITHOUT YOU?
...GO BACK DOWN THE RABBIT HOLE, BRUCE...
...YOU'LL KNOW WHAT...TO DO...
FLOP

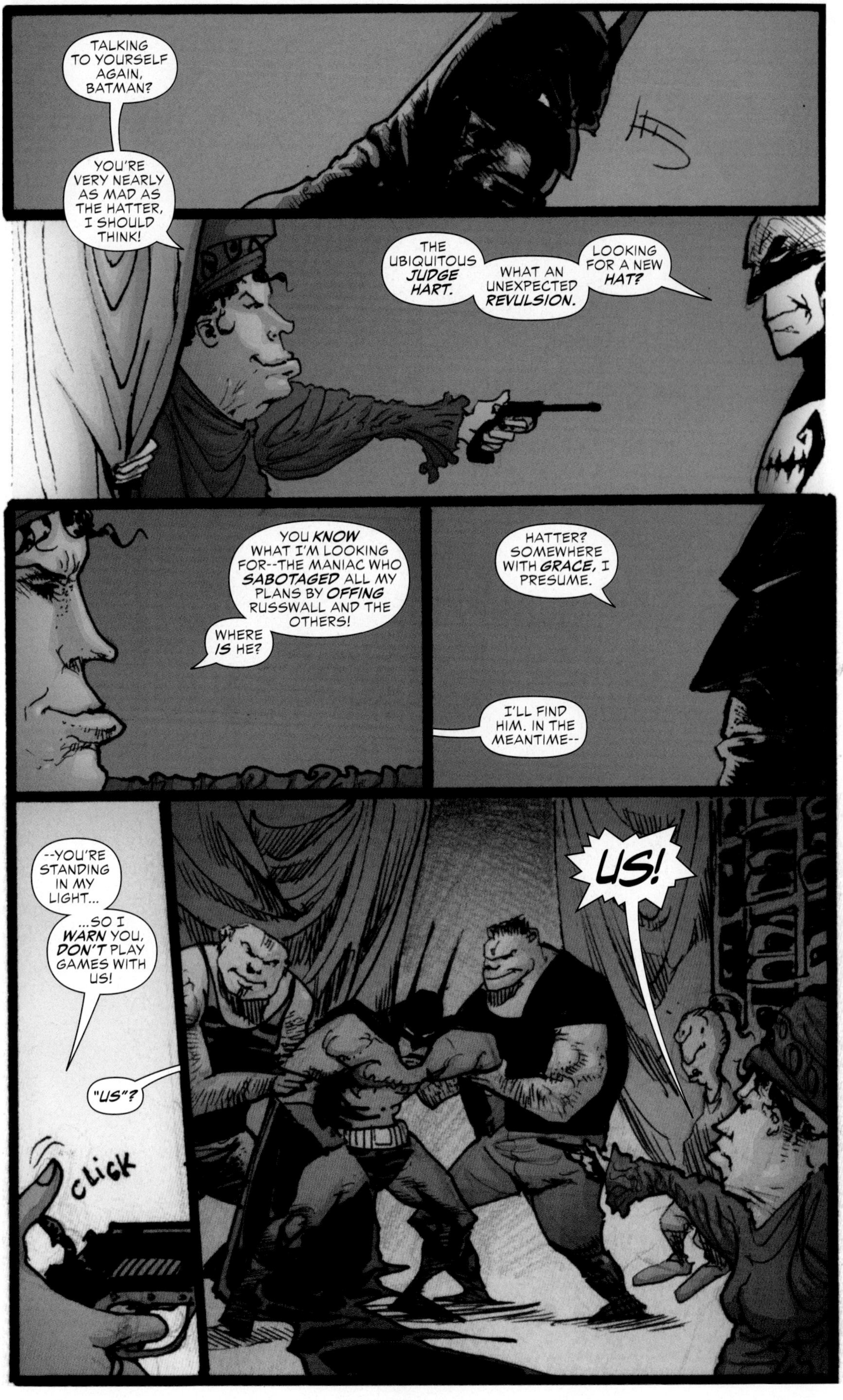

TALKING TO YOURSELF AGAIN, BATMAN?
YOU'RE VERY NEARLY AS MAD AS THE HATTER, I SHOULD THINK!
THE UBIQUITOUS JUDGE HART.
WHAT AN UNEXPECTED REVULSION.
LOOKING FOR A NEW HAT?
YOU KNOW WHAT I'M LOOKING FOR--THE MANIAC WHO SABOTAGED ALL MY PLANS BY OFFING RUSSWALL AND THE OTHERS!
WHERE IS HE?
HATTER? SOMEWHERE WITH GRACE, I PRESUME.
I'LL FIND HIM. IN THE MEANTIME--
--YOU'RE STANDING IN MY LIGHT...
...SO I WARN YOU, DON'T PLAY GAMES WITH US!
"US"?
CLICK
US!

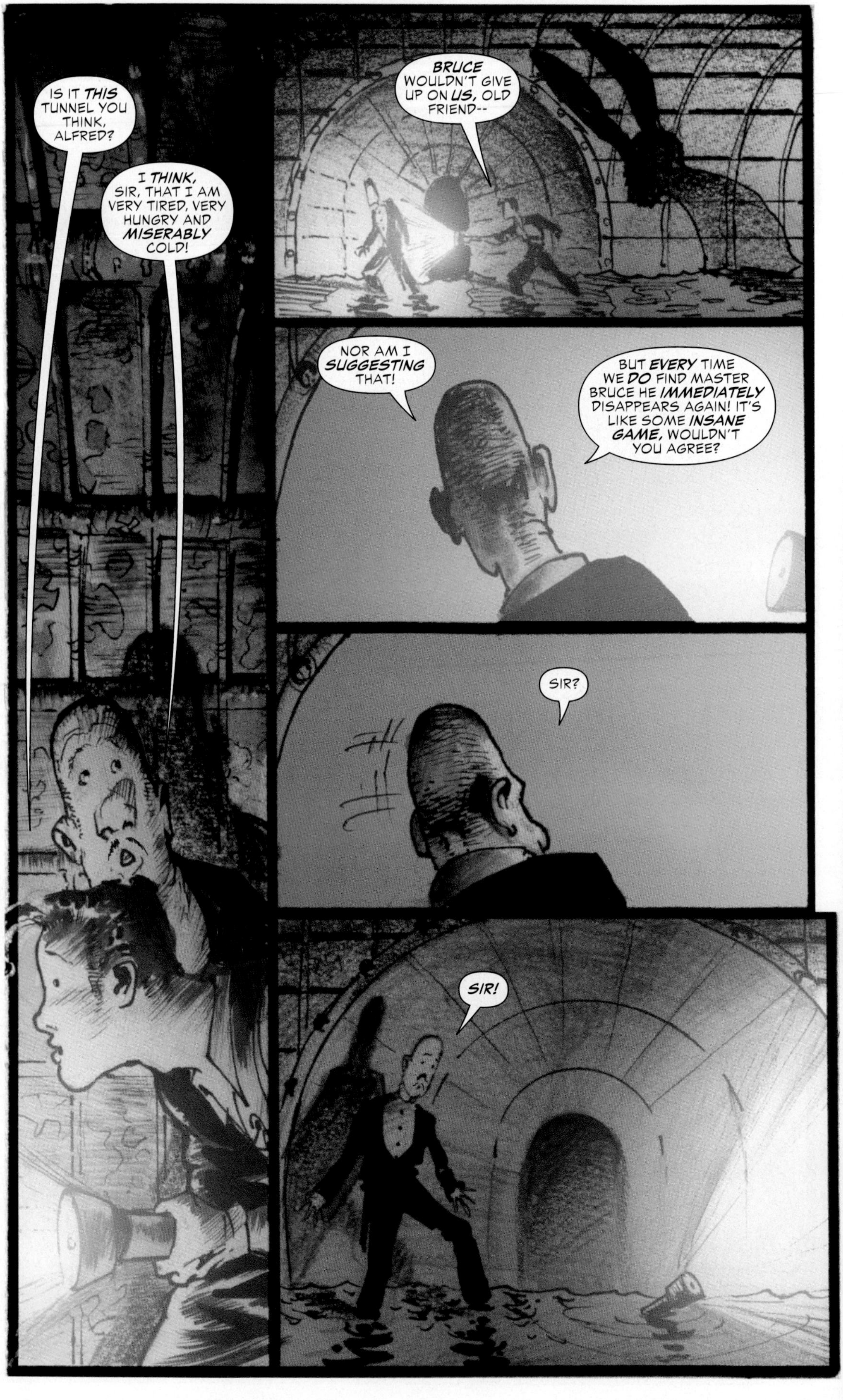

IS IT THIS TUNNEL YOU THINK, ALFRED?
I THINK, SIR, THAT I AM VERY TIRED, VERY HUNGRY AND MISERABLY COLD!
BRUCE WOULDN'T GIVE UP ON US, OLD FRIEND--
NOR AM I SUGGESTING THAT!
BUT EVERY TIME WE DO FIND MASTER BRUCE HE IMMEDIATELY DISAPPEARS AGAIN! IT'S LIKE SOME INSANE GAME, WOULDN'T YOU AGREE?
SIR?
SIR!

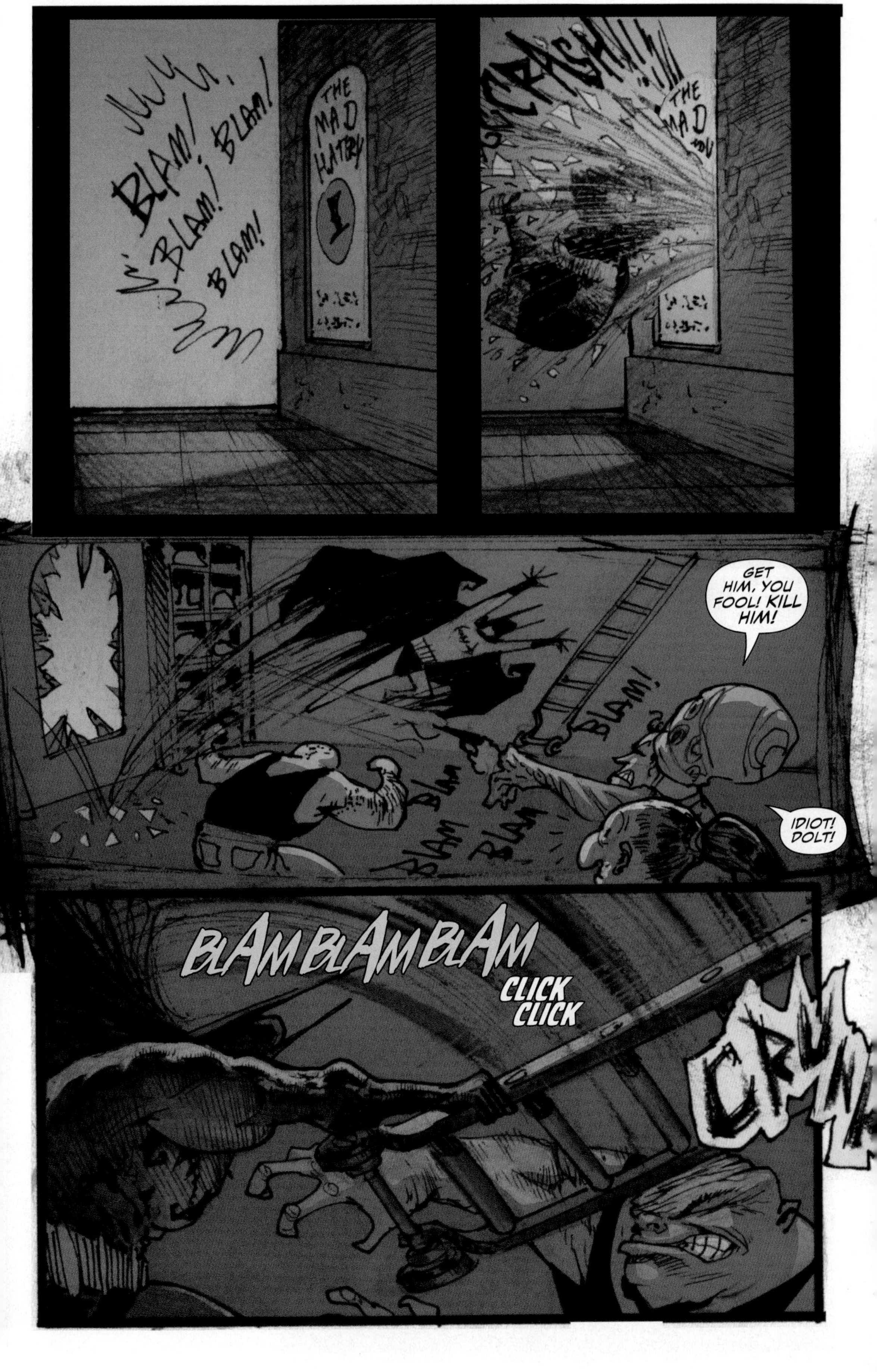
BLAM! BLAM! BLAM! BLAM! BLAM!
THE MAD HATTER
CRASH!
GET HIM, YOU FOOL! KILL HIM!
BLAM! BLAM BLAM BLAM
IDIOT! DOLT!
BLAM BLAM BLAM
CLICK CLICK
CRUN

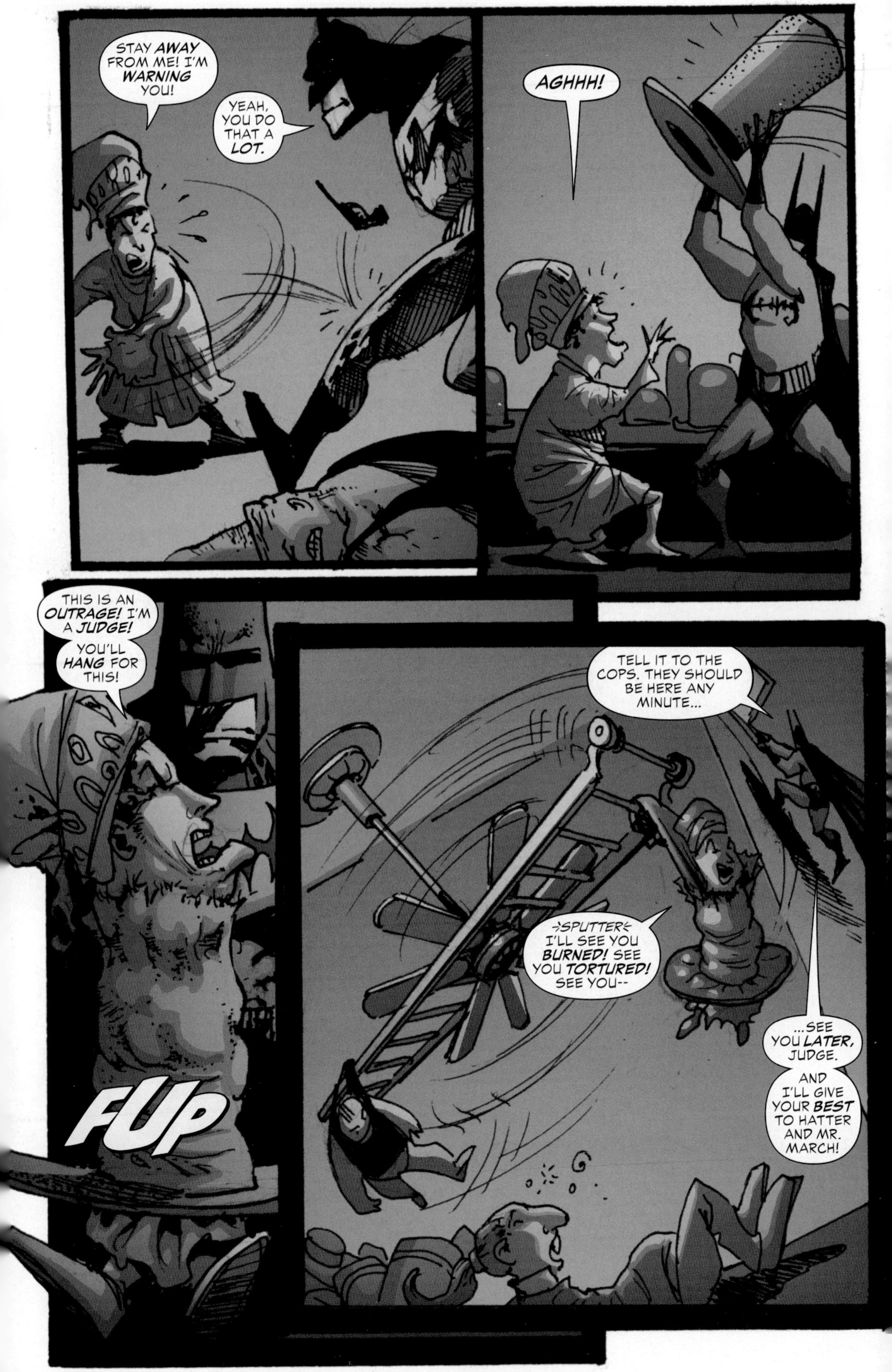
STAY AWAY FROM ME! I'M WARNING YOU!
YEAH, YOU DO THAT A LOT.
AGHHH!
THIS IS AN OUTRAGE! I'M A JUDGE!
YOU'LL HANG FOR THIS!
FUP
TELL IT TO THE COPS. THEY SHOULD BE HERE ANY MINUTE...
SPUTTER I'LL SEE YOU BURNED! SEE YOU TORTURED! SEE YOU--
...SEE YOU LATER, JUDGE.
AND I'LL GIVE YOUR BEST TO HATTER AND MR. MARCH!

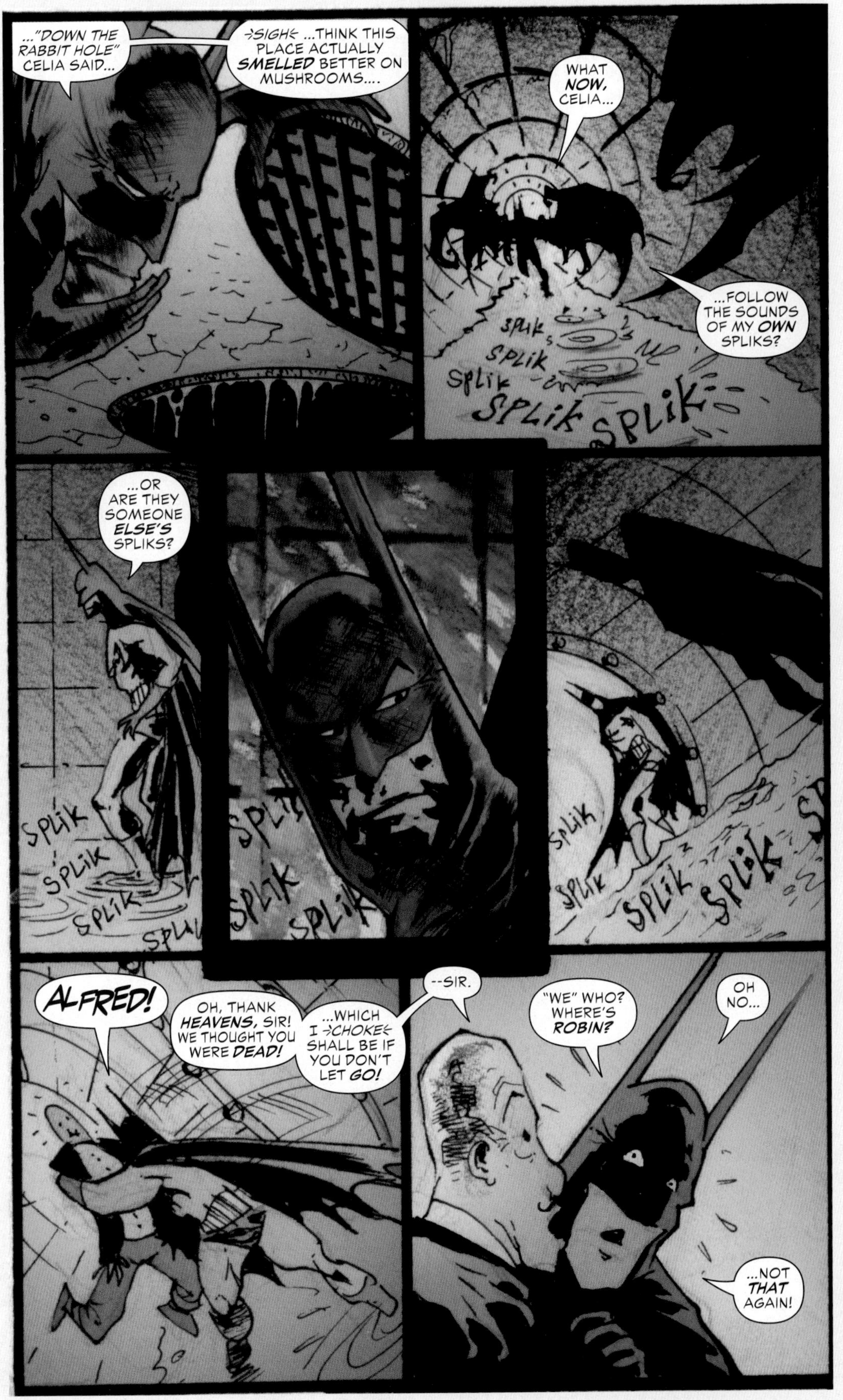

..."DOWN THE RABBIT HOLE" CELIA SAID...
-SIGH- ...THINK THIS PLACE ACTUALLY SMELLED BETTER ON MUSHROOMS....
WHAT NOW, CELIA...
...FOLLOW THE SOUNDS OF MY OWN SPLIKS?
SPLIK SPLIK SPLIK SPLIK SPLIK
...OR ARE THEY SOMEONE ELSE'S SPLIKS?
SPLIK SPLIK SPLIK
SPLIK SPLIK
SPLIK SPLIK SPLIK SPLIK
ALFRED!
OH, THANK HEAVENS, SIR! WE THOUGHT YOU WERE DEAD!
...WHICH I -CHOKE- SHALL BE IF YOU DON'T LET GO!
--SIR.
"WE" WHO? WHERE'S ROBIN?
OH NO...
...NOT THAT AGAIN!

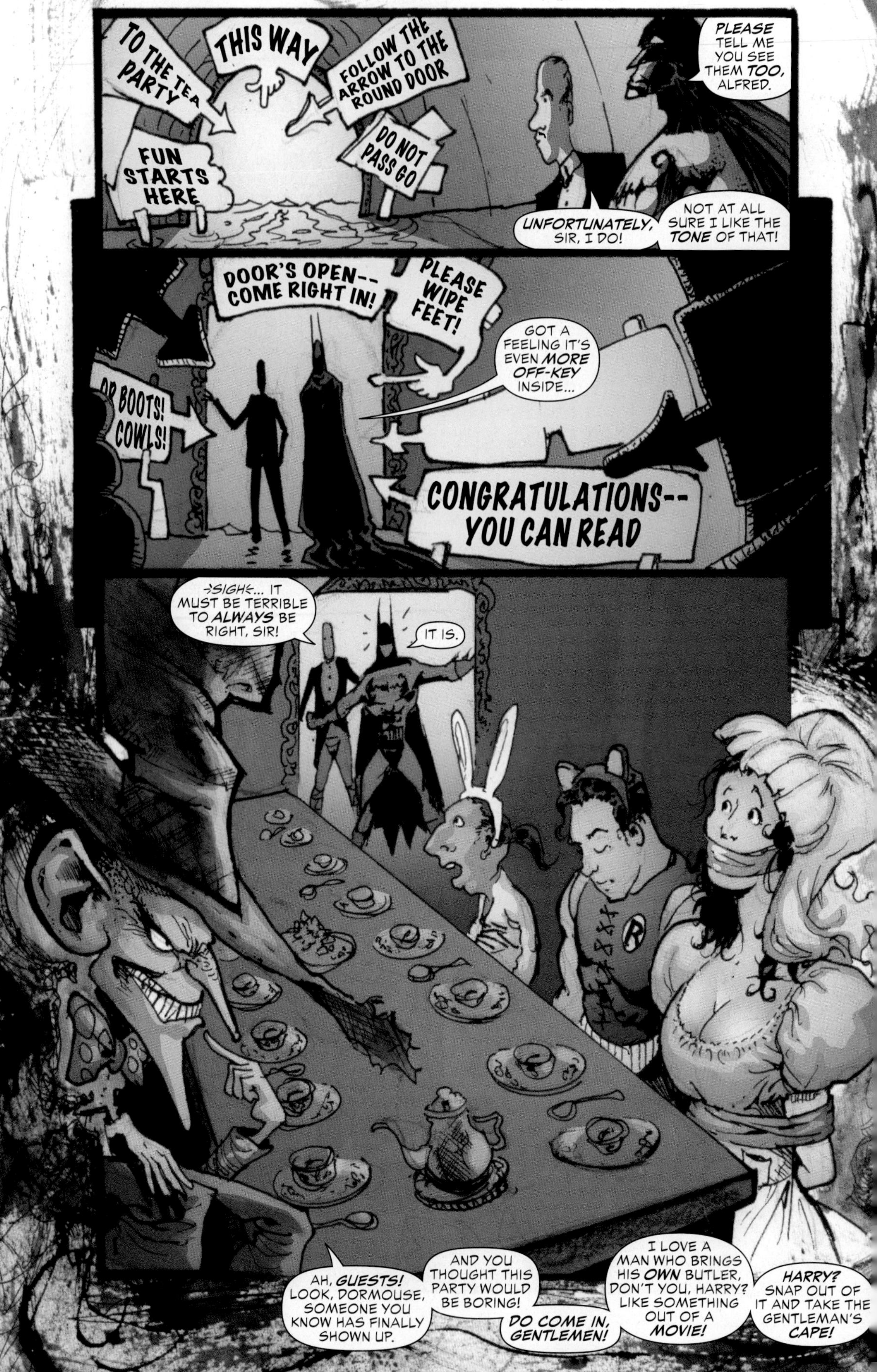
TO THE TEA PARTY
THIS WAY
FOLLOW THE ARROW TO THE ROUND DOOR
FUN STARTS HERE
DO NOT PASS GO
PLEASE TELL ME YOU SEE THEM TOO, ALFRED.
UNFORTUNATELY, SIR, I DO!
NOT AT ALL SURE I LIKE THE TONE OF THAT!
DOOR'S OPEN-- COME RIGHT IN!
PLEASE WIPE FEET!
OR BOOTS!
COWLS!
GOT A FEELING IT'S EVEN MORE OFF-KEY INSIDE...
CONGRATULATIONS-- YOU CAN READ
SIGH... IT MUST BE TERRIBLE TO ALWAYS BE RIGHT, SIR!
IT IS.
AH, GUESTS! LOOK, DORMOUSE, SOMEONE YOU KNOW HAS FINALLY SHOWN UP.
AND YOU THOUGHT THIS PARTY WOULD BE BORING!
DO COME IN, GENTLEMEN!
I LOVE A MAN WHO BRINGS HIS OWN BUTLER, DON'T YOU, HARRY? LIKE SOMETHING OUT OF A MOVIE!
HARRY? SNAP OUT OF IT AND TAKE THE GENTLEMAN'S CAPE!

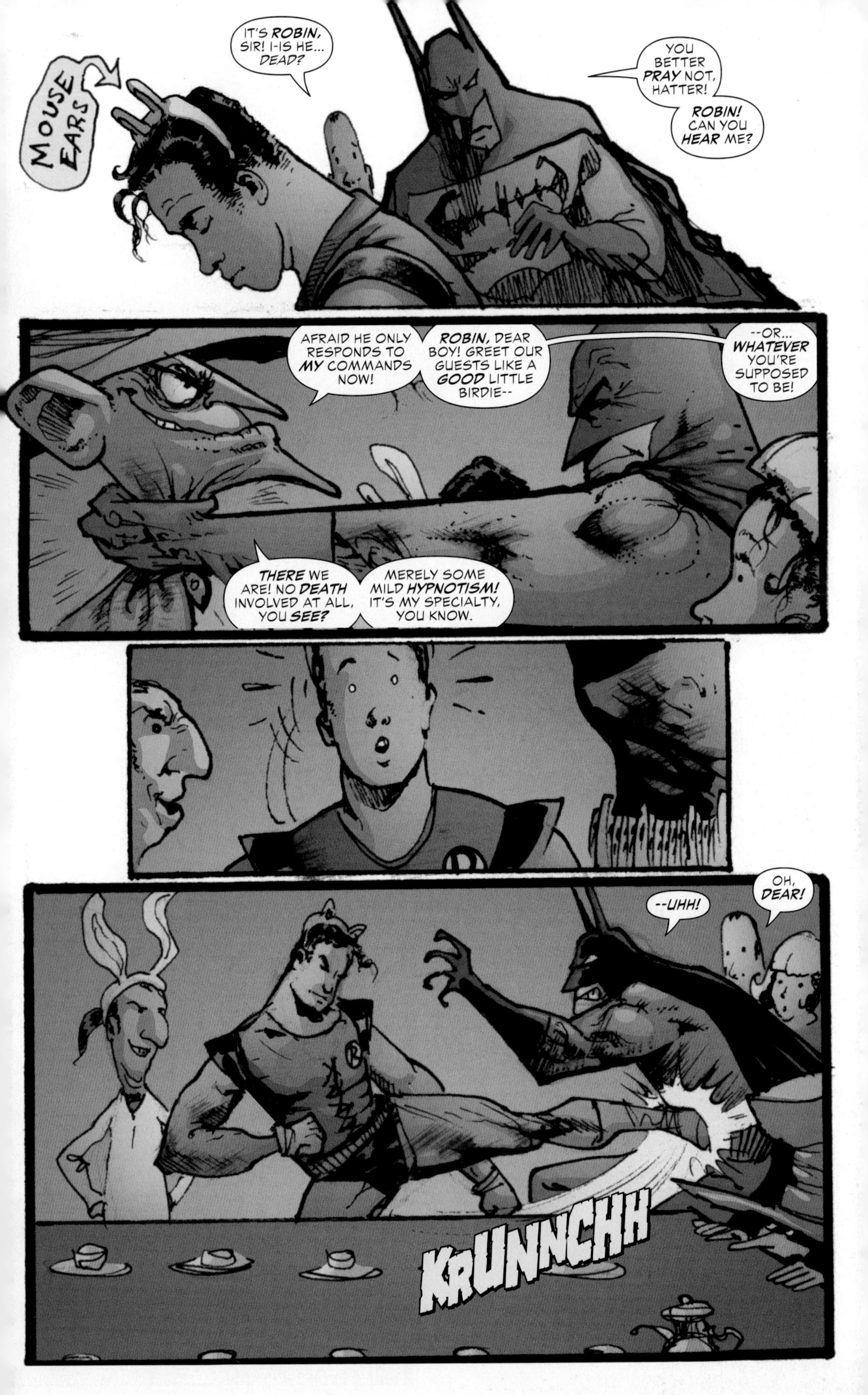
MOUSE EARS
IT'S ROBIN, SIR! I-IS HE... DEAD?
YOU BETTER PRAY NOT, HATTER!
ROBIN! CAN YOU HEAR ME?
AFRAID HE ONLY RESPONDS TO MY COMMANDS NOW!
ROBIN, DEAR BOY! GREET OUR GUESTS LIKE A GOOD LITTLE BIRDIE--
--OR... WHATEVER YOU'RE SUPPOSED TO BE!
THERE WE ARE! NO DEATH INVOLVED AT ALL, YOU SEE?
MERELY SOME MILD HYPNOTISM! IT'S MY SPECIALTY, YOU KNOW.
--UHH!
OH, DEAR!
KRUNNCHH

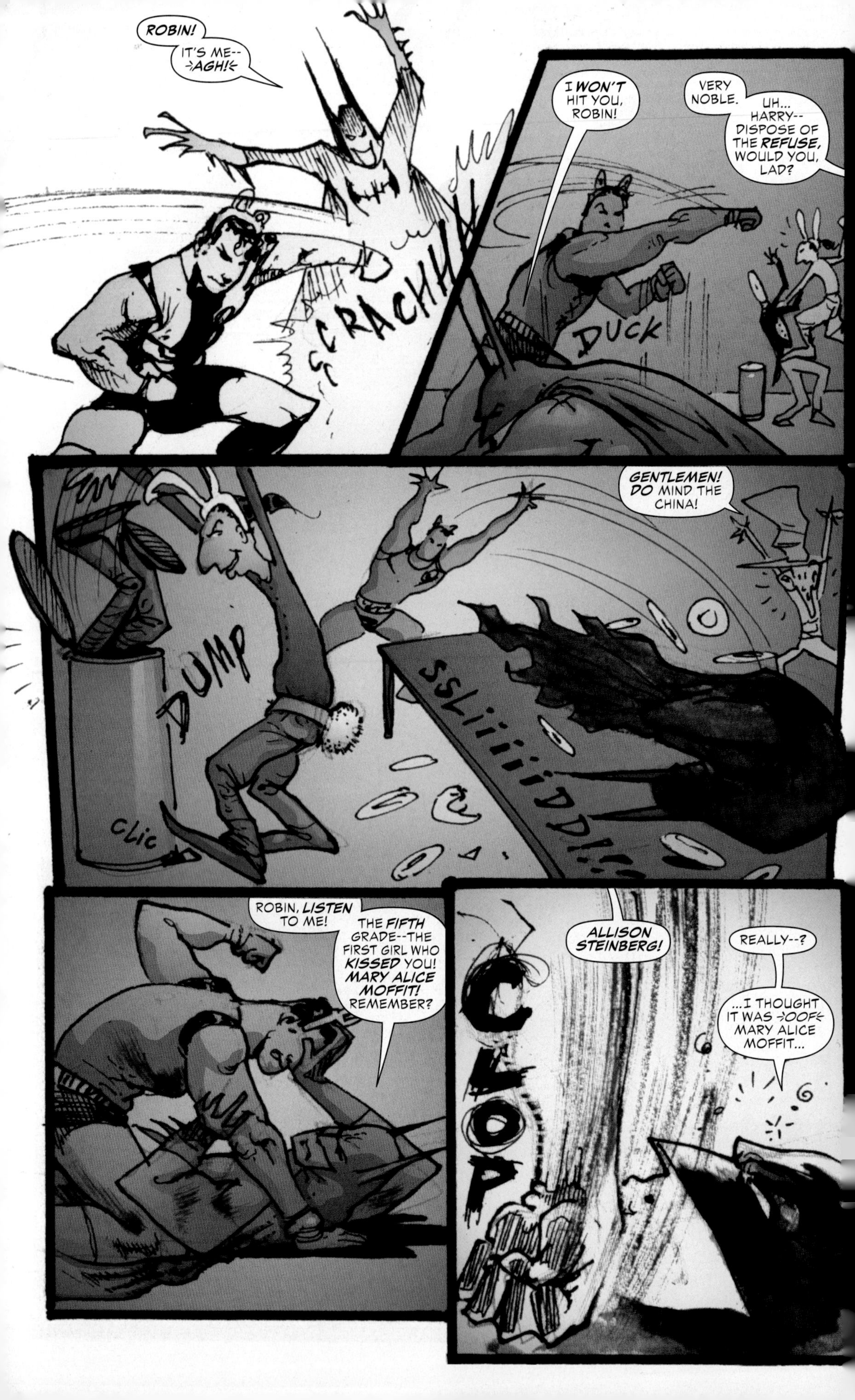
ROBIN!
IT'S ME-- AGH!
CRACHH
I WON'T HIT YOU, ROBIN!
DUCK
VERY NOBLE.
UH... HARRY-- DISPOSE OF THE REFUSE, WOULD YOU, LAD?
GENTLEMEN! DO MIND THE CHINA!
DUMP
CLIC
SSLIIIIIDD!!
ROBIN, LISTEN TO ME!
THE FIFTH GRADE--THE FIRST GIRL WHO KISSED YOU! MARY ALICE MOFFIT! REMEMBER?
ALLISON STEINBERG!
REALLY--?
...I THOUGHT IT WAS OOF MARY ALICE MOFFIT...
CLOP

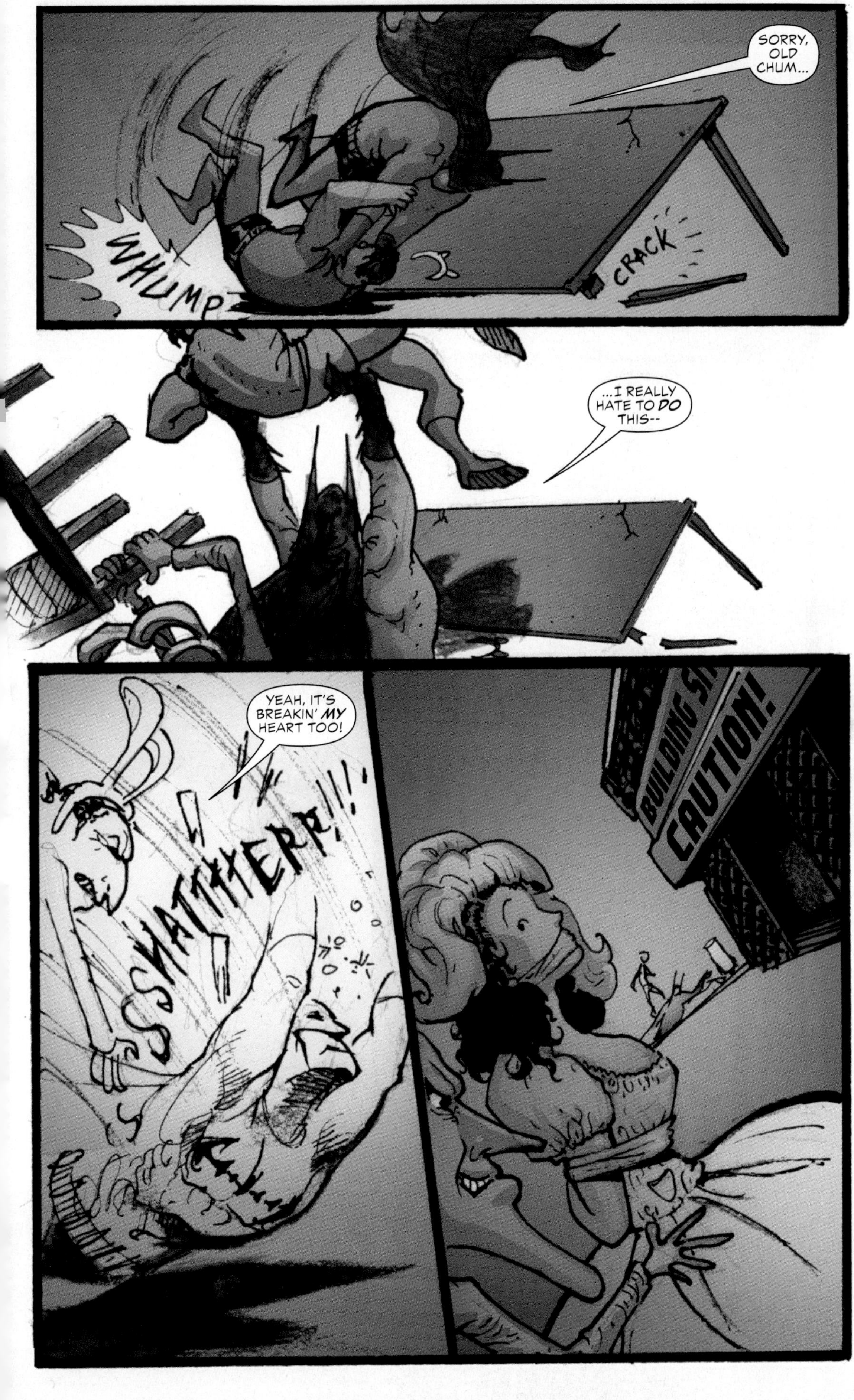

SORRY, OLD CHUM...
WHUMP
CRACK
...I REALLY HATE TO DO THIS--
YEAH, IT'S BREAKIN' MY HEART TOO!
SSHATTTERR!!!
CAUTION!

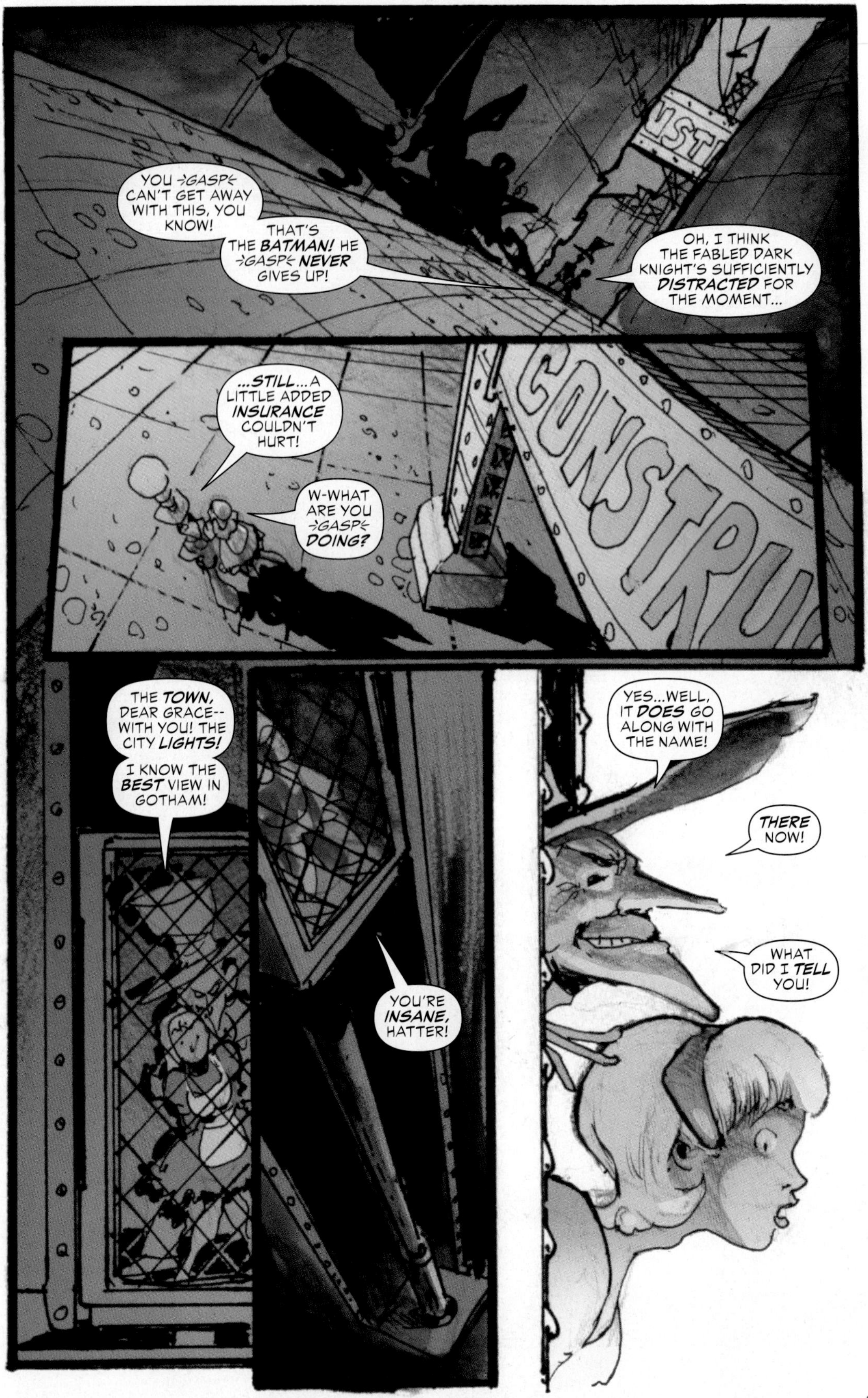
YOU ≯GASP≮ CAN'T GET AWAY WITH THIS, YOU KNOW!
THAT'S THE BATMAN! HE ≯GASP≮ NEVER GIVES UP!
OH, I THINK THE FABLED DARK KNIGHT'S SUFFICIENTLY DISTRACTED FOR THE MOMENT...
...STILL...A LITTLE ADDED INSURANCE COULDN'T HURT!
W-WHAT ARE YOU ≯GASP≮ DOING?
CONSTRU
THE TOWN, DEAR GRACE-- WITH YOU! THE CITY LIGHTS!
I KNOW THE BEST VIEW IN GOTHAM!
YOU'RE INSANE, HATTER!
YES...WELL, IT DOES GO ALONG WITH THE NAME!
THERE NOW!
WHAT DID I TELL YOU!

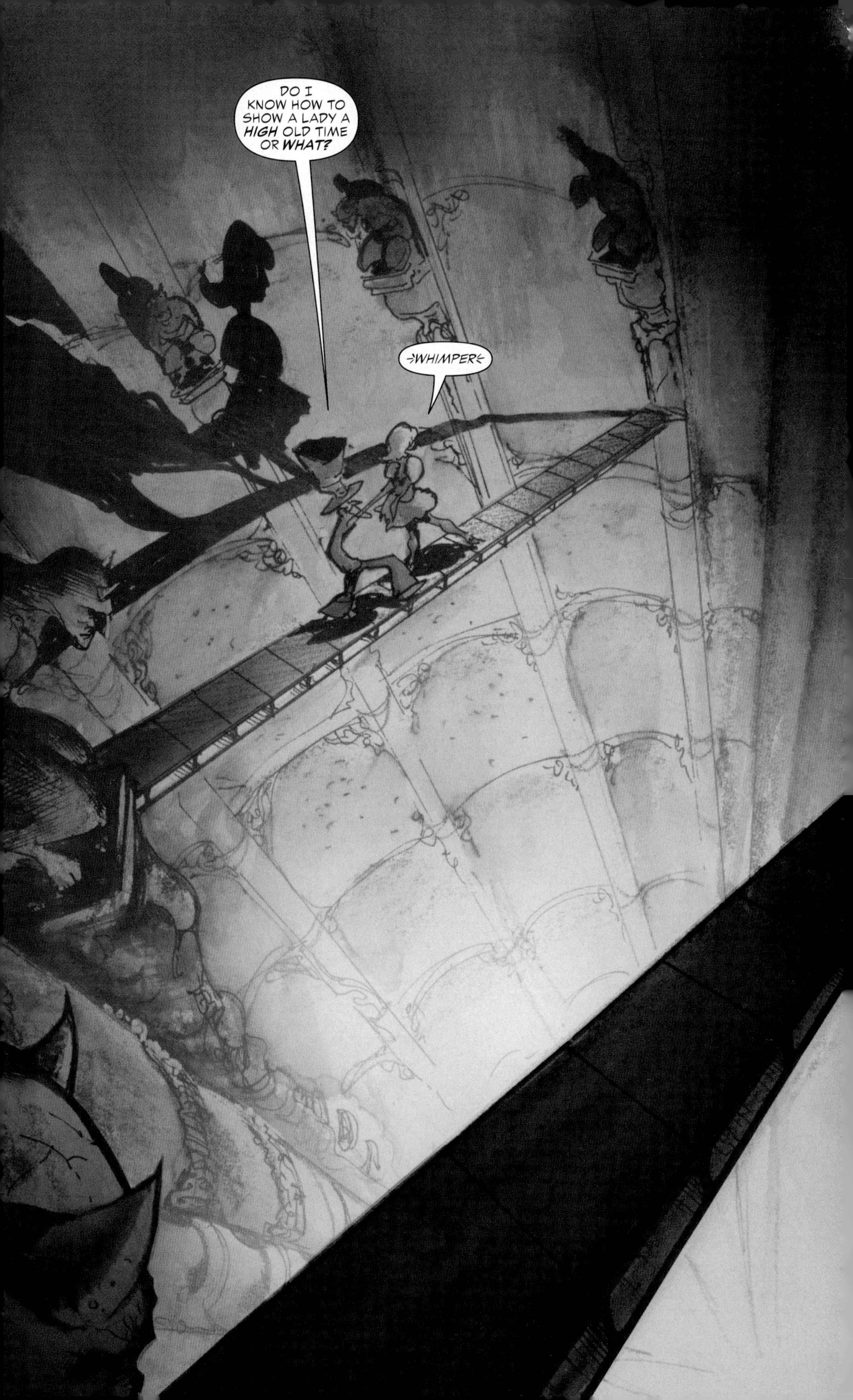
DO I KNOW HOW TO SHOW A LADY A HIGH OLD TIME OR WHAT?
WHIMPER

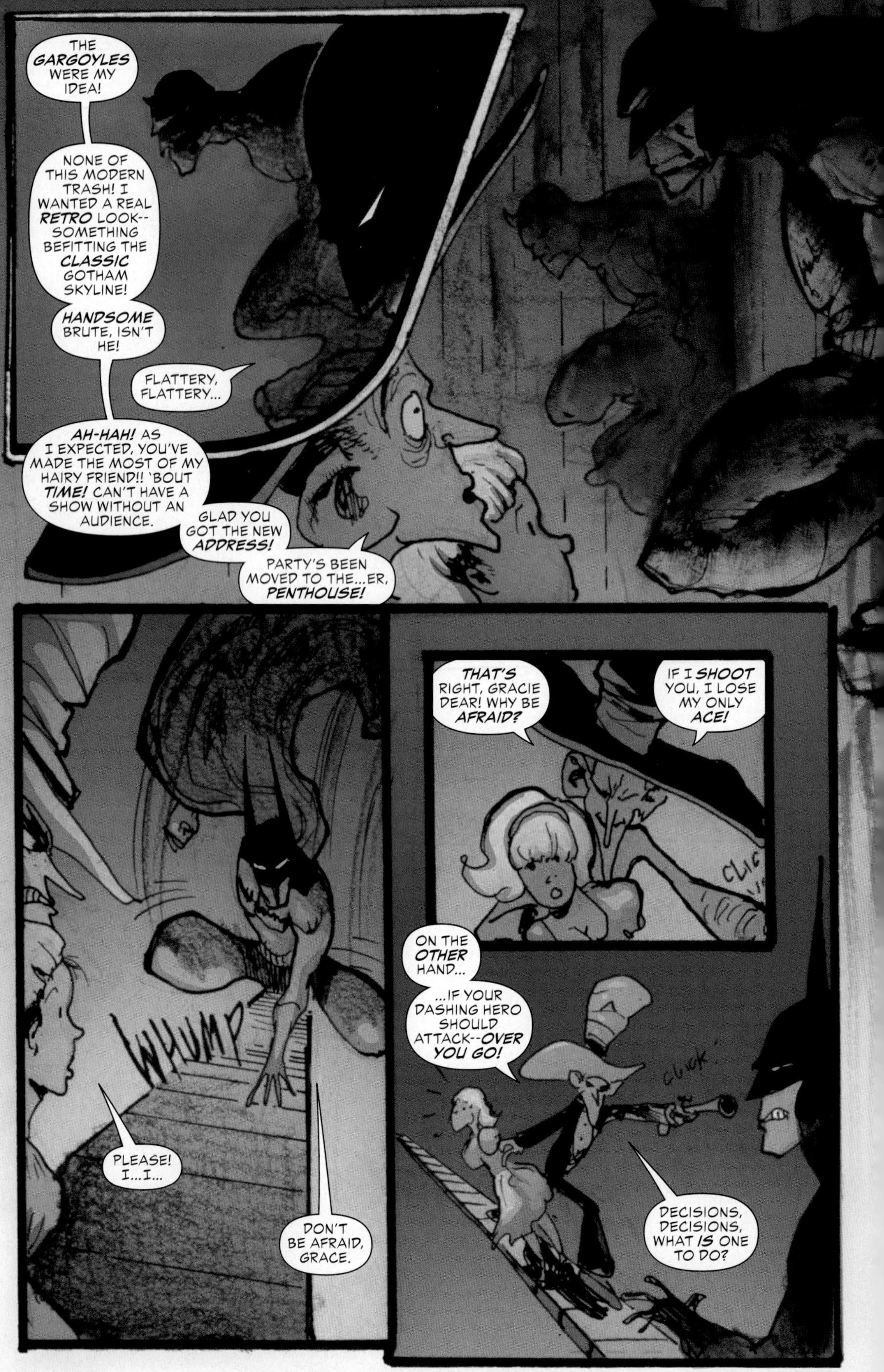

THE GARGOYLES WERE MY IDEA!
NONE OF THIS MODERN TRASH! I WANTED A REAL RETRO LOOK--SOMETHING BEFITTING THE CLASSIC GOTHAM SKYLINE!
HANDSOME BRUTE, ISN'T HE!
FLATTERY, FLATTERY...
AH-HAH! AS I EXPECTED, YOU'VE MADE THE MOST OF MY HAIRY FRIEND!! 'BOUT TIME! CAN'T HAVE A SHOW WITHOUT AN AUDIENCE.
GLAD YOU GOT THE NEW ADDRESS!
PARTY'S BEEN MOVED TO THE...ER, PENTHOUSE!
WHUMP
PLEASE! I...I...
DON'T BE AFRAID, GRACE.
THAT'S RIGHT, GRACIE DEAR! WHY BE AFRAID?
IF I SHOOT YOU, I LOSE MY ONLY ACE!
ON THE OTHER HAND...
...IF YOUR DASHING HERO SHOULD ATTACK--OVER YOU GO!
CLICK!
DECISIONS, DECISIONS, WHAT IS ONE TO DO?

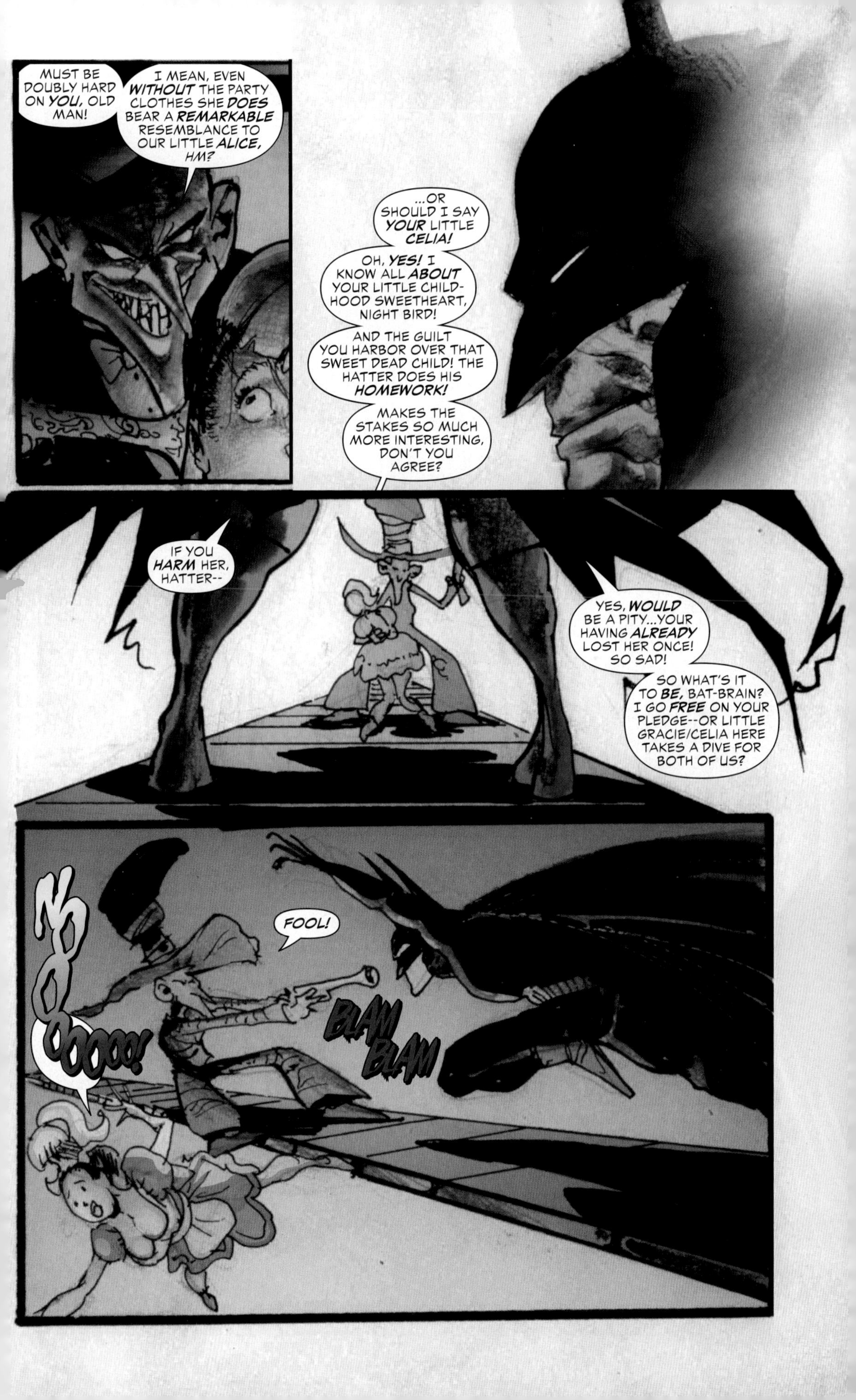
MUST BE DOUBLY HARD ON YOU, OLD MAN!
I MEAN, EVEN WITHOUT THE PARTY CLOTHES SHE DOES BEAR A REMARKABLE RESEMBLANCE TO OUR LITTLE ALICE, HM?
...OR SHOULD I SAY YOUR LITTLE CELIA!
OH, YES! I KNOW ALL ABOUT YOUR LITTLE CHILD-HOOD SWEETHEART, NIGHT BIRD!
AND THE GUILT YOU HARBOR OVER THAT SWEET DEAD CHILD! THE HATTER DOES HIS HOMEWORK!
MAKES THE STAKES SO MUCH MORE INTERESTING, DON'T YOU AGREE?
IF YOU HARM HER, HATTER--
YES, WOULD BE A PITY...YOUR HAVING ALREADY LOST HER ONCE! SO SAD!
SO WHAT'S IT TO BE, BAT-BRAIN? I GO FREE ON YOUR PLEDGE--OR LITTLE GRACIE/CELIA HERE TAKES A DIVE FOR BOTH OF US?
FOOL!
BLAM BLAM
NOOOOOOO!

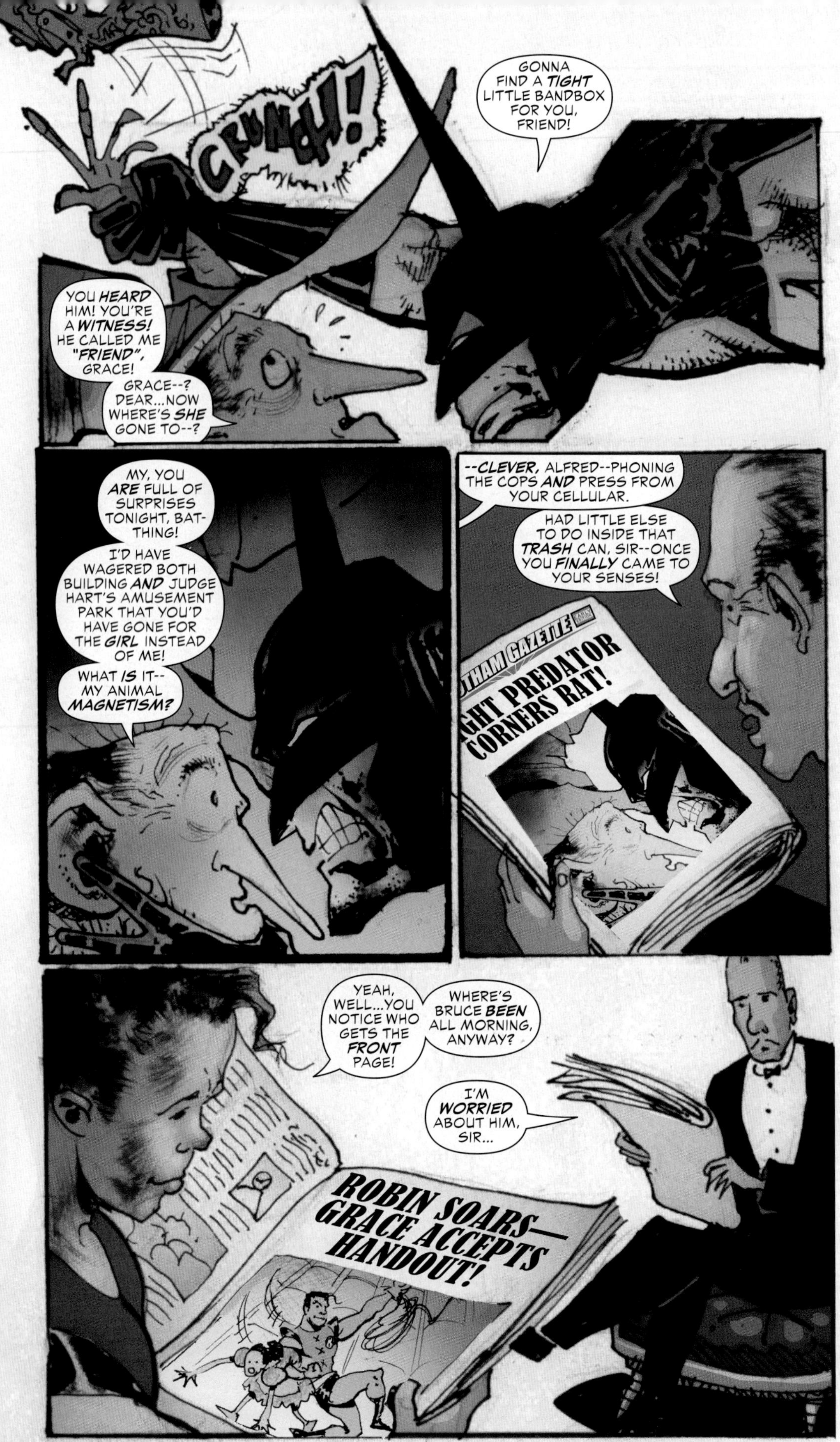
CRUNCH!
GONNA FIND A *TIGHT* LITTLE BANDBOX FOR YOU, FRIEND!
YOU *HEARD* HIM! YOU'RE A *WITNESS!* HE CALLED ME *"FRIEND"*, GRACE!
GRACE--? DEAR...NOW WHERE'S *SHE* GONE TO--?
MY, YOU *ARE* FULL OF SURPRISES TONIGHT, BAT-THING!
I'D HAVE WAGERED BOTH BUILDING *AND* JUDGE HART'S AMUSEMENT PARK THAT YOU'D HAVE GONE FOR THE *GIRL* INSTEAD OF ME!
WHAT *IS* IT--MY ANIMAL *MAGNETISM?*
--*CLEVER,* ALFRED--PHONING THE COPS *AND* PRESS FROM YOUR CELLULAR.
HAD LITTLE ELSE TO DO INSIDE THAT *TRASH* CAN, SIR--ONCE YOU *FINALLY* CAME TO YOUR SENSES!
THAM GAZETTE
GHT PREDATOR CORNERS RAT!
YEAH, WELL...YOU NOTICE WHO GETS THE *FRONT* PAGE!
WHERE'S BRUCE *BEEN* ALL MORNING, ANYWAY?
I'M *WORRIED* ABOUT HIM, SIR...
ROBIN SOARS— GRACE ACCEPTS HANDOUT!

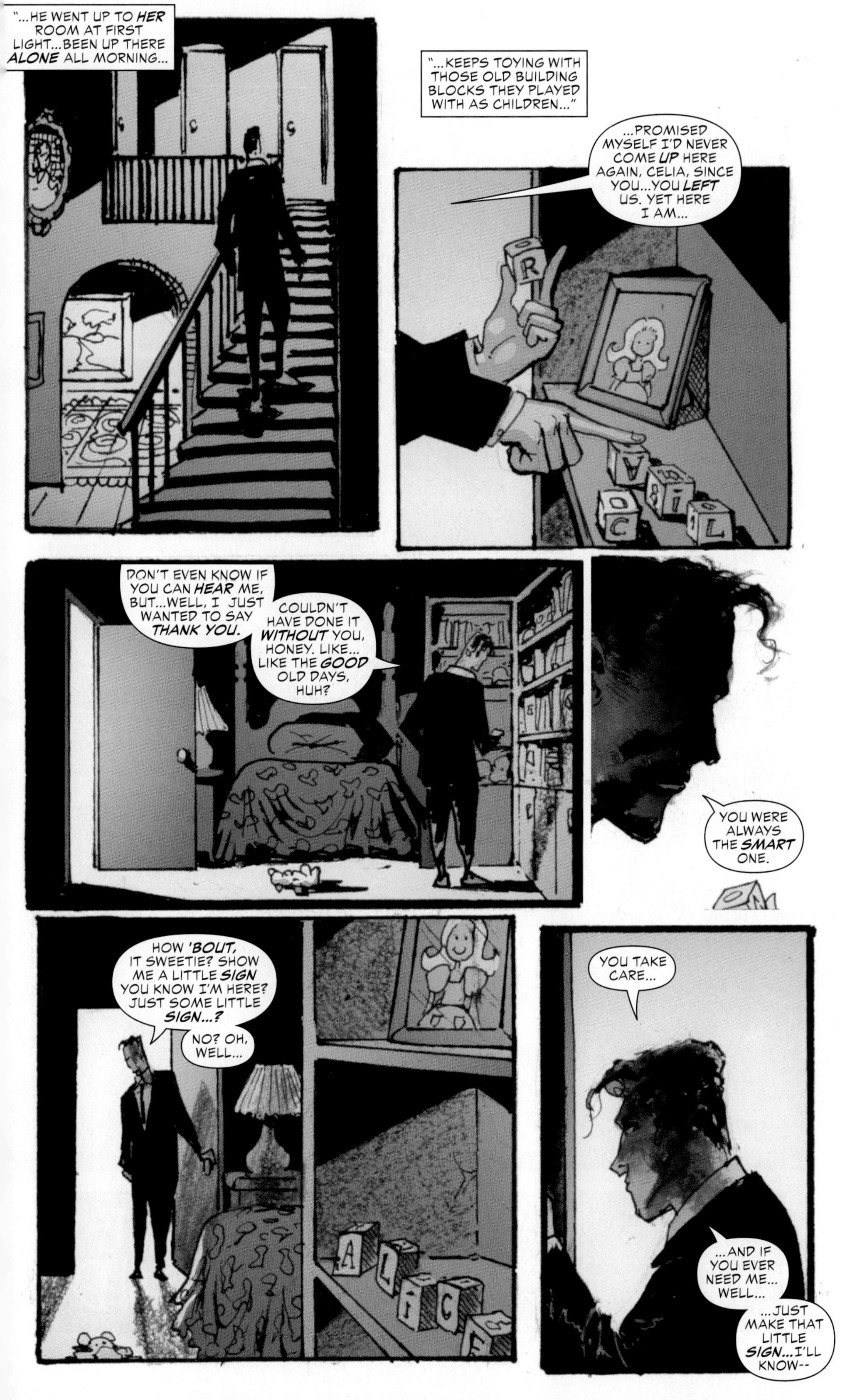
"...HE WENT UP TO HER ROOM AT FIRST LIGHT...BEEN UP THERE ALONE ALL MORNING...
"...KEEPS TOYING WITH THOSE OLD BUILDING BLOCKS THEY PLAYED WITH AS CHILDREN..."
...PROMISED MYSELF I'D NEVER COME UP HERE AGAIN, CELIA, SINCE YOU...YOU LEFT US. YET HERE I AM...
DON'T EVEN KNOW IF YOU CAN HEAR ME, BUT...WELL, I JUST WANTED TO SAY THANK YOU.
COULDN'T HAVE DONE IT WITHOUT YOU, HONEY. LIKE... LIKE THE GOOD OLD DAYS, HUH?
YOU WERE ALWAYS THE SMART ONE.
HOW 'BOUT, IT SWEETIE? SHOW ME A LITTLE SIGN YOU KNOW I'M HERE? JUST SOME LITTLE SIGN...?
NO? OH, WELL...
YOU TAKE CARE...
...AND IF YOU EVER NEED ME... WELL...
...JUST MAKE THAT LITTLE SIGN...I'LL KNOW--

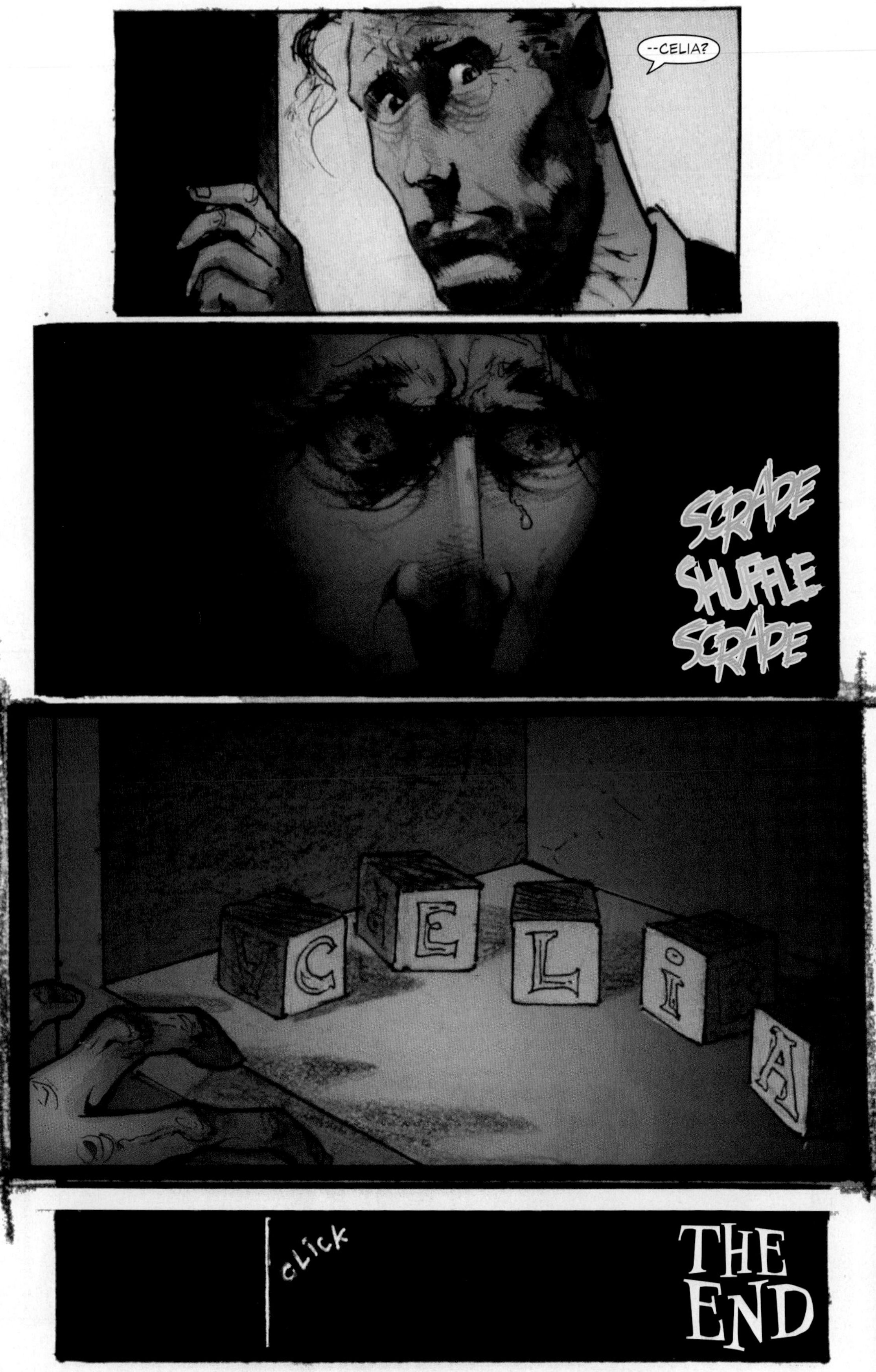
--CELIA?
SCRAPE
SHUFFLE
SCRAPE
C
E
L
I
A
click
THE END

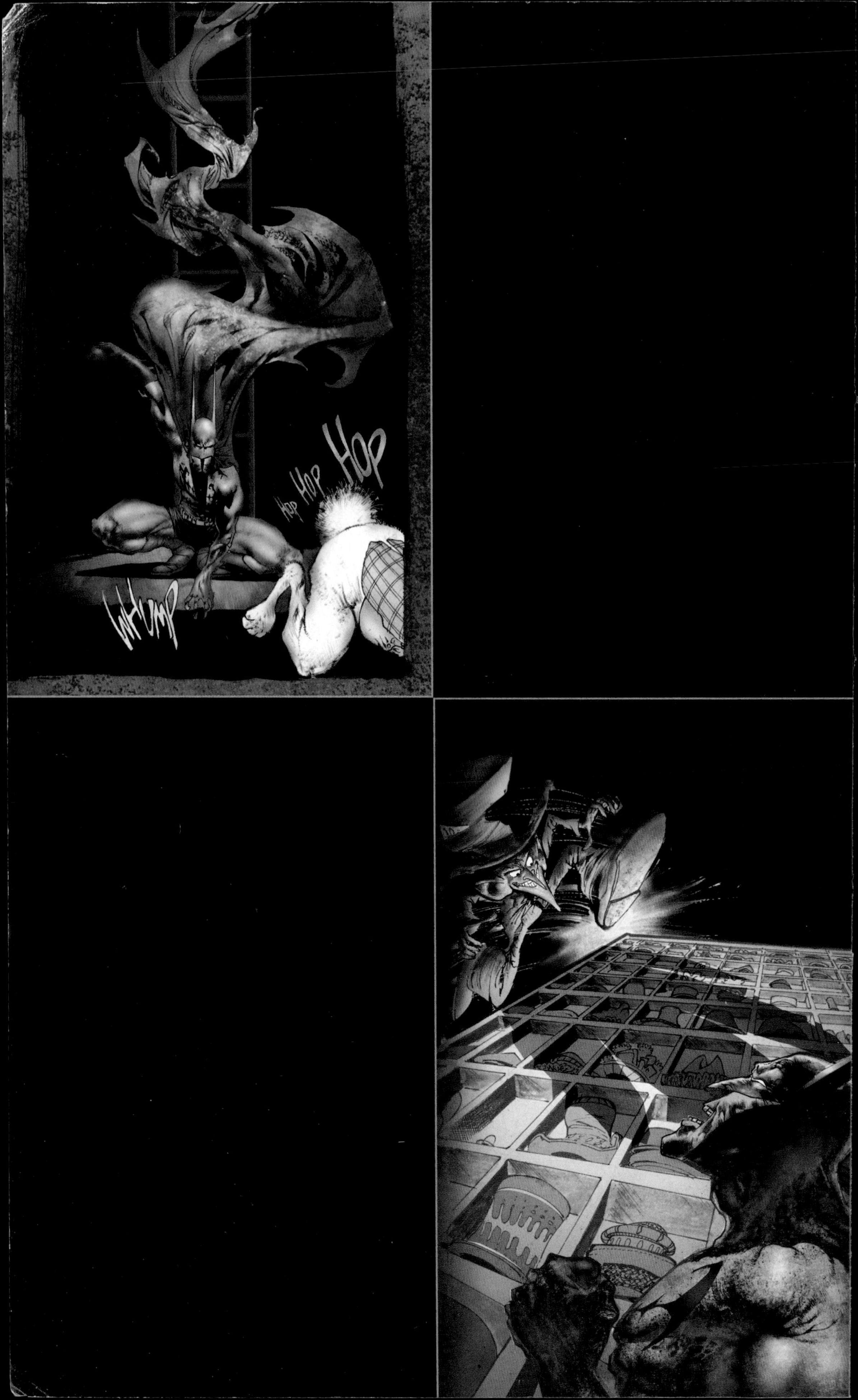
HOP HOP HOP
WHUMP